Leigh Bowery

Sue Tilley

Leigh Bowery

The Life and Times of an Icon

With 25 illustrations

First published in the United Kingdom in 1997
by Hodder and Stoughton

This new edition published in the United Kingdom in 2025 by
Thames & Hudson, 181a High Holborn, London WCIV 7QX

British Library Cataloguing-in-Publication Data
A catalogue record for this book is available
from the British Library

ISBN 078-0-500-29855-8

Impression 01

Printed and bound in the UK by Bell & Bain Ltd.

MIX
Paper | Supporting
responsible forestry
FSC
www.fsc.org FSC® C007785

Be the first to know about our new releases,
exclusive content and author events by visiting
thamesandhudson.com
thamesandhudsonusa.com
thamesandhudson.com.au

Contents

Preface to the 1997 edition

I first met Leigh in the nightclubs of London in 1982. We became best friends, which some people thought was rather strange, as I was an ordinary kind of girl and he was an extraordinary kind of man. But we laughed at the same things and he knew I could understand what he was doing and could keep up with his quick wit and intelligence. I kept him in touch with everyday reality, and he gave plenty of excitement to my life.

Leigh always wanted to be famous, and we spent many happy hours discussing what would happen when he was. There was no doubt in either of our minds that he would be, we just didn't know in which field he would make the big break. He tried fashion, art, dance, acting, television presenting and music and was successful, in varying degrees, in all of them. No one who saw him performing will ever forget the experience.

Leigh liked to keep his friends separate, so most of them only knew one facet of Leigh's life. But he used to tell me everything that was going on and gradually I came to know all of the people in his life and became involved (if only in a small way) with most of his projects.

There was a turning point in our relationship in 1988, when Leigh discovered he was HIV positive. It ruined his plans for world fame, as he knew his time was limited. He worked much harder and became much more serious about his work. I was the only person he told, so I was the only one he could confide in and let out his emotions with. He sent me a postcard from New York in December 1993, apologizing for his behaviour: 'I'm sorry I've caused so much upset and grief during the year – I'll try to change for 1994. You know I don't really mean it. I'm just deflecting the pain and torture of my own life onto you.' He definitely changed, becoming more focused and more determined to succeed; he didn't mind so much who he upset, although he could still be the kindest and most thoughtful person. When he was being vile, it wasn't really meant in a vindictive way, but more for effect and to get a reaction.

When Leigh died, the *Guardian* wanted someone to write his obituary. My friend Angus Cook suggested that I should do it. I refused, thinking I wouldn't be able to. But then I thought about it some more and knew that Leigh would want me to have a go. He was always telling me to take challenges and try new things. So I wrote it in about three hours and it was, surprisingly, very well received. Various people, after reading it, suggested I should write a book about Leigh. They said I had a good memory and could tell a story, but I never had the self-motivation to do it.

Last year I met Robert Violette, who had previously worked at the Anthony d'Offay Gallery, and was preparing a coffee-table book about Leigh, mainly with photographs and written contributions from friends, admirers and collaborators. He had contacted me for pictures and information. Simon Prosser at Hodder & Stoughton heard of this book and, as he had always been fascinated with Leigh, he called Robert in to have a look at what he had done. It was not the kind of book Hodder & Stoughton publish, so Simon asked Robert if he knew of anyone who could write the story of Leigh.

Robert asked around, and once again Angus Cook and his boyfriend Jonathan Kaplan suggested me. I thought that I had better do it, as I knew that Leigh would have wanted me to, and would be proud that I had finally done something creative.

So I set to work, listening to a soundtrack of early eighties music to put me into the mood. It was weird, re-living old memories; sometimes I was laughing so much I couldn't type, or I would start crying remembering the horrible times at the hospital when Leigh was dying. When I was writing about Leigh and Trojan getting ready to go out, I could almost smell their heady blend of make-up, cheap perfume and vodka.

It was a thoroughly enjoyable experience and not nearly as difficult as I had imagined. It was lovely talking to friends about Leigh. They were all incredibly helpful and frank and I'm very grateful to them all. Big thanks to Alison Atkinson, Charlie Atlas, Rachel Auburn, Lee Benjamin, Steve Blame, Bronwyn Bowery, Nicola Bowery, Tom Bowery, Leslie Bryant, Lady Bunny, Michael Clark, Angus Cook, Anthony d'Offay, Malcolm Duffy, Angus Fairhurst, Sophie Fiennes, Julia Fodor, Lucian Freud, Boy George, Peter-Paul Hartnett, Jeffrey Hinton, Simon Hinton, Damien Hirst, David Holah, Adrian Howells, Michael Kostiff, John Maybury, Louise Neel, Lorcan O'Neill, Rifat Ozbek, Jimmy Payne, Colin Ross, Wayne Shires, Stella Stein, Graham Stevens, Dave Swindells, Sheila Tequila, Richard Torry, Jimmy Trindy, David Walls, Baillie Walsh, Cerith Wyn Evans and Yvette for giving up their time to talk to me and also for giving me encouragement and confidence to carry on, despite it being sometimes very painful for them to remember Leigh.

I would like to thank Paul Hoy for being the first one to read the whole book and letting me know where it didn't make sense.

Thanks also to Robert and Sandy Violette and their assistant Zoë Manzi for all their help in making this possible. And a final thanks to Simon Prosser and Anna-Maria Watters at Hodder & Stoughton for giving a complete novice a chance and for showing me how a book is written!

January 1997

30 November 1988

Leigh called me at work to say he had to come round because he had something important to tell me. I told him that I was going to Julia and Jeffrey's, so could it wait. He said it couldn't, so I knew that it had to be something serious, because he didn't visit me that often. My mind kept wandering, thinking what it could be. I came up with loads of different ideas – he was in love, he had been caught cottaging, he was being sent back to Australia – but deep down I knew what it was. Sadly, I was right. He had just received a letter from the clap clinic asking how he was coping with his HIV-positive status. He had been tested a couple of years earlier, but decided not to go back for the results because he preferred to live in ignorance. He had been back to the clinic that afternoon to confirm that it was true. I thought maybe it was one of his terrible lies, but he knew that I would think that, so he had brought the letter to show me.

We had a good old cry: it reminded me of the night he had come round after Trojan had died, when we both had a sob together. His main concern was that he would never have sex again, and he was laughing through his tears, saying, 'How on earth am I going to cope? How are the cottages of London going to manage without my constant presence?' He made me promise not to tell anyone else, because he couldn't bear the thought of do-gooders being nice to him all the time.

I asked if he wanted to stay the night, but he said that he would be fine. I gave him a big kiss and he left knowing that nothing would ever be the same again.

1

Sunshine

Leigh Bowery was born on 26 March 1961 in the small, working-class town of Sunshine, Australia. It was a sleepy little town where not much happened. There were a lot of immigrant families, mainly working in blue-collar occupations. The main entertainment was the church, although there was a cinema, but it was only a ten or fifteen minute drive to the big city of Melbourne.

Leigh's childhood was pretty uneventful, and there was little sign that he would turn out to be one of Australia's most fantastic exports and one of the most innovative people of the late twentieth century.

His mother and father were very pleasant, caring, upwardly mobile people. They had both come from poor families with seven children in each. However, they had been brought up very well. Both had been taught good manners and had been regular attenders at Sunday School, and from those humble roots they developed the hopes and aspirations of the middle classes. They had left manual work behind them and Leigh's father, Tom, worked as an accountant.

His mother, Evelyn, was born in Morris Street, Sunshine. When she was twenty-one, the family moved to the house next door, and when she got married her two brothers built a cream-bricked house for the newlyweds on the plot of land opposite. By comparison Leigh's father, Tom, was very widely travelled, having lived in various towns in the state of Victoria. He was born in Marohawk and then moved to a suburb of Mildura. During the Second World War his father worked in the refugee camps in Rushworth, so they had moved there. The family then moved to Bendigo, where his mother lived, for a couple of years in the early 1950s. Tom moved to Melbourne in 1957 and then to Sunshine in September 1959 when he married Evelyn.

When Evelyn became pregnant Tom felt sure it was going to be a boy, although his wife wanted a girl. Tom was right and Evelyn gave birth to a son. Leigh was a big, bonny baby with beautiful blond curls. Up until his second birthday, people always remarked on what a lovely little girl he was. Unfortunately his sister, Bronwyn, who was born twenty months later, had the opposite trouble. Everyone thought she was a boy because she looked bald due to her fine blonde hair.

Leigh was always larger than the other kids, who called him 'Big Leigh'. I often used to tease Leigh and ask why he looked so old for his age. He couldn't understand it himself, and said that he had been tall as a child and that he expected to be much taller when he grew up, but in fact had stopped growing when he was about fourteen. We fantasized that he had been born four years earlier than his parents said, and because they were ashamed that they weren't married they had locked him up until he was about five and then brought him out and pretended he was only one. Of course this was rubbish, but it kept us amused for several years pretending that it was true. Leigh always lied about his age anyway: in interviews his birth date varied between 1950 and 1965, depending on what mood he was in.

The two children were brought up fairly strictly. Their parents put great emphasis on manners and how to behave in public. They were taught to respect their elders and other people's property. Their father wouldn't let them watch soap operas on the television and only allowed them to see the news, current affairs, documentaries and films that weren't smutty. Perhaps this childhood deprivation was the reason why in later life Leigh adored anything filthy. When they were in their late teens, Tom asked the children what they had thought of their upbringing. 'They said that I was too strict in regards to manners but they were glad that they knew how to behave and never felt uncomfortable in formal social occasions.' In the last couple of years of his life, Leigh often told me the same thing and said that he would always be grateful to his parents for bringing him up properly.

His father used to expect more of Leigh because he was so big. He thought that he should act in a more mature way and be even further ahead at school, forgetting that he was only a young boy. 'Evelyn often used to go crook [get angry] and tell me he was only a boy, not a man.' Leigh was a strong-willed boy, and his father soon realized that you couldn't just tell him off. It was better to reason with him and explain what he had done wrong. 'You couldn't use force with him. Bronwyn, on the other hand, was completely different; you only had to growl at her and she would be in tears.'

When he was five Leigh went to the local primary school, where he excelled at most subjects. He was very intelligent and as most of the children came from working-class backgrounds he stood out. There were a lot of Italian and Greek immigrants in the area, and some of the parents couldn't speak English, so they were unable to help their children as much as the Bowerys. Tom and Evelyn often took Leigh and Bronwyn to museums and places of historical interest. They also went to classical music concerts – their favourite was Gilbert and Sullivan. Some of the local children thought that Leigh and Bronwyn were a bit stuck-up, but they didn't mind that at all. There weren't many children of their age in their neighbourhood, and so they tended to play with each other and, according to Tom, 'did not mix with the run of the mill people.'

While at junior school Leigh showed no extrovert qualities at all, which is rather strange given the way his personality developed when he came to London. He wasn't introverted, but he just kept his head down and got on with his work. He was always well behaved and his parents had no trouble with him at all. He had his own circle of friends and got on well with his sister. According to Bronwyn he had one strange ambition as a child: 'He wanted to be a comedian, a very rich comedian.'

Evelyn and Tom were very involved with the Salvation Army (and later both ended up working for them). Leigh used to go along to meetings sometimes, but it wasn't really his cup of tea. His father explained that it was because he didn't like the band music they played there: 'he found it too brassy.' Mostly he liked classical music, because this is what he was exposed to at home. In the mid-seventies he began to like some of the pop music around at the time, mainly X-Ray Spex, but only because of the way Poly Styrene dressed.

When he was eleven, Leigh went to the Sunshine West High School. He was such a good pupil that when his parents attended Open Evenings the teachers shooed them away because Leigh was doing so well and was so very well behaved. Leigh was always desperate to learn new things, and although he was not particularly keen on mundane work, he would do anything that he knew would impress. He was very talented musically and was an excellent pianist. From an early age he produced and directed the school's end-of-term musicals. He was a confident child and he gained the respect of his classmates by his endless enthusiasm.

There was one area, however, where he didn't shine, and that was sport. His father had been a very keen sportsman in his youth, playing cricket and football, but when he married he stopped playing, and although he watched sport on television he didn't actively encourage Leigh. Leigh tried soccer at school, but when he didn't immediately score ten goals he gave up. His father was disappointed in Leigh's lack of sporting prowess because he had the ideal build for Australian rules football or rugby.

His father now wishes that he had encouraged Leigh more in sporting pursuits so that they could have had a more typical father–son relationship. They did some things together, such as tending the garden, but while they got along they were never particularly close. Leigh always got on better with women and had a much closer relationship with his mother. Bronwyn, meanwhile, was always a 'daddy's girl'.

Instead of sport, Leigh took up more womanly hobbies, such as crochet and tatting (a kind of lace-making). He had to have several operations as a child because his testicles didn't drop. While he was recuperating, his aunt used to come and sit with him and while away the hours doing her crochet. Leigh was fascinated by this, so she showed him how to do it. He was hooked and was soon doing all types of complicated stitches. At one stage his grandmother wanted to know how to do a particular kind of stitch and was delighted when her eldest grandson was able to show her (years later she was still using the handwritten notes Leigh gave her). After a while Leigh decided he should learn to knit, but he didn't just start off with a simple piece, he knitted himself a beautiful jumper with cable stitch down the front. Even his dad was impressed: 'It was the perfect job when he finished and he'd never knitted before in his life.'

The family had another house about sixty kilometres away from their home in a small village called Macedon. Evelyn's mother had bought the land and given an acre to each of her children. When Leigh and Bronwyn were small, there was just a small two-roomed shack on the land, but they still spent all their holidays there. As the children grew up they needed more space, so the family built a brick-veneer place that was much more sturdy and comfortable. It was situated on a mountain in a pine forest, with a lake nearby. It was an idyllic playground for the two children, and since their cousins stayed in the houses nearby, there was always someone to play with. When they were older they also brought their school friends to stay for weeks at a time. They packed a picnic, got on their bikes and cycled to the lake to spend all day swimming and floating on logs. Leigh adored it there and often used to talk about it to his friends in London. It was the only part of Australia he missed. The church youth group often had summer camps up there and slept out in tents. Their father used to join them for the Australian summer holidays in December and January.

Once, Leigh was helping his father in the garden. They wanted to prune a eucalyptus tree, but it was full of koala bears. To get them down they gave the tree a massive shake. One of them took a liking to Leigh's leg and dug its claws into his shorts, hanging on for dear life thinking it had found another cosy tree. Leigh's dad had to shoo it away with a garden spade.

They would have a marvellous, traditional time at Christmas with all the grandparents, aunts, uncles and cousins together. Often they would invite a couple of people they didn't know very well but who would be on their own otherwise. Leigh didn't really like the visitors, because it meant you had to be on your best behaviour all day, but he still eagerly looked forward to Christmas with the special food and presents, although he usually felt sick by the end of the day because he had stuffed himself so much. When he came to England he never enjoyed Christmas because he could never recreate the magic he felt as a child.

When Leigh was thirteen his teachers suggested that he apply for a scholarship to Melbourne High School. There was an entrance exam, and of 400 applicants only 100 passed. Leigh and only one other boy from Sunshine were accepted. It was quite a long journey to school and every day Leigh set off to the station with his birth certificate in his pocket because the railway staff would not believe he was a half fare.

Leigh was still a very keen learner, and his father was very impressed with his thirst for knowledge: 'Almost anything he would set his mind to, he would do. He seemed to have that knack of being able to do anything he wanted to do. He was quite well read and I have never seen him read a book without a dictionary with him. He had a fantastic memory, if he found a word he couldn't understand he'd look it up and then never forget it.'

Leigh's new school was very musically orientated, which suited Leigh. The school was divided into four houses of 250 boys and every year there was a choral competition between them. Leigh was chosen to conduct his house in the set piece. Tom remembered: 'Leigh brought the music home and played it and played it and played it until he knew that music note perfect, if he was here today he could sit down and play it perfectly. On the night of the competition all four conductors came out in their evening suits. Three came out with their music stands and sheet music, but not Leigh. He was able to dispense with the music because he knew it so well and because of this his house won the competition.' Leigh was also talented at art and his family were amazed that he could just pick up a pen or pencil and produce a brilliant picture. Neither of his parents had any artistic ability, so they wondered where their son had found his talent.

Rehearsing for concerts after school gave Leigh the ideal alibi for what was to become his new hobby. At about the age of twelve, Leigh realized that he was attracted to other men, and although as far as he knew there were no other gay kids in Sunshine, it didn't really worry him. He had a couple of fumblings with some boys from his school, and often said that he once caught his mother spying on them through a keyhole (although this is probably a figment of his very fertile imagination). While waiting for the train home from school at Melbourne Central Station, however, he soon discovered the delights of older men. He must have been their dream come true: a well-built, cherubic-looking schoolboy desperate to learn and to experiment. He was soon hanging round the gentlemen's toilets every day. He reckoned that he had had at least a thousand men before he left school. Of course, he sometimes bumped into the same man more than once, but these never turned into relationships, probably because most of them were married. This started a pattern that Leigh was to follow for the rest of his adult life.

At his new school, Leigh was rather shocked to find that he was no longer the brightest boy in the class, and as a result he did not try so hard. He knew he couldn't be top, because the competition was now much fiercer. His parents were rather disappointed, especially when he told them that he only needed 50 per cent to pass his High School Examination, so that is what he would aim for. Instead of giving him brilliant reports, his teachers now said that he could do better and he tended to be rather lazy when he was not interested in a lesson. Leigh didn't care about his drop in performance because he still worked very hard when a subject interested him.

When he was about fifteen Leigh began to show signs of his wilful personality. He was now very keen on gardening, and his parents would get home from shopping to find all the plants moved in the garden because Leigh thought that they would look better his way – and invariably they did. As his father remembers, he did the same thing inside the house: 'We'd get home and you almost had to get your street directory out to find where to walk as all the furniture had been moved.'

I asked Tom whether he had thought there was anything odd in this behaviour. 'No, it didn't seem unusual. He seemed to be doing all the things boys do. He used to help mow the lawn and help me out with the garden at Macedon. He used to ride his bike and by and large he was just a normal boy growing up. I don't know if there was anything different about him. Others may say so. It wasn't until he started going to university and moved into the design area that I noticed anything different.'

After he passed his High School Examination, Leigh surprised his parents by deciding to pursue a career in design. They had always assumed (and hoped) that he would continue to study music. Leigh, however, had different ideas and enrolled in the Royal Melbourne Institute of Technology to study fashion. Here, he was at a distinct disadvantage because he had never used a sewing machine before. There was only one other boy in his class and they both had a lot of catching up to do. But in true Leigh Bowery style, he slaved over his machine until he could do a better buttonhole than all the girls. He continued to study sewing for the rest of his life and pored over dressmaking books, delighting in finding new techniques that would help him to create his superb designs.

Leigh made some good friends at college who he wrote to when he was in England. He seemed to get on best with people he could show off intellectually with. He liked to expound on his theories of life and fashion, and wanted friends who could appreciate his quick brain and brilliance. Hamish was the friend he most admired because he shared Leigh's enthusiasms and understood his ideas. He was a flashy dresser and Leigh took inspiration from him.

Leigh was now beginning to show the more flamboyant side of his character. He grew his hair into a blond bob (which was quite difficult: it was the bane of his life that his hair grew so slowly). Once he had started college he moved into a bedsit in the city and his father used to get reports of his son wearing 'lary' clothes:

People would come up to me in the street and say 'Oh I saw your son walking down the street with yellow trousers on.' We were fairly conservative, especially me. Men didn't wear colourful things of that nature, they'd wear coloured shirts but not so much in the trousers. He had a knitted suit that he had made which was a great heavy thing hanging all over the place. I liked my shirts with the shoulders where my shoulders were but he made them for me with raglan sleeves and all sorts, his things seemed to be way, way out, but after he left Australia things he had been wearing came into fashion about five years later. So where he got his designs from I don't know. Most likely his head.

Even though Leigh had left home, he was still no worry to his parents. He didn't try alcohol until he was about eighteen, and even then he didn't like it. He never even thought of taking drugs until he came to England and, of course, there was no trouble with girls. By comparison to later life he didn't even dress too shockingly. When someone asked him if he dressed up a lot in Australia he was horrified: 'I was never a juvenile transvestite, although I may have thrown on the odd towel and worn it as a turban.'

In the second year of college Leigh began to get bored. The students had to learn how to make ladies' underwear and children's clothes and he was just not interested in this. The college were also finding him too much to handle, as he later explained to *LAM* magazine, a freebie given away at tube stations: 'I didn't last there too long, they'd always say "Oh, that's very nice Leigh, I could imagine you wearing it, but let's be practical, these garments are supposed to sell."' He wanted to leap ahead and make one-off creative designs. He began to realize that there was no outlet for his talents in downtown Melbourne. He was now eighteen and had begun to take an interest in punk music, avidly reading all the music press. He once described his feelings to the *Herald*:

The thing which made everything click for me was the punk movement where people used themselves and their appearance to describe so much and I just loved Busby Berkeley movies – all those sequins and feathers – and I would always have my nose in a *National Geographic* magazine, gazing at women with stretched necks and rings going in strange places.

He also used to read all he could about the London club scene and designers. It seemed that there was only one place he could possibly go: London.

> I wanted to hang out with the art and fashion people. I wanted to go to nightclubs and look at the clothes in the shops. I loved the idea of punk and the New Romantics. England seemed the only place to go, I considered New York but that just seemed full of cheap copies of London. I don't think I made a mistake.

He approached his parents and asked if he could go to London. (He was so well brought up he would not have dreamt of just getting up and going.) They were rather disappointed, because they would miss him while he was gone, but they said he could go. There were conditions, however. He had to save up his return fare, because they did not want him to be stuck in a strange city, miserable and unable to get home. They also insisted that he save $1,000 in case he was unable to get a job as soon as he arrived, though he would be able to work in England because both sets of grandparents were British.

Surprisingly, perhaps, Leigh agreed to this. He deferred from college and got himself a job in a department store in Melbourne. He hated the job but he stuck to it as it was a means to an end. He returned to live at home but his parents said that he had to pay them rent as he would have to pay rent in England, so he had better get used to it. He was not happy with this at all because he wanted to save the money as soon as possible. He made a deal with his mother that in return for paying half rent he would do all the household's ironing. Unsurprisingly, his mother quickly agreed to this (and of course he got most of the money back that he paid in rent because every week his mum would buy him some new underpants or socks ready to take on his big trip to England). He didn't go out in the evenings because he was desperate to save the money. Instead, he stayed in, chatting with his mum and doing her hair while his dad sat watching the sports on the television.

Leigh arranged to meet his great friend from school, Peter Koutsoumbas, in England. He was going to arrive a few weeks before Leigh. They were very, very excited, and believed that as soon as they arrived in London their lives would change and they would be out every night partying with the 'in crowd'. They would be on the phone for hours planning their trip, arguing about very trivial things such as which was the best club to go to and then making up. Leigh was his usual bossy self and always tried to have the last word.

Leigh's parents thought that at the most he would be gone a year and he would then return and resume his studies. So in October 1980, aged nineteen, he set off on his big adventure with his suitcase in one hand and his portable sewing machine in the other.

2

London

In 1980, the club scene in London changed. Punk had finished and the New Romantics were the new trendsetters. This was a movement started by a group of students at St Martin's College of Art. Instead of dressing down, they dressed right up. Nothing was too fancy: frilly shirts, velvet knickerbockers, satin gowns, patent leather shoes with big buckles and, of course, plenty of make-up for both sexes. Steve Strange was the King of the Scene. He opened the Blitz Club, which became the home of the new crowd, in Covent Garden. This was the first time that a normal club was taken over by a promoter on a once-a-week basis and it was to set the style of clubbing for future generations.

This was London when Leigh arrived in the damp October of 1980. He was excited but very tired after the long journey. Peter had already found a bedsit for them to share. It was at the top of a house just off the Fulham Palace Road, with the landlady, Mrs Sedley, living downstairs. The two boys went sightseeing and visited all the museums and galleries. Because they were together all the time, they didn't make any friends. Not that they were particularly trying to, since they were happy with each other's company.

Leigh worshipped Peter. He found him bright, witty and amusing, although sometimes 'lacking in dress sense' – Peter dressed like a normal person in jeans and T-shirts, which Leigh tried to rectify because he thought that people were judged by who they hung around with, and he didn't want to be thought unfashionable just because his companion wasn't quite trendy enough. He realized that Peter was better looking than he was and had a far more 'acceptable' physique, which he thought would impress prospective friends.

Soon Leigh began trying to initiate a sexual affair with Peter. He thought that they would make a marvellous partnership, complementing each other perfectly, and would try to introduce the subject by wandering around naked in front of Peter, playing with his cock, giving him the perfect opportunity to join in. But Peter could not be swayed, even when Leigh started sticking things up his bum in front of him. Peter just laughed and Leigh finally realized that a sexual relationship was never going to take place.

In early December, Peter had to go to Greece to see some of his family. He assured Leigh that he would be back before Christmas. On Christmas Eve he still hadn't returned and Leigh had heard no word from him. He prepared to have a lonely holiday. He told the landlady he was going away, so she wouldn't feel sorry for him, and set about cooking his own dinner. He listed in his diary (a very pretentious journal written in the style of Jane Austen) the menu and the recipes that he was going to prepare. There were to be roast potatoes, pumpkin, carrots, roast onion and kale and a quiche made with feta cheese and filo pastry. He made his own Christmas pudding and served it with a sweet wine sauce. He was desperately homesick and told his diary he was 'missing Mum, Dad, Bronwyn and Spotty'. Spotty was his grey cat. He wondered if he would be in Sunshine for the next Christmas, but realized that whenever he imagined the future he saw it in England.

He was even more depressed on New Year's Eve when he still hadn't heard from Peter. He had written to him several times, trying different ploys to make him come back. He had implied that he was very independent and doing very well on his own, which he thought would make Peter want to return because Leigh would not be so dependent on him. But still there was no response from Peter.

Despite his depression, Leigh managed to make four resolutions:

1. Get his weight down to twelve stone.
2. Learn as much as possible.
3. Establish himself in either fashion, art or writing.
4. Wear make-up every day.

Leigh's first resolution was never achieved, despite his constantly going on crash diets: as soon as they were over he would stuff his face with about ten burgers, which undid all his good work. He thought that if he was thinner, Peter might fancy him more. The second resolution was kept for the rest of Leigh's life: he never lost his thirst for learning and he soaked up knowledge at every opportunity. He began to realize the third resolution later in the year when he got involved in fashion, and as for the fourth resolution, he stuck to it rigidly. Even if you thought Leigh had no make-up on, if you took a closer look you would see traces of blusher, powder and white eyeliner.

At the beginning of January 1981, Leigh suspected he had pubic crabs. He was terribly worried and didn't know what to do, but finally plucked up the courage to go along to the clap clinic at St Mary's Hospital, Paddington. He liked the no-nonsense English way in which he was dealt with, but suffered the most devastating embarrassment of his life when he had to pick up the lotion from the hospital pharmacy. The pharmacist decided to explain in a very loud voice, so that everybody could hear, exactly what Leigh should do with the lotion: 'Rub it into [your] hairy and bushy parts and leave it there for a couple of hours.' It seems strange now that Leigh could be embarrassed by such a simple statement, considering what he was to go on to do in later life. He also suffered further humiliation when he was handed another bottle for 'his girlfriend'. Despite his embarrassment, Leigh felt that he had really achieved something by going and wrote to all his friends back home boasting of his infestation.

On 20 January, Leigh finally ventured to one of the nightclubs he had longed to go to. He was too scared to go to the Blitz, as he thought he might not get in, so he went to the Great Wall which, he had read in *Time Out*, had taken over from the Blitz as the home of the New Romantics. It was a poor copy, though, because nothing is ever as good as the original. He saw a couple of the faces that he had read about, including stylist Kim Bowen and the designer Stephen Linard, who were original Blitz kids, but they looked bored and the club was not brimming with atmosphere. Leigh wore a stunning outfit of a gold brocade blouse, grey breeches, white stockings and black slippers. But he was particularly proud of his hair, which at this stage was bleached blond. He had rolled up the sides so that they made a curl on either side of his head, like two sausages, and had finished the look off with a black velvet headband. He was very pleased to have been photographed twice, but for all the two and a half hours he was there he didn't speak to anyone. He decided that in the future he 'shouldn't drink so much' because it made him tired and lethargic. At this time he was very unused to alcohol and a couple of pints would make him sleepy.

The next day he decided to do something more cultural, so he went to the National Gallery. He joined a tour led by Maggi Hambling, who was the artist-in-residence at the time. Leigh found it very informative as she talked about her favourite paintings and explained some of her own. She said that she had painted one of the wardens, and Leigh decided he too would like to be an artist's model. But that was not to come to pass until several years later, and then for an artist a lot more famous than Maggi Hambling.

By now Leigh's money was beginning to run out and he decided that he really had to get a job, although he used every excuse he could think of to put it off. He also thought that having a job would be a way of making friends. He was really missing human company now that Peter had gone. His ideal job would have been to work in the costume department of the National Opera or the BBC, but those jobs were hard to come by, so he settled for a job at Burger King in the Strand. He joined as a crew member and had to do all the basic cooking and serving. He thoroughly enjoyed his first day, although he found his mind wandering during training when they were shown five films extolling the virtues of Burger King. He soon picked up the work and found that the first day went very quickly and that he really enjoyed talking to people again even if they weren't quite his intellectual match.

By the third day the novelty was beginning to wear off and Leigh was bemoaning the fact that he wasn't working in the fashion industry and the people he worked with had no idea about fashion or style. But he stuck it out and even made a few friends. Most of the people who worked there seemed to be in the same boat as Leigh. They were alone in London, foreign, and even if they had lived in London for a while they couldn't seem to get jobs anywhere else.

After a couple of weeks another Australian who worked there, Peter Miller, asked Leigh to share his bedsit. Leigh had by now found out that Peter Koutsoumbas was in America and would not be returning, so he decided he might as well take up the offer, although he was rather nervous of sharing with a more or less total stranger. He wanted to get his deposit back from his landlady, so he told her that his dad had had a heart attack and he had to return to Australia immediately.

He then moved into the bedsit at 133 Gloucester Terrace, Bayswater, with his new friend. It was very cramped: two single beds in one room with just a small kitchen and bathroom off the main room. He soon settled in and because he worked the night shift at Burger King and Peter worked days they hardly saw each other, and it gave Leigh the chance to do his sewing in the daytime.

Leigh was never sure if he liked Peter or not, because he thought he was rather boring but they got on in a superficial kind of way. His main worry was going to the toilet when Peter was in. He was very worried that Peter might be able to hear him, so he decided to train himself to go without feeling embarrassed. (His training obviously worked, as his behaviour in the next few years showed.) Meanwhile, the flat became a refuge for the waifs and strays of Burger King. Leigh had become friendly with a couple of girls who worked there. One of them was having terrible trouble with her flatmate, who Leigh was shocked to discover got drunk on half a bottle of vodka and brought strange men home for a shag. One night when Leigh got home from his shift he found her on the doorstep, so he let her come into the flat. He kindly slept on the floor while she slept in his bed. The next night when he got in, he was very surprised to find her in bed with Peter.

For the next month he got on with his job, just mixing with the people there. He made friends with a Malaysian couple and liked to go to their house so that he could practise the Malayan he had learnt at school. Sometimes he went to the cinema and one night he went with two of the girls to an all-night showing of John Waters' films at the Scala in Goodge Street, where he saw *Female Trouble*, *Pink Flamingos* and *Desperate Living*. This was the first time he had seen Divine, the brilliant drag actor and singer, who was to be a great influence for the rest of his life. Several years later we went round to Michael and Gerlinde Kostiff's house to see Gerlinde's slides of India. To our great excitement Divine was there, dressed in a floor-length mink coat. I had to sit at his feet but the slides had sent him to sleep and as he dreamt, he kept kicking my back. He only woke up when Michael mentioned there was a cake in the kitchen: I have never seen a person so big move so fast. Eventually all of John Waters' films came out on video and you knew when Leigh had been watching them because for the next three days he would practically become Divine.

Leigh still wasn't happy with the calibre of his friends. Although he quite liked them, they weren't the people he had come all the way to England to mix with. He wanted to meet the arty, trendy crowd who knew what was happening and where the action was. He later told an Australian newspaper about his arrival in London: 'I spent all my time finding out which were the most interesting clubs; I'd even ask interesting-looking people on buses where they went! They must have thought I was a loony.'

At this time Leigh was very keen on saving money and he took to shoplifting. He stole books from the National Gallery bookshop to feed his hunger for knowledge. He liked the thrill and never worried about the moral issue. It was only when he got caught a couple of years later that he stopped. He also nicked little things he needed, such as a couple of blank tapes from Woolworths to send messages back to his parents. But when he had taped the message he played it back and realized he couldn't send it because he sounded too 'queeny'.

He hadn't discussed his sexuality with any of his new friends and was surprised when a girl at work made a move on him. He only wanted friendship and he made this clear, yet he was jealous when she turned her affections to another crew member. One night on the late shift a girl asked him if he was gay, and he admitted that he was. She had never met a homosexual before and was very interested in what they actually did. Leigh told her in full detail but then he felt a bit ashamed, so, to make himself seem less of a pervert, he invented terrible stories about all the other staff there, particulariy a black lad who Leigh was interested in because he had never met a black person before. He invented stories of incest and bestiality, lesbianism and troilism. When he got home he wondered what had come over him and dreaded the other staff finding out what he had said about them.

Leigh was still doing all he could to save money, and was con-tinually pinching his flatmate's food. When Peter confronted him about the missing breakfast cereal, he admitted he had taken a handful once – though in reality he had eaten about half of every box that had been bought. He also devised a way to pay only 40p for his tube journey home rather than £1.40. It made the journey three times as long and involved changing at several different stations but he thought it was worth it.

At the beginning of April, Leigh at last received a letter from Peter Koutsoumbas. He was friendly in the letter and although it confirmed that he wasn't coming back, at least Leigh felt that it was Peter's parents that had dragged him home rather than Leigh driving him there. This made him feel much better and motivated him to write a letter back begging Peter to return to London.

Something quite exciting was about to happen in Leigh's otherwise dreary life. As he worked the night shift he hadn't returned to any nightclubs since his visit to the Great Wall. Peter Miller had decided that they should go to Paris to celebrate his birthday, and they planned the trip with another girl from work. Leigh realized that there was a branch of Burger King in the Champs-Elysées and decided he wanted to work there. This would be the answer to all his problems. He went to bed excited at the prospect of his new life in Paris, but when he woke up he thought about it in greater depth and realized he would be worse off than in London, where he had made hardly any friends but at least he could speak the language. He imagined that he would have even less luck if he had to speak in a strange tongue.

Despite not transferring his job, the trip to Paris went ahead as planned. Leigh was thrilled by the size of the ferry and thoroughly enjoyed the trip across the Channel. It was the first time he had been to a city where they didn't speak English and it was new and exciting. He trudged around the streets for twelve hours a day looking at everything and soaking up all the sounds and smells of this new culture.

Sadly, it was soon time to return to his humdrum life in England, and he realized that things would have to change, so he made four more resolutions:

5. Apply to St Martin's School of Art for a fashion course.
6. Get a new job in a wardrobe department.
7. Write a romantic novel.
8. Learn to drive so he could explore the rest of England, Scotland and Wales.

He discovered that he was eligible to apply for St Martin's but he would have to pay his own fees and he wouldn't get a grant because he had been in England less than three years. He decided to apply anyway and threw together a very flimsy portfolio in less than two weeks. Should he have been accepted, he would have deferred for three years. But the problem did not arise, as his work failed to impress the interviewers. The other resolutions he failed to implement.

Things at the flat were getting worse. Leigh was really beginning to hate Peter, not for any particular reason except that he got on his nerves, and he often wrote in his diary about his loathing of him. Whenever Peter wasn't at home Leigh nosed through all his belongings and read all his mail. He was horrified when Peter accused him of this, but even more horrified when Peter admitted to reading Leigh's diary. Leigh did not think that it was possible, because if it had been the other way round and he had read what he had written about Peter, about himself, he would never have talked to the other person again, let alone in a perfectly civil manner. Leigh really did not want to believe he had read it, because all his innermost thoughts were in there – all his pretentiousness about the fashion scene, all his hopes for the future, all his misery in the present. But Peter had read it, as he proved when he quoted great chunks from it.

Leigh decided it was time to change his living arrangements. In July 1981 he moved to Queensborough Terrace, a few streets away from the room he shared with Peter Miller. It was much more stylish than his old place and had attractive wooden panelling on the walls and fairly substantial furniture. Although he had moved away from Peter he still had to work with him, and was even a bit jealous of him as he had been made assistant manager. Leigh was then offered a trainee management position himself. It was at this point that he realized he had better leave Burger King. He had got no further in his quest for fame and fortune and if he became a manager he might stay there forever and never fulfil his dreams. However, he decided to stay on a bit longer as a trusted crew member because he had discovered a way of fiddling the till so that he made an extra £50 a night, and that amount of money was hard to give up.

An event was soon to take place that would change Leigh's life and set him on the path that he wanted to follow. While he was scouring the listings magazines for hip and happening events he stumbled across an advert for the Alternative Miss World Competition. This was an event that was held every other year by the artist Andrew Logan. Entrants (usually Andrew's friends) would dress up in a variety of outlandish costumes hoping to be crowned the winner. Leigh decided that he must go, as he would be bound to meet all the people he had read about. He got dressed up and set off on his own. He was a bit lost at first, but loved looking at the costumes and the London 'in' crowd enjoying themselves. While

Leigh was in the toilets he was approached by a man in drag who was actually friendly to him. It was Yvette the Conqueror, who was well-known on the alternative cabaret circuit. Yvette was a friendly kind of chap and he let Leigh wander around the club with him. He gave him his phone number and invited him to dinner. A week later, Leigh went round to Yvette's house dressed in flared trousers and clutching a gent's handbag. It was a pleasant evening, with Yvette playing the grand host and Leigh feeling nervous, but trying to be as charming as possible.

Yvette enjoyed Leigh's company, and after a couple of dinner dates took him to Club for Heroes. This club was held at the Barracuda in Baker Street. It was hosted by Steve Strange and was his latest venture after the closure of the Blitz in summer 1981. Years later Leigh told his musical collaborator, Richard Torry, how excited he was to finally discover the scene he had been looking for.

> Steve Strange was my number one idol, we arrived at the club and Kim Bowen was at the door looking fantastic, a bit like Queen Elizabeth the First. Steve was downstairs and I couldn't believe it when Yvette introduced me to him. All my fantasies had come true. After half an hour Yvette said we were off, so we got into a cab. Even that I thought was really exciting and we drove past all the famous sights of London until we reached a dirty alley near Charing Cross Station. I thought I was going to be mugged but instead we went into the best place I had ever been – ChaChas. I spotted lots of the people I had only read about, Stephen Linard again and Judy Blame the jewellery designer. It was even more amazing than I had imagined. Then to cap it all Yvette took me through a door into the most spectacular place – the main nightclub itself – Heaven.

Heaven is Europe's most famous gay club and is situated beneath Charing Cross Station. It is a cavernous club that is always heaving with people (mainly men) dancing to loud disco beats. There was a permanent sexual tension as the men eyed each other up to see who they could take home that night, or even have in one of the darker corners of the club. Leigh was in Heaven in more than one sense of the word. He had finally found where all the people he aspired to know hung out. People who had the same ideas as him, the same dress sense and the same twisted sense of humour. Yvette had no idea that this meeting was so important in Leigh's life. 'I didn't think much about it. I just thought that he was a nice, trendy young man; it wasn't until years later when I saw him talk about it in a magazine that I realized what a big event it was in his life. He was so ordinary then, nothing like the work of art that he was to become.'

3

Nightclubs

ChaChas was in the back room at Heaven. Instead of using the main entrance in Villiers Street, you had to queue up in Hungerford Lane, which was a very dark and dingy alley and added to the excitement of getting in. It was run by Scarlett Bordello and Maria Malla Pasta. Scarlett was a very thin girl with loads of attitude and styled herself in such an incredible way that she always looked stunning. Her hair was sometimes shaved off with just a cross left instead of a fringe, or it was bleached blonde and styled into the most incredibly high flat-top shaped into the New York skyline. Or sometimes she went more feminine and had a demi-wave effect. She was married to her hairdresser, a tall, thin, gay New Zealander called Ross who also helped run the club. Her make-up, although extreme, was always perfect, her cupid's bow lips beautifully painted in a deep shade of red we later christened 'Irresistible To Men'. She dressed in very stylish clothes that were usually made for her. Grey muslin was all the rage then, and she had a very long dress that draped around her body and dragged along the floor. She was also fond of the black studded leather jacket look. One of her trademarks was to wear dead chicken's feet as earrings, and she was usually accompanied by Cerberus, her lame dog. But despite her startling looks she was really just a normal girl from Sutton, looking for romance.

In the early eighties ChaChas was *the* place to be. It was held in an industrial type of space with scaffolding and metal staircases and had a mixed-gay clientele. These were the new young gays who liked girls and didn't want to hang out at exclusively gay bars with some dodgy drag act. Straight men liked the club because it had an easy-going atmosphere and it was much easier to get off with girls who hung around with gay men because they were usually much more open-minded about sex and were quite happy to have no-strings-attached one-night stands.

Leigh soon dropped Yvette and became a regular at ChaChas. He went along every Tuesday night. He was still working at Burger King and nicking from the till, so for once he had plenty of money. He formed an obsession with Scarlett and did everything he could to be her friend, although it didn't last long and he soon moved on to other people. He was new to the scene and was finding his feet, deciding which people he could get along best with and who could get along best with him. He found new friends of his own age and mentality, and it was here that he met Trojan, who was to become his greatest friend.

Trojan had been taken to the club by Wayne Shires (later a successful club promoter), who had met him at the Gay Teenage Group in Holloway. This was a weekly meeting where teenagers who thought they might be gay could discuss their feelings with each other and make new friends. He hadn't invented the name Trojan then, and was plain old Gary Barnes from near Croydon. Wayne was a bit embarrassed to take him along, as he looked a bit naff with his wedge haircut and Bowie peg trousers, but he had a very beautiful face and big brown eyes, loved things that were very extreme and soon became one of the most outrageous dressers in

London. Within a couple of months Leigh had persuaded Trojan to go out with Scarlett so he could get to know her better. But it all ended in tears: Scarlett hit Trojan over the head with a saucepan when she realized he was really gay.

David Walls met Leigh at ChaChas in 1982. Leigh was standing on a balcony with a very tall Canadian friend called John; they were screwing up scraps of newspaper into little balls, setting fire to them and throwing them onto the crowd below. David thought that this was very bizarre behaviour, but he ended up talking to Leigh anyway. 'We got on quite well as I had lived in Australia as a child, so Leigh saw me as a link to his past.'

By now Leigh was spending all his evenings in nightclubs. He had finally lost his job in Burger King when they discovered he was fiddling the till. As the management liked him and he had worked there for over a year, they decided not to prosecute him. He was very poor and living on the dole, which he supplemented by doing odd one-off commissions, making clothes for his friends. Before going out he would get ready, put on loud disco music, prance around the front room and have a few drinks to get himself into the mood. No one really went to the pub before going out, as it was much cheaper to go to Sainsbury's and buy whatever booze was on special offer.

All the New Romantics became fed up with making such an effort to go out, and the fashion look of the moment became its opposite – Hard Times. It was chic to be on the dole and to flaunt your newfound poverty. Ripped jeans and faded T-shirts were *de rigueur*, and it was perfectly all right to go out in your pyjamas. If you had nothing to wear that night it was easy to knock something up. I often chopped up a table cloth or a sheet and made them into a dress just before going out. For an extra-special look, or to cover up the stains, I would tie-dye them. Tailoring was no longer 'in', and neither was hemming – it was the height of fashion to slash the neck of your T-shirt or cut off the sleeves. One boy I knew carefully cut off the round necks of his T-shirts and saved them up to wear as necklaces or wristbands. The main designers at this time were Sue Clowes at the Foundry and Melissa Caplan, but mostly people made their own clothes. The look was copied by Dexys Midnight Runners for their number one single 'Come on Eileen', but they were mocked by people in the know as mere pretenders.

At this time Leigh was wearing very high-waisted baggy trousers that finished above the ankle teamed with a sweatshirt that he had made himself. His hair was short, with the ubiquitous shaved sides and a blond, spikey, back-combed fringe. This was a very popular hairstyle, especially with a sailor hat or straw trilby jauntily perched on the back of the head. At this time there was a lot of back-combing going on because there were hardly any products on the market designed to give your hair height and staying power, unlike today. Boots stocked the only setting gel available, which was a strongly scented green gloop called Country Born, but even that was often sold out. If you made the effort to go to Kensington Market you could sometimes pick up some Black and White, but that was rather greasy. Hairspray was not very sophisticated either. If you used Boots Economy it left great white flakes in your hair, so if you had come into a bit of extra cash you splashed out on a long gold can of Elnett, the queen of hairsprays.

Leigh was introduced to me by some friends I'd met a few weeks earlier, John Talbot, an antiques dealer, and his boyfriend Stephen Luscombe, a musician who was soon to find chart success with his electronic pop duo Blancmange. I had a typical shallow nightclub conversation with Leigh and didn't take much notice of him. I certainly didn't think it would be the start of such a long-lasting friendship. I think we asked each other what we did. I always had a bit of novelty value because instead of being on the dole I worked there, helping people back to work! I was impressed that Leigh was a fashion designer because that is what I had always wanted to be but had never had enough drive, ambition or talent to give it a go. Leigh was doing his favourite dance with his friend David ('Daisy') Walls: they would face each other holding their hands up in a pat-a-cake style and sway from side to side. I hadn't been going out in London long and it was a very exciting time meeting all sorts of new people.

At this time I was living in a big housing association house in Kentish Town. About six or seven of us lived there, but there were always people moving in or out, staying for periods of time ranging from a couple of days to several months. My best friend in the house was Rics, a nice-looking boy who was four years younger than me. We often used to snog but it never went further than that – we had more of a brother–sister relationship and sometimes told people we were siblings, although we looked nothing alike. He was tall, very thin and blond and I was tall, fat and brunette.

One night Rics and I and a few other friends went to Bolts, a more traditional gay disco situated in the insalubrious area of Turnpike Lane, in a club called Lasers. It was mostly frequented by queens from North London and the suburbs who couldn't be bothered to travel into the West End. The clientele were generally very neat and tidy, favouring tight jeans clinched in at the waist with a belt and maybe a checked shirt tucked in over a white T-shirt. It was hard to get checked shirts back then, so they were usually workmen's shirts from Millets, which as well as being fashionable were very cheap (of course the Hard Timers wore them with the sleeves ripped off). They tended to wear very thin-soled, grey slip-on shoes with towelling socks underneath, or if they were a bit daring they might wear a pair of highly polished Doc Martens.

At Bolts all the trendy people and Goths congregated at the front, to the right of the stage. There was a rather stout middle-aged DJ called Norman Scott (not the lover of the Liberal MP Jeremy Thorpe) who was very keen on telling the crowd to 'shake their lallies'. Most people did shake their lallies to his mixture of pop and hi-energy music, though each week the records were the same – the whole Hazell Dean repertoire, 'Mighty Real' by Sylvester and 'Menergy' by Patrick Cowley. There was none of this standing-around-looking-cool business. Everyone got off their heads as quickly as possible, and if they couldn't afford drinks, they pinched them from the out-of-towners. It couldn't be classed as a good night out unless you fell over at least once. Hangovers are not nearly so bad when you're in your early twenties. There weren't many drugs around at this time – maybe a bit of cheap speed or acid, but in general people relied on alcohol for their kicks. The 'snakebite', a delicious mix of lager and cider (sometimes made even more sophisticated by the addition of blackcurrant and, for really special occasions, Pernod), was very popular because it was relatively cheap and you got pissed very quickly.

On this particular night Rics and I had drunk about four pints each and were lying on the floor, snogging. Leigh was there, dancing in the corner, wearing an orange sweatshirt with a row of studs on the front. He couldn't believe his eyes, because he thought we were brother and sister. He was really shocked that two relatives could do such a thing, but of course he loved shocking things, so he took a shine to me and came over to chat. He didn't stand out as being particularly outrageous; he was dressed the same as all his friends and he hadn't covered his cheery, dimpled face with obvious make-up. I took an instant liking to him as he was nice and big and he seemed quite sensible and very polite.

After that we often bumped into each other at various nightclubs. It wasn't nearly such a big scene then as it is now, and you bumped into the same people about three times a week as there were only limited places to go. I gave Leigh my phone number and he called me a couple of times to see if I was going out and we arranged to meet up. He also introduced me to his best friend Trojan.

At this time I moved with Rics to a two-bedroomed council flat near Mornington Crescent. It was round the corner from where Princess Julia and Jeffrey Hinton (two stalwarts of the club scene that we had become friendly with) lived with Stephen Jones the milliner, and across the road from Stephen Linard's flat. Everyone seemed to be getting council flats at this time; they were much easier to get then, as the councils hadn't started selling them off. I got mine by sheer luck: I had phoned the housing association about a leaky sink and someone had just turned my flat down, so they asked me if I wanted it. Most people had to put a bit of effort into getting their flats, but it usually only involved a couple of visits to the doctor complaining of depression and you were soon given somewhere. Some people went to more dramatic lengths and sales of aspirin must have soared as people took overdoses just to get a flat. Trojan used arson to get him, Leigh and Daisy Walls a three-bedroomed flat in Stepney.

The three of them had just started dressing up at this point. Sheila Rock wanted to photograph them for an article in the

Face, but couldn't get hold of them. She had asked Tasty Tim (a very thin, glamorous, blond boy who recorded a glam-rock cover version of 'Sugar Sugar', which had originally been sung by the Archies) if he knew where to find them, so Tasty phoned me to see if I could get hold of them. As they had just moved they hadn't yet had a telephone installed, so I wasn't sure what to do. Should I write, as I had their address, or go round there? I had started to really like Leigh by now and decided that I wanted him to be a good friend, so after some deliberation I decided to go round to their new flat to tell them about the photo shoot. I very rarely called on people unannounced, so I was a bit nervous about just turning up. Luckily, they were in, and they were very excited by the news. The fact that I had bothered to go over there cemented our friendship and as soon as Leigh got his phone connected we chatted for hours every day, discussing the previous night's antics.

In 1983 ChaChas had reached its sell-by date, so it closed down. But its place was taken by two new clubs, the Palace and Asylum. Steve Strange, self-styled King of the New Romantics, and his partner Rusty Egan had taken over the Music Machine in Camden Town and it opened in a blaze of publicity. Steve Strange gave an unintentionally hilarious speech, saying that it was 'The People's Palace, a place for all the trendy young things to call their own'. Of course it was far too big a venue to appeal to the trendy crowd every night, and anyway those people quickly got bored and didn't want to go to the same place all the time, so it soon became a Sharon and Tracy disco, except on Tuesdays when it became the club night Slum it in Style, hosted by Steve and Rusty, with Scarlett employed to do the guest list on the door.

The Hard Times look still prevailed. It was very popular as it was very cheap and easy to wear. Studded belts and wristbands made a comeback and no one was considered properly dressed without at least one belt slung around their hips. Mesh was everywhere and girls and boys styled tops out of dyed dishcloths. String vests were very groovy worn with bleached jeans. The main colours were black, grey and white as the Hard Times look began to merge with the Goth look. Girls tended to wear straight, long jersey skirts or cotton skirts gathered at the waist and going down to mid-calf. Make-up was very pale with dark eyes and either red or black lips. If you could afford it, you might buy one piece of Vivienne Westwood to make the look even more stylish. Buffalo hats were very popular, but if you couldn't afford one it was just as glamorous to wrap a long cotton rag around your back-combed or crimped home-dyed locks. Of course, some people still took things to extremes. For a couple of months Jeffrey Hinton had false, floor-length blond extensions that twirled around him as he threw himself around the dance floor. On one occasion Jimmy Fox, who was one half of the Trindys along with Paul Darberson, once turned up completely covered in mud. Their act was made all the more bizarre by their differences in height: Jimmy was about five foot three and Paul was a good twelve inches taller. They did fantastic cover versions of popular songs, like 'Can't Keep the Pressure Cooker On', a parody of the old Spandau Ballet classic.

Leigh and Trojan were regular attenders at the Palace and enjoyed the attention they got from their freaky fashions. They had moved on from Hard Times and returned to a more glamorous look. Leigh had been too scared to wear the new look out at first, and had made Trojan debut it. Leigh dressed and styled him. Trojan wore a long satin robe with a big star on the front, stripy tights, painted platform boots and a tall hat with a bit of hair from an old wig he had found stuck on the back to make it look like he had flowing locks. He covered his whole face in blue, green or red make-up and stuck sequins on top, or he would sometimes paint extra features on, like a Picasso painting. He might paint a profile of a nose in green paint next to his real nose or extend his mouth about an inch to one side. He would complete the look with various bits of cheap Indian jewelry that they bought down Brick Lane, such as stick-on nose rings with a chain that went to the ear. (This was about ten years before facial piercings became ordinary.) Cameras always started flashing when Trojan was dressed in this fantastic new style. Leigh got a bit jealous and thought that as he had developed the look he should get the credit, so about two weeks after Trojan he too became what he famously dubbed a 'Paki from Outer Space'. (He chose the name as a tribute to Brick Lane, where he gained most of his inspiration.) Leigh still hadn't developed his later truly outrageous personality and tended to wander around the Palace clutching his pint of weak lager while Trojan trailed behind drinking a Bacardi and Coke, which he liked to think was a little bit more sophisticated.

The Palace's stage often featured such acts as Divine, Frankie Goes to Hollywood and Malcolm McLaren's Double Dutch Dancers. Every other week there seemed to be an appearance from Rusty Egan's androgynous protégée 'Ronnie', but despite all this free publicity, she still failed to have a hit. Leigh loved to torment her by shouting 'Ronnie' every time she paraded past him with her nose in the air.

One week there was a fashion show, and Leigh was asked to show his latest collection. He had kept a stall in Kensington Market for a while, but he hated repetition, so he had given it up to make one-off garments mainly for himself and his friends. His collection basically consisted of what he and Trojan had worn the previous few weeks. Leigh tended to leave everything to the last minute because he was always so worn out from the previous night's exertions and he rolled up at about 11.30 p.m., after everyone had given up on him, clutching armfuls of clothes. His friends acted as models and they strutted their stuff on the runway to the acclaim of the crowd. It wasn't meant as a chance to sell anything, just a chance to show off. However, he was upstaged at the end, when the very drunk comedian Peter Cook clambered onto the empty catwalk and did some exotic dancing to the loud cheers and jeers of the crowd.

Sometimes there was a talent night for various alternative cabaret acts. One week it was won by 'Fat Tony', a rather plump and very confident fifteen-year-old. He had started a drag act called the 'Diana Dogg Show', which involved him and his cohorts miming on a certain theme to old pop records. As he did not want to be the fattest person in the show he coerced me into joining in and we soon became regular performers. He worked hard to make the shows entertaining and for the grand sum of £10 each (if we were lucky) we entertained the cheering crowds with 'The Indian Show', 'The Sixties Show', 'The Hawaiian Show' and the marvellous 'Disco Show', which featured Princess Julia and I body-popping while wearing dresses made out of shower curtains and pill-box hats made from Rank Xerox boxes. Leigh and Trojan were always in the crowd, clapping and whooping with the others.

The magazine *i-D* was the self-proclaimed style bible of the day, and for me it is like a personal diary of these times. Every month it was full of pictures of friends, and once you had appeared in its pages you could feel that you had really arrived on the scene! Leigh first appeared in Issue 18 in September 1984. He and Trojan are shown with Victoria Fernandez at DoDo's, which was a monthly Monday club held at Busby's in the Charing Cross Road. It was run by Vaughn Toulouse (who had a chart hit in 1981 with his group Department S) and Nick Trulocke (a professional entrepreneur). The door girls were Caryn Franklin, who was to go on to present the BBC's *Clothes Show*, and Kathryn Flett, who became associate editor of the *Observer* magazine and later starred in the BBC's *Grumpy Old Women*. This was less of a place for posing, more for having a good time dancing to disco classics. The *i-D* photographers would snap people they thought looked interesting and then ask them a couple of questions about themselves. In their *i-D* debut, Trojan says he 'takes his influences from Leigh Bowery and values nothing'. Leigh says he is 'Very spiritual. The cosmic and I are one.' In the photograph he is looking particularly cosmic, wearing an orange shirt with massive pockets and collar. His face is painted blue with massive false gold eyelashes stuck to his eyebrows. He has a line of Indian bindis beneath each eye and a pearl chain going from his nose to his ear. His podgy, beringed fingers are clutching a can of Heineken.

In 1985, *i-D* had their fifth anniversary party at the Institute of Contemporary Arts. There were lots of rooms with different things going on in them. Upstairs there was a free Smirnoff bar that seemed to have been deserted. Leigh and I crept round the back and found several cases of vodka. We grabbed one each and handed them out to our friends, Judy Blame, Richard Habberley (Boy George's flatmate) and Louise Neel, who had been arguing with Leigh. He didn't like her because she was my friend and he did his best to dislike as many of my friends as he could. He also hated the way she argued back when he picked on her. We hit the dance floor big time, and were running all over the place to the retro sounds of Vaughn Toulouse, who was spinning the discs. Leigh then decided to listen to the jazz band who were playing in one of the upstairs rooms. But it was too quiet and civilized in there for Leigh, who decided to make things go with a swing, jumping up on the stage, getting his dick out and masturbating furiously. Unfortunately, because he had drunk so much he was unable to control his bladder, and a stream of piss showered over the audience. An ICA official witnessed all this, grabbed him and escorted him from the building, banning him for life. He later did many art performances involving piss and was asked back to the ICA as a celebrity speaker on art and fashion.

Heaven had noticed the success of ChaChas, so they decided to make the whole of Heaven 'alternative' on a Thursday night. They called the night Asylum. It was very popular with the same people who went to the Camden Palace on a Tuesday, though it was much darker than the Palace and had a different, less sophisticated atmosphere, so there weren't so many of the pop stars. But it was still great fun and it was a better place to dance because the lights were more technically advanced. They also sold poppers at the club. As soon as you sniffed from the little bottle of amyl nitrate you entered a different plane, and you thought that you were the greatest dancer on the planet. The music filled every cell of your body and for a couple of minutes you could do anything. As the bottle was passed around, the dancing got more and more frantic and you felt an enormous warmth for the people you were dancing with. My friend Louise Neel, who was quite plump like me, and

I perfected a fantastic dance called the 'Double Deckers', which really just involved us dancing madly and then bashing into each other with our bountiful hips. This always made Leigh scream with laughter and he would encourage me to bump into Louise a bit harder, as they never really got on.

This was still the early eighties and no one was really overly concerned about their careers. It was completely normal to dance all night, get up at about eleven or twelve the next day, do a bit of work and then go out again. Many of the regular nightclubbers of these times have since become very successful in their chosen careers, but in those days work ethic was hardly at the front of most people's minds. I was about the only person I knew with a proper job, and I still don't know how I managed to get up to go to work on time.

Iain R. Webb, the fashion journalist, was a regular at Asylum, as were his friends Paul Bernstock the milliner and Greg Davis the fashion designer. The BodyMap duo of David Holah and Stevie Stewart were always on the dance floor. I was thrilled to become friends with David because before I knew who he was I used to see him working every weekend on his stall in Camden Lock, where I used to stare at him and think that he was one of the best-looking boys I had ever seen. He had long hair, which was unusual then, and plaited it so that instead of going down his back it went the other way, making a kind of quiff on top of his head. He was short and slight and had a lovely smile with beautiful white teeth. He and his friend Lesley Chilkes (who became a top make-up artist) were very fond of the poppers. At this time David was going out with John Maybury, another very good-looking man who won the MTV best overall video award in 1990 for directing Sinead

O'Connor's 'Nothing Compares 2 U' and went on to make prize-winning underground films.

Among the other regulars at Asylum were Cerith Wyn Evans (now a renowned installation artist, who shows at London's White Cube Gallery), who is tall and lanky, very well-spoken and used to be particularly keen on wearing a striped pair of Stephen Linard dungarees. Stephen Linard was himself an avid clubber. He was very skinny with particularly round eyes that popped out of his head as he told you about his days as a superstud at the Goldmine Disco on Canvey Island, his home town. He became a successful designer in the UK and Japan and used to enjoy boasting that he earned more than Mrs Thatcher. Princess Julia was a very beautiful girl who wore her own special Hard Times look. She wore about three stripy skirts of different lengths with little muslin blouses and old cardigans knotted over the top. She had incredible hair, which she back-combed so much that it formed a coconut on top of her head. Eventually she had to shave it off as it was impossible to brush out. She always had lovely make-up, beautifully applied. Her voluminous skirts came in very handy: she didn't want to get scabs around her nose from sniffing poppers, so she used to put the ragged hem of her skirt over the neck of the bottle and then inhale the noxious fumes through her mouth. Baillie Walsh (a top male model at the time) used to go to Heaven and the Palace. He was always a bit fancy, as he used to walk around in flashy Antony Price suits with a blond wedge, but everyone liked him because he was so good-looking and he was quick to take the mickey out of himself. (He is now a brilliant director and filmmaker who has recently directed the amazing ABBA Voyage.)

Leigh was delighted to meet and befriend all these people, who had been at the top of the club hierarchy since their days as the original Blitz Kids who started the New Romantic movement. In time, many of them involved Leigh in their work and cited him as an influence. Leigh also ended up collaborating with them on many of his future projects.

Probably the most influential person he met at this time was the angel-faced darling of the dance world, Michael Clark. Michael first became aware of Leigh and his friends at the Circus. This was a party night run by Patrick Lilley, Annie Le Paz and Jeremy Healy (from pop band Haysi Fantayzee) at a variety of venues. A huge effort was put into finding different and new locations, and a lot of time and imagination went into the Circus's decoration. They liked to make it difficult to get hold of tickets so it seemed more special when you were there. There were various phone numbers to ring to find out the exact venue, a trick borrowed for the M25 rave parties in the early nineties. On the night when Leigh met Michael, the Circus was held at a disused barracks in Victoria. Leigh, Trojan and David Walls arrived accompanied by Space Princess (a dancer whose real name was Peter Hammond), who had been on the club scene longer and therefore held more clout with the so-called 'in' crowd. They were all dressed alike in long robes and tall hats. The photographers went crazy as they arrived, and their pictures appeared in the *Evening Standard* and various teen magazines.

Honey magazine printed the first picture of the four of them together with the caption:

They said it could never happen, but this picture provides conclusive proof that the glam revival is just around the corner. These four bright young things were snapped at London's hipper than hip Circus. What the well-dressed street socialite will soon be wearing may come as a shock, though. Platforms should be no lower than three inches and preferably snakeskin or glitter-encrusted. Lurex tights are optional, as are the wet-look plastic jackets, but seemingly *de rigueur* for '84 is that oversized, painted or studded plastic cap.

Michael was at the party with his friend Leslie Bryant, a dancer who was usually called Les Child due to the way he addressed everyone as 'child'. He was short, black, camp and very witty and friendly. He didn't know who these strangely dressed people were, thinking them 'a bit naff', and only took any notice at all because Space Princess was with them. Michael, on the other hand, was mesmerized. He thought they looked truly fantastic and was desperate to meet them, especially Leigh. He and Les went over to speak to them and Les was soon won over when he realized how polite and intelligent Leigh was, expecting him to be a typically queeny show-off with nothing to say except bitchy remarks. Leigh and Michael became firm friends. They were thrilled to find in each other a willing partner to shock not only their friends but the establishment too.

Michael had recently left the Ballet Rambert and was establishing himself as the greatest new dancer Britain had seen for a long time. As well as dancing, he was beginning to choreograph revolutionary new pieces for himself and other performers.

Michael and Leigh soon began to hang out together, freaking out on the dance floors of the various clubs. In those days everywhere shut by 3 a.m., which seemed way too early because most people didn't arrive until past midnight. When the lights went up, you were left with nowhere to go unless you went and hung out at someone's house. Then somebody discovered a fantastic place that stayed open until 7 a.m. It was above a seedy peep-show parlour in Wardour Street and was called the Pink Panther. You had to climb up three rickety flights of stairs and then pay your £1 entry fee to a dubious-looking man on the door. You then found yourself in a tiny, shabby room with a bar at one end (where a can of Pils only cost £1), a dance floor in the middle and a DJ box at the other end. The DJ was a chubby, plain bloke with a Gary Glitter fetish who did Gary impressions on a makeshift stage made of two milk crates.

The Pink Panther had a very mixed clientele because it was originally a rent boy hang-out, and they still stood about, leaning against the walls in their tight jeans and blond wedge hairdos. Then the trendy crowd took over and danced the night away to disco classics. It was a fantastic venue and the fact that it was regularly raided gave it an added glamour.

A typical night out with Leigh might involve walking there after Asylum. On one night I remember, Leigh, Trojan and Michael had taken acid and were still tripping on the way there. For once the club wasn't particularly full, so there was plenty of room to dance. Leigh was desperate to go to the toilet, but as usual the loos were full of couples having sex, so Leigh ripped a poster of the eighties pop band Kajagoogoo from the wall, put it on the floor, squatted over it, crapped on Limahl's face and then called it a work of art. This was the first time he had defecated in public and it was a precursor of his later acclaimed work as a performance artist.

One night, Lisa the Teaser, a Vietnamese trans woman who was at all the clubs, was treating the audience to a special cabaret performance. At about 6 a.m. the manager decided to shut up because there were only about twenty people left. Michael didn't want to go home, so he led the dregs that were still there in a rousing chorus of caterwauling, after which the manager got so sick of us we were all banned for two weeks.

We sat in the gutter outside wondering what to do next. Fat Tony found some pills in a puddle, so he stuffed them into his mouth. Luckily they were only bran tablets. Then Michael and Les Child started dancing down the street as if they were in a Hollywood movie, leaping and pirouetting in and out of the parked cars in perfect unison. It was one of the most beautiful things I have ever seen. Leigh and Trojan were screaming with joy at the excitement of the performance. Unfortunately, later, when Michael slid down the metal section between the escalators to get the first tube home, he damaged his back on the 'Keep to the Right' signs and was unable to dance for a couple of months.

The Pink Panther stayed open over Christmas 1983, and most of the regular clubbers were there on both Christmas and Boxing Day nights. Somehow or other we found our way into the peep-show booths and Leigh did a marvellous striptease for everyone's entertainment. Then he and Fat Tony found the drinks cupboard. Leigh kicked it in with one of his platforms and whisked a couple of crates of lager into the back of someone's car.

By early 1984 there were plenty of other club nights going on. On Fridays, Philip Sallon ran the Mud Club. Philip liked to appeal to the trendy folk, but his club was usually full of rock-a-billy types from the suburbs. Sometimes Leigh and Trojan went anyway because they liked dancing to the old disco records played by Mark Moore (who would later form dance act S-Express). It was on the way there one night, when I had known Leigh a couple of months, that I discovered he was Australian. Because he thought it was so uncool to come from Australia he had quickly learnt to speak in a cockney accent, and he'd done such a good job I hadn't noticed. But he was gabbling really quickly and I suddenly heard the Australian slip out. I was very shocked that I hadn't noticed before and for ten minutes he tried to deny it, but eventually told me the story of his arrival from Sunshine.

Another popular night spot was White Trash at Planets in Piccadilly, on Saturday nights. Small and intimate, it gave you the chance to chat to people; it was run by Dencil Williams and Paul Bernstock. You used to get an interesting mix of people down there: trendies, some rich Arabs who got the day wrong, and a number of celebrities. It was here that Leigh famously (and probably apocryphally) bumped into Mick Jagger on the dance floor. When Jagger rudely commented 'Fuck off Freak', Leigh snapped back with 'Fuck off Fossil'.

Throughout these times, there were always one-off clubs and parties. One Friday night we heard of a club being held at the Camden Tiger in Kentish Town Road. The venue was a health club and the party was to be held in the saunas and Jacuzzis. This sounded exciting, so Trojan, Leigh, Michael Clark, his boyfriend Richard Habberley and I piled into a cab. It was wonderful sitting in the sauna, jumping into the cold-dip bath, then relaxing in the Jacuzzi. As we got drunker we got less inhibited and by the end of the night all five of us had stripped off and were lying naked in the bubbles, with Leigh and Trojan's false eyelashes and sequins bobbing up and down on the top of the, by now, very dirty water. Needless to say we had frightened everyone else away.

Leigh inevitably began to think about opening a club of his own, having been to so many and thinking that since he spent practically every evening in a club he might as well earn some money by running one himself. He was just waiting for the right opportunity to arise.

4

Taboo

Early in January 1985, Leigh was approached by Tony Gordon to open a club night with him. Tony had tried to run some nightclubs before, but they weren't very successful. He was a very short, light-skinned black man, always smartly dressed, with a penchant for large overcoats. He had a strange way of speaking, almost lisping but not quite. He wanted to open a club but he knew that he didn't have enough clout on his own to make a go of it, so he enlisted the help of Leigh, who would be the public face of the club. Leigh was very excited by Tony's proposition because it seemed to tie in exactly with what he had been thinking about. Tony also involved a girl called Angela, who was commonly known as Angela Frankie because she had danced with Frankie Goes to Hollywood. She had been in the original, banned video for 'Relax', and anywhere or any time it was played she would get up and dance to it.

Tony had discovered a small nightclub in Leicester Square. It hadn't been used for a fashionable club night before and it seemed the ideal premises. It was centrally situated, and it was exactly the right size – not too big but not pokey. It also had extremely and perfectly tacky decor. There was an entrance lobby, then a flight of stairs down to the cloakroom and toilets. When you entered the club it had everything you could want from a disco: tatty red velour banquettes, mirrors everywhere, strange light effects on the walls, three bars and a central dance floor with several cheap lights and a mirror ball.

The opening night was set for 31 January. Leigh was very excited and as neither he nor Tony had any money to get flyers printed, he decided to make them himself. He cut out photos of naked men from his vast supply of pornographic magazines, stuck them onto bits of card, then stencilled Taboo over the top in gold paint. They had picked the name Taboo because it epitomized everything that Leigh loved. On the back of the card he printed the time and place using a John Bull printing set. He distributed these to his friends at the many clubs he attended before the opening night.

Mark Lawrence, Jeffrey Hinton and Rachel Auburn were the DJs. Jeffrey had worked as a DJ for a long time and was well known for his video scratch mixing. He enjoyed a drink and liked to throw himself around the dance floors of London. Mark Lawrence was a handsome boy and a gifted tailor. Mark Vaultier was chosen to do the door. He had a very extreme look and was fond of wearing cheap, woollen wigs teamed with Leigh's garish clothes, which because he was tall and thin always seemed to hang off him. He was thrilled to be on the London club circuit, which was very different from his background as the son of a high-ranking army officer. A girl called Alex who worked with Rachel was on the till. Princess Julia and Malcolm Duffy worked in the cloakroom and were allowed to keep all the money they made, often going home with about £50 each, the only problem being that it was all in 50p pieces. Both went on to be very successful DJs. The only friend of Tony Gordon's who worked there was Max, who did the lights. Leigh's idea, naturally, was to make it the place to be seen. The policy was simple: 'Dress as though your life depends on it, or don't bother. We'll only let in fabulous, over-the-top dressers and stars. We can sniff out phonies and weekend trendies a mile away.'

Tony had negotiated a very good deal with the management of the club. They had to pay them £315 per night, and after that all the takings were Leigh's, Tony's and Angela's. All the people they employed were to be paid about £50 total, which was very generous at the time. Before the opening night Leigh's excitement reached fever pitch. He was constantly on the phone telling me the latest developments and who had promised to come down.

I had been ill for the whole of January and didn't really know what was wrong with me, so I doubted if I would be well enough to go to the opening night. The matter was resolved for me when I collapsed and was whisked into hospital, so that at the very moment the club opened I was under the surgeon's knife having a cyst the size of a grapefruit removed from my ovary.

By all accounts the first night was quite a success and although not incredibly full, the trash disco music being played was very popular and everyone got down and boogied. Later Les Child said, 'It was all right but I didn't like the space and there certainly wasn't the buzz that came about two months later.'

Even if it wasn't a mega success, Leigh was still thrilled, as he had made some money. He came to see me in the hospital the next day with such a bad hangover he tried to get in the bed with me to sleep it off. He was also excited because *i-D* magazine had called him and wanted to do a photo shoot of him and his crowd for their 'Flesh and Blood' issue in April 1985. So Leigh rounded up a group of his friends, including Trojan, David Walls, Rachel, Mark, Annie

Le Paz, a French girl called Valerie, Jimmy Payne and George Gallagher. They all dressed up in Leigh's creations and gave their opinions on life and make-up.

RACHEL: I'm wearing the glamour look – foundation cover stick, aquacolour and powder. My lips are brown stage light pencil filled in with three different shades of lipstick. Pink powder, a little mascara with eye pencil and violet powder. In general men have no idea of how to look beautiful. Lipstick is the most versatile make-up piece and you should never be without it – you can use it for eyeshadow, blusher, shadow and of course for your lips.

TROJAN: If I had a big spot I'd squeeze it and then cover it with make-up. At the moment I am wearing foundation, black aquacolour and lip seal. I wear make-up very well, but most men do it very tackily … [Greta] Garbo used it best. Clinique is the best skin preparation – believe me I need it – I've got really bad skin.

This article was one of many that began to appear in the press, which led to the great success of Taboo. Originally the club night was only going to be held every other week, but it soon became so successful that it took place every Thursday. The queues outside would get longer and longer, so that by 10.30 p.m. there would be a big gaggle of Japanese girls hanging around outside along with fashion victims who hadn't yet realized that it was not cool to be at a club before midnight. Mark had started giving out a lot of atti-tude on the door and if he didn't like the look of someone he would hold up a mirror to their face and say, 'Would you let yourself in?' Terrible stories used to go around about people being crushed to death in the queue, and it was once rumoured that a girl had died of starvation on the steps because she had been on a crash diet to make herself beautiful enough to be allowed in.

After the first couple of weeks Leigh and Tony decided to sack Angela because they thought that they could manage perfectly well without her and they would make more money if there wasn't a third partner. Leigh was not the money-grabbing type, though, and if they made a lot of money on the door, he gave all the staff bonuses, so they often used to earn about £100 a night, which in those dole-queue times seemed like a fortune.

When one of the club's regular bouncers left, Leigh decided to employ Nicky Crane, a very tough bisexual skinhead. He was often at Heaven showing off his massive tattooed torso and flirting with all the boys. He had been leader of a very big gang and had a scrapbook full of newspaper cuttings about his misdemeanours. He was half Italian and his first name was Nicola, so many of the reports said that he was a she, which made his exploits seem even more shocking. He had tattoos all over his body, including an 'S' on his penis; it was originally going to say 'Suck on This' but it was too painful to continue. Nicky was thrilled to have a proper job and I went with him to Lawrence Corner to buy a cheap tuxedo. However, when *City Limits* magazine found out he was working for Taboo, they wrote a very derogatory article about the club saying they employed fascists, which thrilled Leigh as he loved controversy and in his book any publicity was good publicity.

By now I was doing the cash till on alternate weeks with Alex. The club opened at about 11 p.m. and I never really knew the first people in. Leigh didn't mind letting in a few unfashionable people because they usually left early and they paid, which was more than most people did. The guest list was incredibly long. I typed it up for Leigh and every week we used to put in joke names just so the bouncers got excited because they really thought that Des O'Connor or Joan Collins might come down. It would not have been that surprising if they had, because the club night soon became a big celebrity hang-out. I would look up and see Boy George, Bryan Ferry, Paul Young or George Michael waiting to come in. After midnight the regulars began to fall in, some not appearing until 2 a.m., if they had been to a party first or had just taken a long time to get ready. People used to come out with every tale under the sun to try to get in free. Sometimes I used to take pity on them. One night Paul Simper came in. He was working as a journalist on the pop magazine *No. 1* at the time, which was a poor person's *Smash Hits*. He had a couple of mates with him and they all pleaded poverty; they offered to get their dicks out if I'd let them in free. I was only too happy to agree and was in hysterics when they unzipped their flies and plonked their plonkers on the desk.

Another bonus of working was that I got paid, and on Friday nights Leigh and I would spend our newfound wealth in what we thought were classy restaurants – Peppermint Park or Café Pacifico. They were very sophisticated compared to our usual haunt of Garfunkel's, which we usually went to because we couldn't afford any better. We would discuss events from the night before – who had got off with whom, who was wearing what, what celebrities had been there, who had been most off their heads.

By 1985 Hard Times was no longer the look. Under Leigh's influence, Glam had made a revival. You could still wear ripped jeans as long as they were teamed with shiny platform shoes, a sequinned top and plenty of diamanté jewelry. Make-up was very garish on both girls and boys. 'Gender-bending' was all the rage among the straight boys. There were three in particular who were at Taboo every week: Simon Hinton, Christopher and Julian, who all worked in banks. They wore full make-up, diamanté earrings and men's suits, although Chris sometimes wore a very becoming dress. Despite their feminine appearance there was no shortage of girls after them. Simon loved those days, eulogizing about them years later:

> The transition from a tarted-up, stall-stomping, wannabe Numanoid to a full on androgynous, glitterati nightclubber, shimmering with diamanté attachments, was for me an obvious and natural evolution. I went off concerts really quickly because all the attention was focused on the stage and I wasn't up there! The decadent, dandyish nightclubs I patronized in the early eighties were gorgeously, eccentrically outrageous. We were weird and wonderful nightclub creations of an underground extravaganza, where a sacrosanct liberality and a taste for the ridiculous were the standard entry requirements in a twilight world of quirky, romantic, open-door elitism. Superficially we weren't deep but we were deeply superficial, and for those who understood the joke it was funny, very funny.

Each week Taboo became more shocking. And the one person everyone wanted to see was Leigh. He would wear a different outfit every week, reflecting his particular favourite look of the moment. At this time all his garments bore some resemblance to normal clothes and he hadn't yet started to distort his body shape. One of his most popular looks was a short pleated skirt teamed with a glittery, denim Chanel-style jacket, scab make-up and a cheap, plastic souvenir policeman's hat. He would arrive about midnight and bounce down the stairs greeting everyone he saw. If there was a film crew present – and by now there invariably was – he would be polite and helpful, but once they had gone he would leap onto the dance floor, grabbing whoever was nearest to him. He might hold them by the arms and spin them round or pull them to the floor in a rugby tackle. There was a marvellous series of photos of him in *i-D*, lying on the floor, passed out with his glorious thunder thighs exposed to the world. His energy would raise the energy level at the club and you could feel the buzz as soon as he arrived. If he was feeling particularly flash he would drink one of the disgusting cocktails that they sold in the back bar. The ceiling of the cocktail bar was fairly low, so with his platforms on Leigh was able to do a high kick and smash the lights above the bar, which he did when he was feeling particularly mischievous and in need of attention. He was usually given a fistful of drinks tickets by the management and if you were one of his favourites that week he would hand you a couple.

There was so much press about the club that it just got fuller and fuller. Alix Sharkey of *i-D* wrote:

These days Thursday night in the West End usually means Taboo – London's sleaziest, campest and bitchiest club of the moment which is stuffed with designers, stylists, models, students, dregs and the hopefully hip, lurching through the lasers and snarfing up amyl. The coolest geezer in here is wearing BodyMap tights and, yup, platform soles. A sudden rush for the toilets could only mean that a camera crew had arrived and were filming, nothing less would penetrate this narcissistic air of self-absorption.

The fame of the club even spread to Leigh's homeland. There was a huge article in one of the daily papers, headlined 'AUSSIE'S CLUB IS HOTTEST FOR ROCK'S ELITE', reporting:

> George Michael and Andrew Ridgeley were in a corner swigging cans of beer – Fosters of course. Boy George and his friend Marilyn were holding court near the dance floor – and just about anyone else who is anybody on the glitzy London club scene was there too. It was a typical Thursday night at Taboo, the mega-trendy London club run by outrageous Australian fashion designer Leigh Bowery. Even he is surprised by its amazing success. At the end of the month it will have been going for a year which is quite something on the London clubscene where 'in' places become 'out' after nine months.

Boy George wrote about the club in his autobiography *Take It Like A Man*:

> New York drug culture had filtered through, and everyone was popping ecstasy and whatever else they could sniff, smoke or swallow. With the drugs came the trash fashions, primed by new disco celebrities like Leigh Bowery and Trojan. I was dismissive when I first saw them, I'd had a blue face years ago, but I had to admit that they did it with unmistakable brilliance. Mark did the door, when the bouncers confiscated drugs they went into his stripy tights. Though he loathed 'pretentious' Leigh and Trojan, Philip Sallon never missed a Taboo. Every week he wandered around counting heads and handing out flyers for the Mud Club. 'Amateurs, amateurs,' Leigh spat back, 'Philip Sallon's so brilliant managing all those stairs at his age.'

Designer John Galliano would arrive giving out invitations to his latest fashion show, which would always be terribly over-attended. As soon as he heard Madonna's 'Into the Groove' he would be up on the dance floor, grooving away with all the others. It was a place to network, to hear about other parties, other gigs, other clubs.

George Michael wasn't nearly as famous then as he is now, but the newspapers still liked writing about him. One week the *Sun* had a massive double-page spread about him and his supposed exploits at Taboo. They described him on the dance floor sniffing poppers. They obviously had no idea what they were writing about, because as the article went on, the bottle of poppers got bigger and bigger until it seemed to reach the size of a litre bottle of vodka. He would have been very popular if it had been true!

Everyone was out of it: ecstasy was just appearing on the scene, but it was quite hard to get hold of, while acid, speed, downers and of course poppers were very popular. There was a bit of cocaine around, though most people couldn't afford it. But as usual the main stimulant was alcohol, and the reason the management let the club so cheaply was because they made so much profit on the bars. As the night went on people's behaviour would get more and more outrageous. The dance floor would disintegrate into something that resembled a collapsed rugby scrum. If someone spilt some poppers everyone scrambled on to the floor to sniff it up. People were rolling all over the floor to the disco music, and sometimes DJ Jeffrey would get so carried away that he would hurl himself onto the dance floor, not managing to get back to the DJ's booth before the record finished, so there would be a long gap in the music, but nobody really noticed or cared. There was also the famous incident when Jeffrey was so drunk he played the slip mat for half an hour.

Jeffrey wasn't a great drug taker, but one night he was feeling really tired. 'Mark Vaultier was in the DJ box cutting up lines of what I thought was coke. I snorted the line Mark offered me and it was only when I began to go all woozy that I realized it was heroin.' A couple of weeks later he was really tripping on acid. 'I thought I was in my bedroom at home so I asked Julia to make me a cup of tea! People longed to DJ there and once when I went onto the dance floor to dance to a record I had chosen, Luke Branson, your lovely flatmate of the time, started putting his records on, I went mad and threw a drink at him!'

David Holah, Lesley Chilkes and the BodyMap gang would be on the dance floor doing carefully choreographed dances that they had put together in Lesley's kitchen. Their favourite records were 'Body Rock' by Maria Vidal and 'After the Rainbow' by Joanne Daniels.

In September 1985 Leigh was asked to do an interview and appear on the cover of *LAM*. The magazine was originally aimed at Australians in London, but it had expanded and was aiming for a general audience. Leigh was thrilled when it came out and went dashing along to all the tube stations, collecting about three hundred copies for himself. He looked very dashing on the front. He was wearing his yellow gingham spotted jacket with matching shirt and face, posing against his *Star Trek* wallpaper and one of Trojan's paintings. In the interview he described his feelings about his club:

> Taboo is a reflection of my clothes and attitudes. The name
> Taboo is a joke really, because there's nothing you can't do
> there. My job at Taboo is as a sort of local cabaret act I suppose
> – the original vaudeville drunkard. If people see me behaving
> in such an outrageous manner, they won't feel inhibited
> themselves. I can hardly call myself a club entrepreneur

because I don't do much. My partner Tony is the exact opposite of me, and it's just as well really, because let's face it – somebody's got to be serious. I started Taboo to amuse myself as well as other people. I was and still am amused by going there. As soon as I stop enjoying it, I'll close it.

AIDS hadn't really been heard of at this time. There were rumours of a horrible disease going round New York that you could catch from drinking from the same glass as someone else, but it didn't seem to pose a threat to the bright young things of London clubland. Going home with a different person each night didn't seem dangerous, just a normal way of life. There were people snogging everywhere – girls and boys, girls and girls, but mainly boys and boys. There were always massive queues for the toilets as the cubicles were used for a quick grope. It was quite an education looking under the doors to see who was with whom, and because everyone knew everyone else the news soon went flying round the club. The toilets were the heart of the club, and some people would stay in there all night adjusting their hair and make-up and passing on gossip. There was a lot of bitchiness around. Lots of people were finally trying to get their careers together and there was a lot of jealousy if something good happened to someone else. Trojan was so jealous of Patrick Cox's (he was just beginning to make it as a shoe designer) new fringed leather jacket he poured poppers down the back and set fire to it.

Strangely, the one person who never pulled at Taboo was Leigh. He had a few snogs, but they were mainly for attention rather than sexual pleasure. Once he had started dressing up in his freaky fashions he gave up on looking for romance in nightclubs and preferred the anonymity of gentlemen's toilets. The nearest he ever got to sex at Taboo was when Molly Parkin, the author, took a shine to him. She insisted on following him around, trying to snog him and shouting that she was delighted to have found a straight freak and they were going to get engaged.

Nonetheless, Leigh met two women at Taboo who were to become important in his life. The first was Nicola Bateman, a young textiles student from Middlesex Polytechnic, who saw in Leigh a soulmate who shared her pleasure in dressing up. Nicola was usually attired in a swimming costume, laddered tights and a pair of bejewelled, bewinged spectacles, while perched on her head would be a creation consisting of three swimming hats stuffed to make a giant helmet decorated with jewels and studded dog collars. One night she had come to the club early and because it was quite empty she decided to sit in the cocktail bar until it filled up. Leigh spotted her and was very flattering: 'Darling, you look divine, where do you come from?' When Nicola told him that she came from Hampshire, Leigh replied, 'Oh, you must be very rich then,' and swanned off to greet an old friend.

Nicola was very taken with Leigh, and thought he was one of the most handsome and sexiest men she had ever seen. She bumped into him later near the toilets and he introduced her to several of his friends. At the end of the evening he scribbled his phone number down with a lipstick. The next day Nicola rang him and was mortified when she had to describe herself, as he couldn't remember her. But she soon jogged his memory and he generously offered to put her (plus one) on the guest list for the following week.

Nicola used to make fantastic cartoon books about her experiences, and on her second trip to Taboo she presented Leigh with one describing their first meeting. Gradually they became firm friends. Leigh invited her to the BodyMap fashion show, where she revelled in the attention they got, the photographers loving this freaky duo. Leigh realized that she would be a willing slave to him, and she was looking for a master, so it was an ideal relationship.

The second fan that became his friend was Fat Gill. She was as wide as she was tall and she usually wore a two-inch-long pair of golden eyelashes. She was so short that when she arrived at the club all you could see were these huge lashes peering at you over the top of the cash desk. She soon became one of Leigh's 'gang' and he loved taking her around to other clubs in London.

One night my twelve-year-old brother was staying with me. I dressed him up in platforms and spiked up his hair, but because he was so short he could only just about pass for fourteen. I sneaked him into the club, and as we went down the stairs he gasped in wonder: 'It's just like Ali Baba's cave.' None of his friends believed that he really went to the legendary Taboo, but he was the youngest-ever guest.

As the club's reputation grew, more and more pop stars were seen there: Depeche Mode, New Order, Erasure, Marc Almond, Bananarama, Sade, Toni Basil and even Leigh's old adversary Mick Jagger made an appearance. Paul Weller came once but left after about fifteen minutes, saying it was the most disgusting place he had ever been. The straight Beat Route crowd, such as Christos Tolera, Dylan Jones, Chris Sullivan and Robert Elms, became regulars. Leigh decided for no good reason that he hated Bob Elms and had him kicked out just because 'he was Robert Elms'. I had read his book *In Search of the Crack* and Leigh decided to borrow it, but I never got it back: 'Sorry, Sue, I was reading it on the tube but it made me feel so sick I had to tear it in half because I was worried that if I just left it there some other poor unsuspecting fool might have the horror of reading that garbage.'

The older, arty crowd came down too: Derek Jarman, Andrew Logan, Luciana Martinez, Duggie Fields, Michael and Gerlinde Kostiff and the marvellous Ula, who had gone out with Frank Sinatra when she had been Miss Sweden. Michael remembers Gerlinde jumping onto Leigh's shoulders and charging around the dance floor until someone came and pushed them over. 'I asked her about it fifteen minutes later and she couldn't even remember it happening.'

The club was extraordinarily successful for well over a year, becoming undoubtedly the most famous of all London's legendary eighties' club nights, but as there began to be more and more tourists, it lost its original exclusivity. It was still good fun, but the novelty was beginning to wear off. Heroin had also raised its ugly head and syringes began to be found in the toilets. Leigh was getting a bit bored, but as he was making money, he didn't really want to close Taboo down.

A teetotal cleanomaniac called Peter-Paul Hartnett (or Powder-Puff Hairnet, as he was sometimes called) was always there documenting the fashions and the crowd with his Polaroid camera. As well as not drinking, he refused to take drugs. Instead, he seemed to take a voyeuristic pleasure in the goings on at the club. He sometimes used to sit with me on the door and as he had been a model in Japan he used to greet the Japanese girls in their own language, which rather fazed them. He took it upon himself to worry about what was happening to the club and decided to take Leigh into a corner for a quick word. He told Leigh that if he liked he could get the club closed. Leigh lifted a white, begloved finger to his lips, as if to say 'Don't tell anyone', and Peter-Paul took this as a sign to put his plan into action.

He decided to contact *You* magazine, which was given away free with the *Mail on Sunday*, and ask them to do an article on the club. He brought them down the next Thursday and told them all about the drug taking and debauchery. The following Sunday an article appeared condemning the club as a den of iniquity.

> In the tradition of English youth night spots, most of the action takes place in the ladies' toilet. You can smell grass everywhere. But Taboo's distinctive drug is ecstasy, a designer drug which in the short term gives you a benign view of humanity and, in the long term, a chance of Parkinson's Disease.
>
> Most people just drink. Cans of Fosters generally. A lot of them. Theirs is a once a week binge. Dole-er-crats Peter-Paul calls them. 'They live like aristocrats,' he says, 'rising late and existing on exotic forms of cheese on toast.' It is 3.30 a.m., last dance time. For some it is their last chance to find a partner for the night. There is an enormous scrum on the dance floor, with Leigh at the centre grinning wildly.

The next day Leigh got a phone call from the management of the club saying that it was to be closed from then on.

This early closure led to part of the legend of Taboo. It stopped when people still wanted more. A few weeks later, when the fuss had died down, the manager contacted Leigh to see if he wanted to open up again, but with his expert judgment Leigh decided that Taboo had had its day and it was time to move on to something else.

For a decade, clubs opened with the pronouncement 'It will be the new Taboo.' But times changed, and it became impossible to recreate the bawdy hedonism that took place every Thursday night for eighteen months of the mid-eighties at a tatty little club in Leicester Square.

5

Men

Leigh realized he was gay when he was about twelve and had no doubts or worries about his sexuality. It was just a fact of his life and one that he could always deal with. He spent his school days hanging around public toilets picking up men and seemed to have no guilty feelings about this at all. In fact he was rather proud of it, and often used to tell me how many men he had been with. Melbourne Central Station was his mecca. Every day after school, he would find another man to have sex with. He didn't really mind what they looked like – in fact the more grotesque, the better. It was part of his philosophy on life not to judge people by their physical attributes. Nothing ever developed into romance, just quickies in the cubicles.

When he came to London, things didn't change. He still spent plenty of his time hanging around toilets; it was probably the only thing he never got bored of. If he heard of a good cottage several miles away he would make the effort to go there, often combining the trip with a more practical purpose. So when he heard that there was an excellent cottage in Southall he set off on the bus to West London, and while he was there found some fantastic Indian fabrics that inspired him to create a whole new look.

One of his first experiences in a London toilet greatly shocked him. He had given a couple of men blow jobs, but still hadn't come himself. The second man had just left when Leigh was startled to notice a middle-aged man with long, straw-like hair peering over the top of the cubicle door. He invited Leigh back to his place for some more sex and to watch a 'blue movie'. Leigh declined to go, partly because the man was so repulsive (he was upset by this reaction in himself, because it went against his principles, but this man was too ugly even for Leigh), but mainly because he had never seen a blue movie before and he didn't think he would like it!

Any toilet, however grotty, was a temple for him. Whichever one he went to, he would end up kneeling at someone's feet. If he was desperate for trade he would pop out to the local toilet in Commercial Road, and he was devastated when council cutbacks forced its closure. Whenever I went to Sainsbury's or Brick Lane with him he would point out at least five plain, middle-aged men, saying he'd had them all. He used to love telling me the stories of his exploits; I could hardly believe that such things went on. He described one gymnastic event when he was in a lavatory with big gaps beneath the cubicle walls. He was in the middle cubicle stretched horizontally across the floor, lying on his back with his legs up the left side. His head was under the cubicle to the right and he was sucking off the man in there, while the man in the cubicle to the left had his head under the gap and was giving Leigh a blow job, so it was a kind of three-way daisy chain.

Another favourite local haunt were the toilets in the London Hospital. He told me that you got a better class of trade in there, and if you really struck lucky, you might get a doctor. On one occasion he was peering through the glory hole into the next cubicle when he saw a man pull up his trouser leg and undo a little plug at the end of a tube. Leigh realized that he must have been emptying his catheter bag and was thrilled when the man tore off a sheet of toilet paper and wiped the end of the tube.

Wherever Leigh was, he would find some action. He once came to stay at my parents' house in Windsor. Before we went back to London we decided to look around the town, and while we were wandering around he announced that he needed to go to the toilet. They were above some souvenir shops at the entrance to the local car park, so you had to walk up some stairs to get to them. Leigh took ages; I was staring into the window of a shop that sold model trains, but I soon exhausted the interest I could find there. I was pacing up and down getting more and more impatient when I looked up and saw a young man running down the stairs of the gent's looking rather flustered. He ran back up, then came down again, this time clutching a handful of carrier bags. I immediately guessed that he had been the object of Leigh's desire. Leigh emerged very smugly and was happy to affirm my presumptions. We then got on the train to London, and sitting in the same compartment was the boy and his mother. He was blushing profusely and Leigh just made him more embarrassed by continually staring at him and calling me 'Darling' as if I were his wife.

Leigh's favourite cottage was at Liverpool Street Station, which reminded him of the happy days of his youth. He usually stopped there in the early evening when it was at its busiest, with commuters returning home to their wives in suburbia who usually had a few minutes to kill, so they went to the gent's to see what fun they could have. Quite often Leigh would have furtive sex with three men in one rush hour. It seemed easy to catch men's eyes at the urinals and they slunk off to the cubicle together. It was easy, uncomplicated sex, and Leigh loved it.

Leigh had an incredible sex drive and masturbated three or four times a day. He was particularly fond of Boris Becker and spent many happy hours fantasizing about his white eyelashes and chunky ginger thighs. Another of his heartthrobs was Marti Pellow from Wet Wet Wet. He had one special video of him that he watched as he wanked, making sure that his orgasm coincided with the climax of Marti's song.

Les Child had to suffer Leigh's sexual frustration when they were on tour with Michael Clark together.

> There were times when we had fights, Leigh would just push you to the edge. It had been going on all week but I knew it was sexual frustration. She [Leigh] gets sexually frustrated if she hasn't had it for twenty-four hours. So she starts getting worked up and starts taking it out on whoever was nearest. It would take you so long to realize what Miss Thing was up to, until you were at breaking point, one time he was chasing me around in Liverpool, waving that big old elephant penis. He told Michael and David I was begging for it and they believed him! Begging him to plunge me, girl! They just lay there laughing. I never trusted him, you could never feel comfortable with him because you didn't know what would come next. To the point of me having to sleep with my tights on in bed. I was sure he was going to interfere with me in the night.

One day in 1991, I got a phone call from Leigh saying he had been arrested. Of course I didn't believe him, as it was a story he had used so many times before as a joke. But because he seemed so genuinely upset and frightened I began to think that maybe it was the truth. He had been caught in a compromising position with another man in the toilets at Liverpool Street Station. They had been found by the toilet attendant who, according to Leigh, had been checking the toilets with a mirror on a stick that he slid under the doors to see what was going on. The attendant had called the police because he had almost caught Leigh before and had given him several prior warnings.

Leigh was truly worried that he might be deported, and he told the painter Lucian Freud, who he had recently started sitting for, of his plight. Lucian kindly paid for his great friend Lord Goodman to defend him. (It was in Lucian's own interest, too, because if Leigh had been sent back to Australia he would have been left with a couple of half-finished paintings.) Leigh was thrilled and boasted that the Queen's solicitor was helping him with his cottaging case. I typed up a list of Leigh's achievements, which he was going to show off in an attempt to impress the magistrates. The other man involved was married and denied all involvement, pretending that Leigh had forced him into it, so in the end Leigh was charged with sexual assault. He had to go to court at the Guildhall in the City. He was advised to plead guilty, which he did. His friend Angus Cook went along to give him moral support. 'Leigh smirked as his lawyer shot him a withering glance as the judge read out his previous convictions for shoplifting, which he had not told his defence about.' He was found guilty but only fined £400, which Lucian kindly paid for him. One may have thought that this incident would put Leigh off cottaging for a while, but the next day he was up to his old tricks again, although it was a couple of weeks before he dared to go back to Liverpool Street

Station. When he did, he changed his wig in the hope that the zealous attendant wouldn't recognize him.

Leigh was also fond of cruising, but this usually took place late at night when all the toilets were closed. If he was feeling adventurous he would make the effort to go to Hampstead Heath and wander around the bushes and undergrowth looking for a partner. It wasn't difficult, because every night the Heath was a hot-bed of passion with semi-dressed men coupling under the trees. Because it was so dark it was difficult to see who you were playing with, but that was a bonus for the not-so-attractive man, who could always be assured of pulling.

Russell Square was a much more conveniently situated cruising area. It was also far smaller than the Heath, so there was no danger of getting lost. Sometimes Leigh went there on his way home from a late-night session at Lucian's. He would wander around in his tatty trousers and wig and if he hadn't had any luck within five minutes he would quickly shove his wig in his pocket, as he found that his bald head attracted the blokes. On a very rare occasion he might take someone home with him, but this always caused difficulties in the wig department. When he was wearing the wig Leigh deluded himself that no one would realize that it wasn't his own hair. Whatever wig he wore was usually skew-whiff and with great big chunks missing. But despite this obvious clue, he could never properly relax in the bedroom because he was worried that his partner might find out it was a wig. So he always had to be on guard in case the bloke decided to run his fingers through his hair. If he felt the man's hand going in that direction, he would quickly grab it and engage him in some other activity. Not surprisingly, his pick-ups hardly ever phoned him for a repeat performance – not that he really wanted them to.

Very occasionally, Leigh would go back to men's houses, but he never really enjoyed it. It just confirmed the dreariness of most people's lives and their complete lack of taste in home furnishings.

When Leigh was in Scotland rehearsing a play, he sent me a hilarious postcard about one of his cruising exploits:

> I had sex in the park with a man who said on completion, 'You're Leigh Bowery aren't you?' I said, 'Guilty as charged.' He said, 'Are you always so slutty, so eager to please?' I said, 'What are you getting at?' He said, 'Nothing, you just seemed so desperate, so hungry.' I said, 'You were my charitable act of the week.' He said, 'Ditto. You were mine.' I said, 'I don't think there's anything left to say.' He said, 'Except goodbye.' As he walked away I shouted 'I love you!'

On one of his cottaging jaunts Leigh met a well-built Nigerian student who was moonlighting as a night security guard. He invited Leigh back to his deserted warehouse and they had fantastic sex on a dirty old mattress on the floor, which was luxury compared to the usual cramped conditions of a cubicle. The man asked for Leigh's number, and Leigh would often pop down to the warehouse for unbridled passion. Leigh considered this guy to be his boyfriend and was thrilled to have regular sex on tap. What he didn't realize was that the student had rung once when he had been out and Trojan had answered the phone, so he had gone to the warehouse instead. Trojan was thrilled to be seeing the security guard behind Leigh's back, and used to snigger whenever Leigh talked about their 'loving sexploits'. In the end Trojan couldn't hold it in any longer, and one day when Leigh was really picking on him he threw his own romance with the man in Leigh's face. Leigh was rather deflated by this news, but they both carried on seeing him for a while. In the end he stopped ringing, and one night Leigh scuttled down to the warehouse only to find that he had left.

Wherever Leigh was – at home or abroad – he would be on the look-out for men. He had an encyclopaedic knowledge of all the cottages in London and would happily pass on the information to his grateful friends. When he first discovered he was HIV positive, his main worry was that he wouldn't be able to have sex again. But that only lasted about a week: he got in a big supply of condoms and carried on cottaging. His last encounter was about six weeks before he died and involved going to the very tidy, beige, semi-detached house of some sad soul he had picked up at Liverpool Street Station.

Even so, when asked by a magazine what his greatest regret was, Leigh replied, 'Having unsafe sex with more than 1,000 men.'

6

Love, Sex and Slavery

Leigh loved to have someone at his beck and call at all times. Because of his charismatic personality, he was usually able to find somebody to fill this position. His first 'slave' in London was a girl called Lorraine. He had met her at ChaChas, where she used to hang about doing her best to try to fit in. She was very short, with a strange, bird-like face, and she dressed in fifties' style suits. Leigh took pity on her and decided to befriend her, which was very easy to do, as she was desperate to be liked. Leigh made her do everything for him – his shopping, his cooking and his cleaning – and if she did something wrong he would furiously tell her off. In return, she got friendship and someone to hang around with. Leigh loved to dress her up and do her make-up. He painted huge, arched eyebrows onto her small budgie face and sometimes he used to style her on Scarlett, which used to enrage Scarlett, who hated Lorraine. Leigh liked to pick on Scarlett because when he first met her she was everything he would like to be – successful and popular on the club scene – and he was jealous of her success.

Rachel Auburn thought that Lorraine was the most subservient person she had ever met in her life and couldn't believe what Leigh did when they spent a weekend in Amsterdam. 'He made her sit outside the Rijksmuseum topless with a handwritten sign hung around her neck saying "Give Me Money". I know it sounds ridiculous but it's completely true. She looked like the grandfather from the *Munsters* as Leigh had cut her hair into a creepy widow's peak.'

Eventually even Leigh got fed up with Lorraine's total devotion, and as he found more fancy, fashionable friends he dropped her. She disappeared to Italy, where she was last heard of happily married and with lots of children.

When Leigh opened Taboo he found his second slave, Fat Gill. She took to slavery like a duck to water and was soon turning up at Leigh's to do his cleaning, but he was so bossy that if she turned up ten minutes early he would make her wait on the doorstep until the appointed hour. He made her go out in the most shocking outfits. He crocheted her a long, see-through dress that he insisted she wear with nothing underneath, and took great joy in encouraging her to appear naked. When Leigh entered her into the Alternative Miss World Competition he made her cycle on stage starkers except for red stars painted over her nipples and a pail on her head, which led to her being called Bucket Gill. He also persuaded her to shave her head so she would look much 'prettier'. To cheer her up after he had done it, he painted her a lovely new hairstyle with black aquacolour.

He once took Fat Gill to dinner at Michael and Gerlinde Kostiff's, but said she wasn't allowed to sit at the table. He opened up all the cupboards until he found the oven cleaner and told her that this was her job for the evening. Gerlinde, being a kind-hearted soul, was horrified, and to Leigh's apparent disgust put her at the head of the table.

He eventually got bored with Gill too, but she found that hanging around with Leigh had given her a lot of confidence. In a way he was being cruel to be kind – by continually being nasty to her it prepared her for when people called her names in the street, and she was well practised in shouting back witty put-downs. She applied for a job as a toilet attendant at the newly opened London Limelight. She became very popular and was eventually offered a television presenter's job on the late-night television youth programme *Club X*. Leigh was very jealous of this and constantly mocked her appearances, in which she was dressed up as a fairy. Sadly, soon after the series ended she died of an asthma attack.

Trojan was the true love of Leigh's life. Leigh adored him and thought he was the most gorgeous man he had ever met. He was thin and about six feet tall, with thick brown hair that he changed the style of on a weekly basis. He was named the 'Face of '84' by the *Observer* magazine. Trojan loved Leigh too, but in a different way. He didn't fancy him, but he admired his quick wit, his intelligence, his ideas and the way he could make things happen. So it was a strange relationship, in which to all intents and purposes Leigh was in charge – he bossed Trojan around and designed all his clothes – but Trojan held the trump card. Leigh fancied him and he couldn't have him. This was a pattern that would repeat itself in Leigh's future relationships, in particular with Lee Benjamin and Malcolm Duffy.

Leigh used to worship Trojan despite constantly belittling him and calling him thick. When they both lived in Ladbroke Grove, Leigh used to give Trojan ten new words to learn every day, and then he had to go round to Rachel's to be tested. Woe betide him if he got any wrong! When I went round to the flat and Trojan was out, Leigh used to confess his love for him and how it was tearing him apart. He tried to coerce Trojan into having sex with him by quoting Sigmund Freud and saying that the only way their relationship could continue was for Trojan to let Leigh fuck him. In early 1984, just after they had moved into Farrell House, they began taking a lot of acid and for three happy weeks they enjoyed some sort of sex life. Leigh phoned me up the day after they first 'did it', delighted that at last his dream had come true.

Their closeness caused a terrible atmosphere in the flat they shared with David Walls, as the pair of them were always picking on David and constantly mocking 'his old granddad ways'. It drove David so mad he had to move out, which was even better for Leigh, as he and Trojan now had the flat to themselves. He worshipped his new lover and constantly made him jump up and down naked to show off his huge 'donkey balls'.

Leigh encouraged Trojan to take acid practically every night so that their affair would continue. Trojan was happy to do so, as he loved drugs. But after a couple of weeks Trojan began to get bored with Leigh's constant sexual demands; Leigh was not really Trojan's type and, to infuriate him, Trojan would call him 'Doughnut', referring to his rotund shape. The sexual side of the relationship soon fizzled out and, much to the fury of Leigh, Trojan returned to his own room.

Despite Trojan ignoring all the moves Leigh made on him, Leigh still adored him. He used to ask me to tell Trojan that he really loved him and wanted to go out with him. This of course just put Trojan in a stronger position and made me feel like a fourteen-year-old girl in the school playground. Trojan embarked upon a new career: he became a rent boy and registered with an agency in Maida Vale. He had no qualms about doing this type of work and enjoyed his newfound wealth. Leigh was torn about it – on one hand he liked the scumminess of it and the hilarious tales of other people's sexual behaviour, but on the other he was jealous of other men going with Trojan. He thought about doing rent himself, because then he would get paid for doing what he liked best, but there was something in his Christian upbringing that held him back and he couldn't bring himself to do it. It was perfectly all right to have sex with dirty old men for free, but if he got paid it would be a different matter entirely.

Sometimes Trojan went to the men's houses or hotels, and sometimes he would meet them at Farrell House. Leigh would phone me up while listening at Trojan's door and report back on all the action. His favourite punter was an old man nicknamed 'Professor Plum Knob'. This is because he thought his penis was too small, so he had engineered a contraption that consisted of a round lump of wood, painted a vivid purple, that he tied to the end of his knob with long lengths of satin ribbon. He just used to wander around the room wearing it while Trojan watched. This seemed a great way of making money. Trojan couldn't believe that he was being paid to watch such entertainment.

Trojan also had an alter-ego called Sandra. She was very pretty and feminine and was very popular with some of the punters. Trojan and Leigh used to spend ages rummaging around second-hand shops finding sophisticated evening dresses and shoes for 'Sandra'.

Leigh, meanwhile, encouraged Trojan to develop his artistic skills. Trojan had first thought of becoming a painter when they had visited John Maybury's exhibition at the B2 Gallery in 1982. Leigh had told Trojan that he could easily paint pictures as good as John's, and this led to Trojan producing a series of paintings to decorate the flat. He used rough materials that he found in the road as canvases, maybe a headboard or a wooden pallet. He painted bright portraits, glueing on various objects such as false nails, radios and even a fake £50 note. They were naive but also powerful, and in 1996 his talent was finally recognized with a posthumous exhibition of his work at the Manchester Metropolitan Gallery.

Trojan began to see himself as an art object, and one evening I got a call from Leigh saying he couldn't believe what had just happened: for a long time Trojan had wanted to perform some sort of permanent mutilation to his body, and he had finally gone ahead and done it. As Leigh called me, Trojan was sitting on the sofa with a towel wrapped around his head soaking up the blood from his ear. He had hacked away at his lobe with a knife so that it was completely cut into two. The bleeding would not stop, but he was frightened to go to the doctor in case they wanted to sew it back together. Michael Clark was living in my flat at this time and we passed the phone between us, screaming, as we listened to the gory details. But in the end it healed and Trojan made a special feature of his split ear by highlighting it with make-up. It gave him a newfound confidence, and he threatened to cut off one of his fingers; he was even tempted to cut off one of his hands with an axe, but luckily he never got round to it. Strangely enough I've now got a split ear, as an earring slowly cut through my lobe without me noticing. I could easily get it repaired, but I keep it as a tribute to Trojan.

Leigh and Trojan used to have terrible rows. Trojan got sick of the way Leigh constantly bossed him around, and it was very hard to win an argument with Leigh, as his mind was so fast he could always have the last word. Trojan wanted to be independent and was sick of being seen as Leigh's sidekick. He began to invent his own 'looks', wearing pastel Chanel-style twin sets with shorts and growing his hair into a bob with an asymmetric fringe, which he highlighted by painting a black line underneath.

In the middle of 1985, Trojan started complaining to the council that he and Leigh were being harassed – which they were. The local boys constantly taunted them for their outrageous dress, which Leigh of course interpreted to mean that they fancied them but couldn't come to terms with their feelings. There was one boy in particular who they both liked; they christened him 'Lips' because of his very inviting mouth. Trojan then did his old trick and put lighted newspaper through his own letter-box then said that queer-bashers had done it. He also went to the doctor's complaining of depression again and in the end managed to get himself a council flat in Notting Hill Gate.

One night at Taboo, Trojan got off with John Maybury. John had just split up with his previous boyfriend, David Holah, who was now going out with Michael Clark. John was feeling very lost at this time because his relationship was over. 'Trojan was looking particularly gorgeous that night, he was working the bob look, he wasn't that kind of fucked up, he looked really beautiful so I said to him "You look gorgeous, will you come home with me tonight?" and he said "Yes" and that opened a whole new can of worms.' On their first proper date John went round to Trojan's flat: 'Trojan opened his box of magic tricks, which was full of pills, silver foil, wraps and syringes. I had never seen so many drugs, and within a few minutes Trojan was injecting heroin into my arm for the first time.'

Leigh was not happy with this relationship at all, but he was always nice to John's face, and the new couple often stayed at Leigh's flat in Trojan's old room, which was exactly as he had left it because Leigh always hoped that someday he would come back. Leigh was worried about the drug taking, because although he used drugs for recreational purposes he never took them in the daytime or if he wasn't going out. He thought that if John and Trojan were in his flat he could keep an eye on them. He used to cook them breakfast and various snacks throughout the day just to keep them in the flat so they didn't go out to find drugs.

John and Trojan had a very intense relationship that lasted for over a year. 'Trojan was so beguiling in every way, Trojan's humour was very different from Leigh's but you had no choice, once you were sucked in, you were sucked in.' In August 1986 Leigh phoned me. I was in the bath at the time, and with his voice shaking he told me that Lee Sheldrick, John's flatmate, had just called him to say that Trojan had been found dead in John's flat in Camden. Leigh refused to believe it and asked me to phone the police to confirm that it was true. Unfortunately, it was.

John was in America at the time working on a video with Genesis P-Orridge, the leader of the avant-garde group Throbbing Gristle. Trojan had been staying at John's flat and by now was heavily into drugs. He had taken some DF118s and Rohypnols that he had conned out of a doctor and had then gone to John's flat and put some pies in the oven for his supper. Lee Sheldrick had got up in the morning and found Trojan dead on the kitchen floor, his dinner burnt in the oven. John returned from America, devastated by his loss. About a week later John was found unconscious from an overdose on a settee at another flat in Crowndale Road. He was luckier than Trojan: he was rushed to Intensive Care and, despite being paralysed for a short while, made a full recovery.

John truly appreciated how kind Leigh was to him at this time.

When Trojan died Leigh was so amazingly brave and incredible and that lovely side of him came out. There was a really loving, deeply sensitive person in there. He understood the situation, he knew that I was in love with Trojan and that Trojan was in love with me, for better or worse. Leigh would come to the hospital at least every other day and also vetted other people, telling them to stay away. That whole thing was very weird because people I didn't even know would come and visit me. I couldn't move, it was like the audience at a play, where there's an audience of one who can't leave the theatre. It keeps on going, it's a fucking nightmare. Leigh would show up at nine o'clock at night and just come and make me laugh and this was the best possible thing.

Leigh was devastated by Trojan's death. When he was interviewed later, he commented, 'He died five years ago today. I can still hardly believe it. He's still so alive in my head. It's the small things – like if someone were to put different weights in my hand, I'd be able to say which one was the weight of his hand.' This was the first time that anyone close to Leigh had died, but it certainly wasn't to be the last. People were shocked when Trojan died, but they didn't realize that over the next decade they would become almost blasé about death as so many friends died from drug overdoses and AIDS. At that time you could never imagine that the deaths of young people would become commonplace and that each year you would be going to several of your friends' funerals.

About four months after Trojan died, Mark Vaultier was found dead from a methadone overdose. He had been hanging around with Boy George and had got into the whole heroin trip. He didn't really have a strong enough personality to keep up with his new, glamorous friends and had discovered that drugs bonded them – if you were all out of it together, no one noticed that you didn't have much to say. A couple of weeks before he died he had called round to my flat but just sat in the corner scratching himself. I have never understood the attraction of heavy drug taking, and found it shocking that a perfectly pleasant young boy had let himself get into this terrible state. No one was allowed to go to his funeral because his family wanted to keep everything private, which was just as well because with the Boy George connection it could easily have turned into a media circus.

When Trojan moved out of Farrell House in July 1985 and started going out with John there was a space left in Leigh's heart, so he found himself a new object of desire, a young Scottish boy called Malcolm Duffy. I had introduced him and Mark Vaultier to Leigh as prospective models for the Performing Clothes Show at the ICA. Malcolm was boyish with his hair shaved at the sides and spiked up on top. He enjoyed the attention from Leigh but yet again did not fancy him, just admired him. He was pleased to be in the company of this person who had such importance on the club scene, and when you are young, hanging around with someone older who is more respected gets you accepted more quickly. Malcolm frequently stayed the night at Leigh's. 'I would often stay there five nights a week, but I could only manage three nights in a row before I went mad and had to go home. Sometimes I would wake up and he would be sucking my cock. I used to lie on my stomach wrapped in a sheet because I didn't want him to do it.'

Their intense friendship lasted about a year, then they drifted apart for a while. Malcolm made other friends and carved a niche for himself. Leigh had encouraged him to become a DJ, which he did, becoming the regular DJ at the very popular all-night club Trade. He had records in the charts and became well-respected on the music scene. After a while, his friendship with Leigh developed into one of equal standing, and when Leigh later started his own musical career he often turned to Malcolm for help.

Several years later Leigh met a talented dressmaker called Lee Benjamin, who held a particular fascination because as a child his babysitter had been Violet Kray. Leigh soon procured him as his assistant. He was very good at cutting and sewing and proved to be a great help to Leigh. When Leigh was busy, Lee more or less lived at his flat. Leigh fed him and paid him as much as he could afford, which wasn't much, but was enough to keep Lee working for him. He was always generous to him and often took him on trips to New York, Japan and Europe. Leigh developed a major crush on Lee but he already had a boyfriend, Jon, who was a member of the drag cabaret act 'The Pleased Wimmin'. Leigh, as usual, did everything he could to break them up. He hated Jon for no particular reason other than that he was Lee's boyfriend, and used to revel in telling the very prudish Jon that he had taken Lee to live sex shows in Amsterdam.

At this time I was working as a cashier in a fashionable gay bar run by Wayne Shires and Rod Lay, called Industria. One night Lee came down and for some unknown reason I made up a story to Leigh that he and his boyfriend Jon had been kissing in the corner. I could never have imagined the effect that this seemingly innocuous fib would have on Leigh, who went ballistic, demanding to know every detail. I couldn't believe his reaction, so carried on with the lie. It was the first and only time that I managed to wind Leigh up. I could only keep up the pretence for an hour or so, and then, to the relief of Leigh, I told him that it wasn't true. He liked to imagine that Lee and his boyfriend had no sex life, to keep alive the hope that one day he and Lee would be lovers.

Leigh realized that his chosen way of life made it hard to have a proper relationship, as he told the *Sunday Times* in 1993: 'It certainly does my sex life no favours and I've had no intimate relationship for many years.' He was most people's idea of a nightmare to go out with: forever controlling, sometimes loving, but deep down feeling that he wasn't attractive enough to deserve a happy relationship.

Leigh always had more luck with his female admirers. He first met Rachel Auburn at her stall in Kensington Market in 1982. Rachel was small and quite dumpy, with bleached blonde hair and enormous breasts, although a couple of years later she became very svelte. She had seen Leigh and Trojan wandering up and down the Portobello Road and had been struck by the strange outfits they wore, Leigh in a home-made, wide-shouldered tweed suit and Trojan in pyjamas clutching a tiny, old-fashioned brown suitcase. They went round to each other's houses and found that they got on quite well. Rachel hadn't known Leigh long when she asked him to go to Corsica with her, not really thinking he'd come. When he did, she found him to be the most interesting travelling companion. They mainly talked about sex and fashion: 'I had never met anyone before who was so sexually open and up-front. He told me all of his cottaging stories and encouraged me to become more sexually open myself.' There was a big French Foreign Legion base where they were staying, so by the end of the holiday, with Leigh's

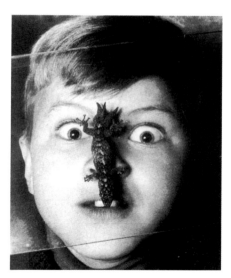

TOP Baby Leigh aged 15 months.

ABOVE Leigh's first publicity photo – for a local paper
when he discovered a three-tailed lizard in his garden.

Leigh and friends, *c.* 1981: Lorraine and Trojan; Leigh and Trojan;
Scarlett and Trojan; Trojan's Sandra; Fat Gill.

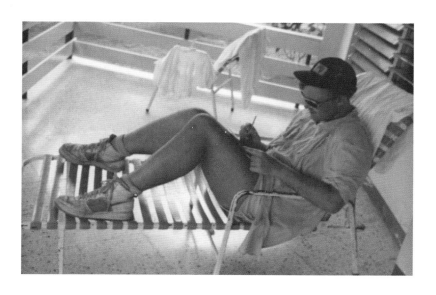

TOP Leigh writing postcards in Jamaica, 1983.

ABOVE Leigh, Richard Habberley and Trojan outside the
U.N. building, New York, 1984.

TOP Leigh trying to look sexy in his flat, *c.* 1983.

ABOVE Leigh waking up in New York after too much vodka and Cran-Grape, 1984.

TOP Leigh, Trojan and Sue on the Isle of Wight ferry, 1984.

ABOVE Leigh and Jeffrey Hinton at the Schonbrunn Palace, Vienna, c. 1986.

ABOVE Leigh and Trojan in the toilets at a Max gig in Brighton, 1985.

OPPOSITE ABOVE Leigh outside the gents at Taboo, 1988.

OPPOSITE BELOW Jeffrey Hinton, Leigh (in casual dress!),
Baillie Walsh and John Maybury, Christmas 1987.

TOP Leigh and Wigan in U4 Disco, Vienna, 1986.
ABOVE Leigh and Nicola at Daisy Chain, 1988.

encouragement, Rachel had slept with several of the gorgeous legionnaires. 'He egged me on to do things I wouldn't normally have done or even have thought of doing.'

After the holiday Rachel hung around with Leigh much more, and they would go to art galleries and the cinema, mainly to watch arty films at the Electric or the Scala. Leigh was still obsessed with John Waters, and any time a Divine film was showing he would be there with a large posse in tow. Rachel began to admire Leigh more and more, excited by his intellect, his open-mindedness and his willingness to experiment. 'I loved how Leigh was twisted, but in a funny way. I liked the way he could verbalize all the sick things you thought of in your mind.'

Rachel fancied Trojan, who was such a perfect, handsome boy. She more or less forced him to have sex with her, although she found the experience less than satisfying. 'He was a typical Virgo – very passive, reflecting in other people's glory. I don't think he really liked sex.' She used to give Leigh full accounts of what had gone on between her and Trojan, and Leigh loved to hear these tales because he wasn't yet obsessed with Trojan himself.

In 1983, when Leigh was between flats for a while, he slept under the cutting-room table in Rachel's flat on the All Saints Road. Because it was very uncomfortable she said that he could share her bed in her flat opposite. Tucked under the covers they used to talk about all their sexual experiences, and Rachel used to ask him why he had never slept with a girl. One night he got a hard on, so they decided to do it. There was not much kissing involved, nor much foreplay, but Rachel was happy because although she didn't physically fancy Leigh she had grown very emotionally attached to him. Years later, Leigh greatly exaggerated the story as part of his only attempt at stand-up comedy at a pub in Holborn, but Rachel took it in good spirit and laughed along with the rest of the audience. They had sex several times after this, but Leigh would taunt her by going off to Holland Park to find a man as soon as they had finished.

The sex between them fizzled out when Rachel realized she was on a road to nowhere. She was an independent woman with her own career and her own life to lead. She eventually had a son with her then boyfriend Dick Jewell, Jack, to whom Leigh was godfather. Leigh was very kind to his godson and often babysat, always remembering his birthday and buying him lovely presents.

When Leigh met Nicola Bateman at Taboo she thought he was the most gorgeous man she had ever met. She had suffered from spina bifida growing up and for most of her teens she had been encased in a plastic corset to correct her back problems. Because of this she started going out with boys later than most girls. When she met Leigh she was ripe and ready to experiment with the newfound glories of sex.

As her relationship with Leigh got stronger, she would go round to his house before they went out, helping him to get ready and having a few drinks. After they had been out she would always get the night bus back to her flat in North London, and it would be a couple of years before she first stayed the night at Leigh's. She really fancied him and was delighted when they got home drunk from a nightclub and he started experimenting with her. Leigh put a rubber glove on and started investigating her vagina. He then got more daring and began to penetrate her, and they had full sex, which Nicola loved. This started a sexual relationship that was to last for several years.

Once Leigh realized the lengths Nicola would go to in order to please him, he made her do more and more outrageous things.

He once asked her to put a carrot up her vagina before they went to the cinema. She happily agreed to this and sat with it up there throughout the film. On the bus home it began to fall out, so he shoved it up again. When they got home he rubbed his hands gleefully and said the carrot was nicely roasted, and proceeded to shag her with it as if it was a dildo. He had a bit of a thing about vegetables. On another occasion they were eating corn on the cob when Rachel called. While he was on the phone to Rachel, Leigh dared Nicola to put the corn on the cob up herself. At first she refused, and the more he pleaded the more she refused, but in the end she decided to do it to shock him as he didn't think she would. Leigh was screaming down the phone to Rachel exactly what Nicola had done. He admired her for her daring and the things she would do. He loved anyone who would act in an extreme way and not mind.

Leigh loved to play his friends off against each other. He often said I should be more daring and open-minded like Nicola, but I couldn't bring myself to be. I still find it difficult to climb up the stairs on a bus because if I was with Leigh he would always follow me and pull my skirt up over my head. If you tried to get your own back on him by pulling off his wig, he would make you look stupid and cruel by talking in a loud voice about his leukemia and imaginary chemotherapy.

Once Leigh found out that he was HIV positive, he stopped making love to Nicola and used dildos instead. He often took her shopping to buy a new one. He bought her a double-ended one that she once wore out underneath a pair of tight trousers. Leigh delighted in showing everyone Nicola's packet. After a while the dildo sex stopped too and their relationship developed into a mutual friendship, although sometimes if he was really drunk he would try to stick his fingers up her fanny in a nightclub just for shock value. He used to tease her in front of other people, saying 'Your pussy is so big it's like throwing a chipolata up Oxford Street.'

Nicola found it hard to talk to Leigh about her emotions, so she drew little books that expressed her true feelings, and gave those to him. A lot of the time Leigh was really horrible to Nicola. Usually she would put up with it, but sometimes she just snapped and started shouting at him. He would pick her up and lock her on the balcony of his flat, and she would shout for a couple of hours, but then she would start laughing at the absurdity of the situation, and once he heard her laugh he would let her back in. Or he would lock her in the bathroom or toilet, and to get her own back she would screech out Whitney Houston songs.

Once Nicola started sequinning for Leigh she spent most of her time at his flat. She was a very diligent worker and would individually sew sequins on for hours at a time. Leigh cruelly told Michael Clark that she had 'no friends so she gave each sequin a name'. When they had been out the night before she would get up early and start sewing and he would lie in his massive bed gossiping on the phone. Every now and then he would shout out 'Bitch, sandwich' and Nicola, knowing that he really meant 'bitch' as a term of affection, would run off and make him whatever he wanted. He never used to gossip to Nicola and he kept all the details of his private life from her; she would never know what he was talking about on the phone except when he was telling his friends how stupid she was, when he made sure she heard every word. He always said she was stupid and he told her he would try to educate her. He started by teaching her the names of the supermodels, but they were all wrong. He would bring Lee

Benjamin into the room, hold up *Vogue* and ask Nicola to name the model. Lee would die when she said Linda Evangelica. Nicola used to get her own back on Leigh when she was lacing him into his corsets for his latest fashion look. She would tie them as tight as she possibly could, putting her knee into his back to get better leverage, thoroughly enjoying his gasps of pain.

However horrible Leigh was to Nicola, he loved the way she loved him. He liked the way she would cuddle him and stroke him; because of his strange sex life in public toilets he missed out on those things, so Nicola fulfilled that part of his life for him. He wanted to keep her happy so that she would continue to look after him. Sometimes he was very kind to her and would take her abroad on trips as his assistant. She had to work hard, but she loved to know that Leigh depended on her.

He hated it if Nicola had a boyfriend, which she sometimes did, because she realized that she could never have a proper relationship with Leigh. At one point she was going out with Alex Binnie, who had pierced Leigh's cheeks and had done a tattoo saying 'MUM' in his mouth. Leigh hated this and did everything he could to split them up. When he knew Nicola had arranged a date with Alex, he would say he had a photo session arranged and could she stay to help him. Of course Nicola would; she sat and waited and nobody turned up. When she asked Leigh why, he replied 'Oh, sorry, I forgot to tell you they phoned and cancelled.'

When I started going out with a new boyfriend, Leigh was desperate to see what he was like so he could mock me. One night the man had come round, and at about midnight there was a sudden, loud banging on the front door. It was Leigh, who had taken two buses just to get a look at him. I couldn't believe it, and screeched at him to go away, although it was quite flattering that he should show such an interest in my business.

Whenever Les Child found a new romance, Leigh would wheedle the details out of him and then spread them all around. 'She hated it when anyone had a man, hated it. Hated anyone to have more sex than she did.' When Michael Clark started going out with choreographer Stephen Petronio, Leigh really hated that too, and he once phoned up Michael only to find that he had left a very romantic message for his new boyfriend as his answerphone greeting in case he rang. Leigh thought that this was truly sick. He phoned up everyone he knew and told them to call Michael just so they could all hear the message. Years later, when he was working with Rifat Ozbek, Leigh did everything he could to get the designer to split up with his boyfriend. 'He always wanted to separate me from my boyfriend. He would go on and on, on the phone and then I'd put the phone down. Then he'd ring again. "If you're gonna start about Barton, Leigh, I'm gonna put the phone down." Then he'd start again; then I'd put the phone down and not pick it up again because I knew it would be him.' Just to be contrary, Leigh would sometimes try to make people who had split up get back together. He hated it when Cerith and Angus split up after many years together and did his best to manoeuvre a reconciliation.

Nicola finished with Alex because she couldn't stand the pressure Leigh put on her. A couple of years later she went out with another man, who was keen on perverted sex involving voyeurism and videos. In Nicola he found someone who was keen to experiment and who would join in his games. He introduced her to the fetishism scene and took her to wife-swapping parties in the suburbs. Leigh really hated this man (for once with good reason, as he was not very pleasant) and again tried to split them up, although he did enjoy the stories of Nicola's scandalous behaviour and loved telling all and sundry of her antics.

Leigh hated the fact that Nicola was not there at his beck and call and that sometimes he had to go out on his own without her to help him dress. He hated the fact that she wasn't there in the morning to make him toast. Most of all he hated the fact that someone took precedence over him. But eventually the relationship ended, much to the relief of Leigh.

He dreaded the thought of Nicola going off with someone else, so eventually he decided to marry her. One night they were coming home in a black cab when he said 'Sorry, this isn't a very romantic place, but will you marry me?' Nicola was amused and sceptical, but of course accepted straight away. He told her she had to arrange it all and he would go along with her plans. Nicola booked a date, but unfortunately Leigh's mother became ill, so he had to return to Australia and the wedding was cancelled. When Leigh returned from Australia he had bought an opal ring in a duty-free shop, which he presented to Nicola, suggesting that they rebook the wedding. It wasn't long until the three months were up, at which point they would lose their licence money, so they looked at the calendar and saw the perfect date – Friday 13 May 1994. Christine, Nicola's sister, was to be the bridesmaid and Cerith was to be best man. Leigh told him he was marrying Nicola for tax purposes, and told Nicola he was marrying her as 'A little private art performance, just between ourselves.' He made it clear that no one was to be told of the impending nuptials.

Leigh wasn't in a great mood on the morning of the wedding, and could not believe that Nicola had taken it so seriously that she was wearing something old, something new, something borrowed and something blue. (But when she told him it was tongue-in-cheek, he cheered up.) She had also bought her own wedding ring and bridal bouquet, and was wearing a simple, long blue dress that she had made herself, with a lacy garter around her thigh. Leigh was wearing a knee-length Jewish-style coat that he had bought in Brick Lane market. He had a fairly long blond wig on and a small amount of make-up, just a dusting of powder and some blusher. Christine was dressed in a very extreme seventies look with a bouffant hairdo and Cerith was in a Yohji suit. The four of them trooped off to Bow Registry Office.

They had to wait in a side room for about twenty minutes. Leigh insisted that Nicola take lots of photos of the cheap clock and the plastic flower arrangements to document this special occasion. Leigh and Cerith had terrible giggles as Nicola kept saying for their amusement that it was the most important day in a woman's life. The registrar heard them giggling, and before she ushered the party into the main room she stressed that it was a very serious event. It was at this point that Cerith realized that they really were getting married. 'It wasn't that Leigh wasn't taking the whole thing seriously, but you got the sense that it was Nicola's day, she was finally getting married to Leigh and it meant really a lot to her.' All the time Nicola was worried that the wedding would be stopped because the registrar would think that Leigh was an illegal immigrant, but it went ahead without a hitch. They were then sent round to the back to have photographs taken. The council had made an effort to make a little garden that could almost pass for the grounds of a country church, but if you looked in the other direction there was a backdrop of tower blocks and a used car lot, which they used for their photographs.

They then went to the West End for the wedding reception. However, Leigh's mood had got worse by now, and he said he had to go to a rehearsal of a musical performance with his friend Richard Torry. So Nicola, Christine and Cerith went to the Angus Steak House in Leicester Square, where Nicola insisted that Cerith eat whatever he liked as it was her wedding day. They then met up with Leigh, who was so hungry that he had his own wedding feast in TGI Fridays while the others carried on drinking. He was in a foul mood, and the false jollity of the waitresses did not make him any happier. Cerith then remembered that there was a James Bond party at the Architectural Association where he worked, so he took the others along. Christine was highly commended for her costume, which she had been wearing all day, and got so drunk that she left the 3-D camera in the ladies' toilets, so the planned exhibition of photos of the event could never take place.

A couple of days later Nicola and Leigh went to Amsterdam to perform with Leigh's band Minty at the Love Ball. Nicola found it very romantic:

> The people who had paid for us to go there had paid for us to go on a canal boat. Leigh was really sweet, he slipped away to the bar and came back with two glasses of wine, which was unusual for him as he never drank in the day, he then toasted me with his glass of red wine and hoped that we'd be very happy.

They returned to London and Nicola found that marriage had changed her feelings towards Leigh. 'I didn't mind doing the washing-up nearly so much, or doing his washing because it seemed proper that a wife should do those things.' Leigh, of course, did not become a conventional husband to Nicola. He still loved her in his own way, but continued to treat her as he had always done.

7

Fashion

When Leigh arrived in London he was determined to be a fashion designer, as he wrote in his journal in 1981:

> I believe that fashion (where all the girls have clear skin, blue eyes, blonde blow-waved hair and a size ten figure and where all the men have clear skin, moustaches, short blow-waved hair and masculine physique and appearance) STINKS. I think that firstly individuality is important, and that there should be no main rules for behaviour and appearance. Therefore I want to look as best as I can, through my means of individuality and expressiveness. I think that the clothes I am interested in are strictly the opposite to what's in mass taste, and that there is a minority that like the same style as me.

For the first year in London, Leigh only made clothes for himself. He made things in the New Romantic style to fit in with the scene that he had almost just missed. He would sometimes make a shirt for a friend or to send back to Bronwyn in Australia as a present. But all the time he was working at Burger King he was desperate to become involved somehow in fashion. After he had been introduced to the London club scene, he met a woman who had a clothes shop in Pembridge Road. He got a job making clothes out of curtains, which he ran up in his flat and then trundled down the road to the shop. He was also able to make more clothes for his friends, who were very eager to wear his unusual designs.

When he met Rachel Auburn she was already quite successful in the fashion business, and as she liked Leigh's clothes she persuaded him to set up a shop in Kensington Market, where she had a stall. Leigh was obsessed by Vivienne Westwood and his first designs were based on her 'Buffalo Girl' collection, as worn by Bow Wow Wow and Adam and the Ants. He made long, brown woolly skirts with big stitches around the bottom to keep the hems up and made lots of shirts and dresses in muted, checked cotton polyester fabric. He was very fond of patchwork and mixing and matching different fabrics. He liked the star motif and perfected a pattern whereby he could insert a star into the front of a garment rather than appliquéing it on later. He employed his slave of the time, Lorraine, to work on the stall, but he hardly ever paid her and in fact he sometimes made her pay him for the privilege of working there. If she didn't make any money on the stall he made her life a misery, but she seemed to enjoyed the humiliation.

Rachel had met Michael and Gerlinde Kostiff in 1981. They were perhaps the trendiest couple around at the time. They were older than most of the people on the scene, but they were very modern: both were tall and thin and usually dressed head to toe in Vivienne Westwood. Michael was a down-to-earth Northerner and Gerlinde was a very glamorous German, and they both liked to encourage new talent. Gerlinde had been buying some clothes from Leigh and Rachel, so she decided to introduce them to her good friend Susanne Bartsch, who put on fashion shows in New York and had a store where she sold British fashion. Susanne arranged for Leigh and Rachel to go to New York to show their clothes. It was here that Leigh decided he didn't want to be a mainstream fashion designer. He loved designing the clothes, but the thought of producing them all was too much to contemplate. He also decided that he would no longer be influenced by Vivienne Westwood or anyone else. He would make what he wanted to make and whether other people liked it or not was their business. It didn't matter to him, as he wasn't trying to sell the garments anyway.

Rachel was really shocked when he came up with his new look. 'It was so unfashionable and not like anything else. It was seventies glitter, satin, stretchy fabrics and fake fur. Everyone else's look was still Hard Times. I dared him to walk down All Saints Road in it, which was still like the front line at the time. He went teetering along with his platform boots on, and all the rastas were shouting out "Botty Man" but he didn't care.' Even though the look didn't make Leigh much money, it did get him a lot of attention. Rachel was even slightly jealous, because Leigh had dared to do exactly what he wanted and had been rewarded with enormous press coverage. It was a two-way jealousy, though, because Leigh was envious of the money Rachel made. He and Trojan would sometimes sneak into her studio and rip up cheques that buyers had given her, as well as nicking any cash that was lying around.

In 1983 Lynne Franks, the absolutely fabulous fashion PR agent, offered to promote Leigh and Rachel for nothing in an attempt to give her company free publicity. She had an office in Long Acre where she stocked a few of their garments. Rachel sold a few, but Leigh wasn't so successful – much to his relief, because he didn't want to keep making the same thing over and over again. These were very exciting days for Leigh and Rachel. She later recalled, 'It was the best time. My mind was being opened, everything was so creative, there was so much energy about. I felt alive and exciting.'

The so-called 'Paki from Outer Space' look that Leigh debuted on the London nightclub scene in 1983 was the first time that he had experimented with a totally made-up face. The look involved red, green or (usually) blue faces, decorated with gold writing and Indian accessories that he had bought in Brick Lane. He had always worn make-up before, but it was applied so subtly you wouldn't spot it unless you looked very hard. But from then on every look was finished off with its own make-up. The next make-up look was to complement his new frilly designs, when he made stockings with frills at the top, paired with pinnies and very detailed blouses covered in pockets, intricate collars and full sleeves. The cutting was very unusual and lots of the garments had uneven sleeves and clever capes and flounces. The colours were pink, brown and white. Most of it was made in pink gingham or synthetic lace, which he was able to buy very cheaply on Brick Lane. He made large, floppy hats to match and even covered shoes in the frills so they resembled very large slippers. The make-up consisted of wide panels of white, brown and pink aquacolour painted onto the face, at first still with some blue round the edge and a couple of bindis in the middle of his forehead so that it wasn't such a big step from his 'Paki' look.

If Leigh was feeling particularly daring, he would wear this look without the frilly knickers, so that his bottom was bare. This caused a furore and he was very pleased when he ended up in one of those celebrity montages at the front of the *Sunday People* magazine. Alexander McQueen was later hailed as a design genius when he put his models into 'bumsters', but Leigh at this earlier time was just seen as an eccentric.

While Leigh was wearing this look he was asked to do a show at the ICA as part of the Performing Clothes Week. He gathered together some models and put them all in his bumless tights and frilly blouses. All the other designers showing took it very seriously and had properly choreographed shows, but Leigh just gave his models vodka, poppers and magic mushrooms and let them do their own thing, so they ran up and down the catwalk stumbling into each other and falling over.

The show was repeated in Manchester at the Hacienda night-club. This was the first time that Adrian Howells, who was later to perform in the play *The Homosexual* with Leigh in 1993, came across him:

> We were very young and someone told us that Leigh needed some more models. We thought that this could be our pathway to fame and fortune, so at about five o'clock in the afternoon we nervously knocked on the dressing-room door. Someone mumbled 'Come in', so we entered the room to see about eight boys practically comatose lying all over the place. We asked for Leigh and this big lump appeared from underneath the dressing table, hardly able to speak. Sadly, he told us that he had enough models. We watched the show and not surprisingly they kept bumping into each other. I think it was too much for Manchester.

In late 1984, Susanne Bartsch took Leigh to Japan to show his frilly clothes. At the same time, Michael Kostiff organized an art show for Trojan. They were joined on this trip by other, more established, designers, including English Eccentrics, Betty Jackson, Wendy Dagworthy, John Richmond, Scott Crolla and Judy Blame. The Japanese were at first horrified at Leigh's show and didn't know what to make of it at all, but once they saw the other English designers laughing and clapping they dared to titter embarrassedly behind their hands. Rachel paraded up and down the catwalk with her bum out and her pubic hair on view, which completely shocked the Japanese. When Leigh and Trojan came out of the lift the hotel staff were scared to look at them and looked at the floor instead. One morning everyone had to get up early to go on a sightseeing coach tour of Tokyo. Leigh got on the coach in his pyjamas and the dressing gown provided by the hotel, which was at least four sizes too small. He had his feet squeezed into the tiny slippers that had been provided, which he kept on by hooking his big toe over the edge. No one was interested in the tour until they came across a running track and saw loads of young boys in tight running shorts taking their daily jog.

From this point on, Leigh changed his look every three months or so. Sometimes the new style would gradually take over from the old one; sometimes he would debut a radical new look. As he once said, 'I've always adored extremes, so that's usually what I incorporate into the "looks". There have been themes running through my work but it is always difficult to say where one ends and another begins.'

The next look was spotty. He changed the colour of his ging-ham to yellow, but he thought it was a bit dull, so he got one of the factories down Brick Lane to print burgundy spots all over it. He made shirts and jackets out of the fabric, and had also got hold of some maroon pinstripe material with which he tailored low-fronted frock coats. The low front was to show off his pierced nipples, from which he sometimes suspended a silver chain. To make his face blend in with the clothes he painted it yellow and covered it in matching burgundy spots, finishing the look with a grey wig. Leigh described his make-up look in *i-D*:

> I never try and conceal a spot. I put a big red circle around it. Most of my make-up I have collected from jumble sales over the years and I got a lot of it from Charles Fox. My make-up is mainly theatrical. This new look is a cross between polka dots and skin rash … simulating infection and disease. I've done it this way because I still like wearing make-up but I don't want to be a gender-bender … basically I never want to look ordinary.

Leigh felt that he wasn't getting enough press coverage at this time, so I sometimes went round to his flat before going out and acted as a photographer. He would pose and I would happily snap away, both of us pretending that I was David Bailey. The next day I would take the film down to Joe's Basement, a photography shop on Wardour Street, hoping that they would think I was a professional, and get a contact sheet printed up. We would pore over these, deciding which images were the best, and then get enlargements made. Surprisingly enough, they have popped up in a variety of magazines and newspapers over the years.

The next move for the yellow gingham was to get swastikas printed on it. This was too much for a lot of people, who could not believe that Leigh would go out as a gay man wearing such a shocking symbol. But as Leigh explained, it is an ancient symbol of the Indian gods, and he stuck to his guns and wore it whenever he wanted to.

In about 1985, the looks started getting even freakier. Leigh had gained extra confidence from running Taboo and just didn't give a damn what anyone thought. Up until now he still had some hair that he tried in vain to grow. When it wouldn't, he shaved it all off. This was a great liberation for him, and his head became another part of his body to decorate. He decided to put drips of paint on his head, changing the colour of them to match what he was wearing. He usually laid them over a white base, but sometimes it would be yellow or green. He loved the fact that at the end of the night you could just peel the drips off in one fell swoop.

At about this time Leigh began to decorate his clothes with fringing made out of Lady Jayne gold hair grips. He used to go to the local chemist and buy up all their packets of them. When they ran out, he would have to travel farther afield, and he found it very hard to find enough supplies to keep up with his demand until I suggested he contact the factory and get them wholesale.

In 1985 he was asked to customize a Levi's jacket for *Blitz* magazine. This was part of a big affair with a show at a West End theatre and an exhibition and auction at the Victoria & Albert museum, with all the profits going to charity. All the top British designers had been asked to take part. Leigh completely covered his jacket with hair grips so that it was almost too heavy to put on. It was a great success and raised several hundred pounds. He also debuted a new make-up look for the auction: the one-eye look. During one of his many trips to professional make-up supplier Charles Fox in Covent Garden he had discovered some theatrical putty, so he decided to cover his whole eye with it. It was a very disturbing look and one he didn't use again, as it was just too uncomfortable to wear.

Holly Johnson of Frankie Goes to Hollywood saw the jacket in *Blitz* and asked Leigh to make him one, which Leigh happily did. Leigh had previously made stage clothes for Blancmange and for the transsexual gender-bender Lanah Pellay. She was a very fussy customer and insisted on wearing Holly's jacket for publicity shots before Leigh gave it to him. Boy George also contacted Leigh to have some stage clothes made. 'The costumes made by Judy Blame and Leigh Bowery were meant to hide my expanding girth, although it was hard to look thin in an A-line smock with angel wings jutting out the back.' Leigh never had much of a head for business and charged ridiculously low prices for his clothes because he felt embarrassed to ask for more. He asked me to come round when Boy George came for a fitting because he would feel nervous on his own with such a megastar. After he had left, Leigh and I went for a ride on the Docklands Light Railway to celebrate his new commission. Leigh always had to sit in the front seat and pretend to be the driver.

Leigh then discovered the bustle, and began to wear long, checked dresses with an enormous protruding silhouette. This was years before Vivienne Westwood came out with her bustle collection. Sometimes he wore them on the outside of his clothes and, as he said, 'It came in very handy when I fell over as it didn't hurt nearly so much.'

Soon enough, Leigh got fed up with the paint drips and decided he wanted a pointy head. He experimented with shaving foam, but it wouldn't stand up to the rough treatment he gave it and had usually flattened within about five minutes. Once, while his mother was staying with him, Leigh asked her to make him some meringues as he was going to a tea party. She happily obliged, but she got home from sightseeing earlier than expected and was appalled to find her son with the lovingly cooked meringues stuck to his head. This idea didn't really work either, so he paid me to make him some painted cardboard helmets.

I started off by making a head shape on a balloon out of papier mâché, then stuck cardboard cones all over it and covered them in strips of newspaper for extra strength. They were then emulsioned and varnished to make quite a sturdy hat. They didn't really fit Leigh's head properly, as it wasn't the same shape as a balloon, so he stuffed the inside with foam to make it more comfortable. As we progressed we decided to make a plaster cast of his head so that it would fit perfectly. He sat on my sitting-room floor as I spread plaster all over his Vaseline-covered head. We then poured fresh plaster into the mould and used the result as a block for the base of the hats. As time went by, the points on the hats got longer and longer, so that he had a lot of trouble going through doors and I was always having to stick stray cones back on.

Leigh's next progression was to wear a strange, strappy harness on his head, to which he attached the tops of aerosol spray cans to cover his ears. He soon got bored with this, though, and wanted something more exciting. By now he had had his cheeks pierced and thought that he should be able to rig up a bulb in his mouth so the light would glow through the holes. Unfortunately, this wasn't really practical, because it meant having batteries in his mouth. Even with his very high pain threshold, he could not stand the taste of battery acid, and thought he might be electrocuted if he drank something. So he rigged up the light bulbs in the same harness as before and attached the batteries inside his clothes. Poor Nicola had to follow him around all night with spares because he didn't want his lights to go out. Charlie Atlas, a long-time friend and collaborator of Michael Clark, remembers going to a nightclub in his home town of New York with Leigh when he was wearing this look. 'It was always a drama as to when he should put the bulbs on. If he did it at home the batteries would run out by the time we reached the club, so we stopped in a parking lot just before the club to connect the batteries. It was disgusting, full of trash and rats, and he was leaping about trying to hide the batteries in his tights.'

Leigh spent hours making up beautiful garments from velvets, satins and other exotic fabrics, but they always ended up with a tide mark of grease paint round the neck that was very hard to remove. Leigh didn't want people to see his face but he was fed up with these greasy marks, so he decided to cover his face with material. In about 1988 he started to design beautiful crewel-work cloaks with an attached total head mask in the same material. There were little holes for his eyes and mouth, and he still had to put make-up on these areas, but at least it didn't ruin the entire garment. By now he had discovered Nicola's talent at sequinning and she used to sit for hours adding adornment to the crewel work. She sewed the sequins on individually, with a little bead in the middle of each one so that there would be no ugly line of cotton going across the sequin. He continued this look for a while because it was so much quicker to get ready, and had a vast number of the hooded capes made in a variety of fabrics.

Leigh then became friendly with Mark Erskine-Pullin, usually known as Mr Pearl, a South African corsetmaker who was very talented at fine detail work and embroidery. Pearl was obsessed with corsetry and gave Leigh a great deal of help and inspiration in this line. Leigh loved the idea of transforming the body into a different shape, and because he had a lot of extra pounds it was much easier for him to distort and sculpt his flesh. The two of them would spend hours poring over Victorian corsetry books to give them new ideas. They developed corsets of every shape, and Leigh loved them so much he started wearing them on their own rather than as under garments. He described his look to *Modern Painters* magazine:

> Because I'm chubby I can pleat the flesh across my chest and hold it in place with heavy-grade gaffer tape. Then, by wearing a specially constructed, under-padded bra, I create the impression of a heaving bosom with a six-inch cleavage. Rather than dance with my penis flopping about I do a tuck and glue job: inverting the penis inward and pushing the balls up into the pelvic cavity. I take a strip of gaffer tape and secure everything into place. I then glue on a pubic wig, using theatrical spirit gum. The effect? – big breasts and a luxurious bush, and I'm still able to do splits and high kicks without anything falling out.
>
> Of course I have to shave my pubes right off to facilitate taping and gluing, and the strips of gaffer tape bound tightly round my tits almost invariably begin to cut into me, finally breaking the skin, leaving quite spectacular marks, as if I'd been whipped across my upper carriage with a riding crop. I shave my legs as well, and my arms, my chest, my pits and all my hair off.

Nicola made him fantastic bugle-beaded headdresses to finish off the look. These covered the head and were shaped to look like bug eyes, with beautiful strands of glass coming over his face, giving it a shimmering glimmer. Leigh made gloves for himself by covering his hands in glue and then sticking them into a tub of glitter and made his pubic wigs out of fun fur, which he set with spirit gum. He used to call them merkins. I wondered how he could survive without going to the toilet, especially as he drank so much. 'If you want something enough,' he replied, 'you can do anything. I dance a lot, so I sweat the liquid out of myself.'

He was only caught out once, when he went to a rather stylish fashion party at a grand house in Islington thrown by the designer Jacques Azagury. He was very generous and there was plenty of drink and food available. When Leigh arrived he was rather out of place, as everyone else was rather sophisticated in a smart, casual kind of way, and he was practically naked. He was a bit nervous about this party, so he had drunk a bottle of vodka before leaving his house. He was manically jumping about and making the ornaments shake. Baillie Walsh and Rifat Ozbek thought that they should calm him down, so they gave him a Rohypnol. Since he didn't usually take drugs, he completely collapsed. He was falling all over the place and was desperate to go to the toilet. He was all of a fluster and didn't know what to do with himself. Mr Pearl ripped off his merkin with an evil look on his face and Leigh dashed into the garden to relieve himself. He was so off his head that he fell onto the front step, cracking his head open. He stumbled up three flights of stairs, dripping blood all over the thick, white shag-pile carpet, and then passed out on the bed, covering several expensive designer coats with his blood. When he came to, he couldn't really remember what had happened, but he phoned Nicola and asked her to come over at once as he needed a nurse. When she saw the extent of his injuries she insisted he go to casualty to get stitches, which he did.

Mr Pearl and Leigh also designed exquisite neck corsets covered in exotic stones or beautiful lace. They were very uncomfortable to wear – when I put one on I thought I might choke to death – but Leigh found them very comfortable and loved the way they improved his posture. Rifat Ozbek used them in one of his shows, and another turned up in a George Michael video.

In August 1990, Leigh decided that he could afford a full-time assistant. He was modelling at Lucian's studio and was earning fairly reasonable money, so he thought he would be able to pay about £30 per day. He originally wanted Jon of the Pleased Wimmin to work for him, because he had seen and admired his work, but Jon didn't really want to do it, as he saw his career developing in other directions. He suggested his boyfriend, Lee Benjamin. Lee wasn't working at the time and £30 seemed like a fortune, so he jumped at the opportunity.

The first job he had to do for Leigh was to knit a massive red dress on very large needles that Leigh was going to wear for a show in Japan. He had been booked to pose as a mannequin in a shop window. Nicola was going to be at his side and would gradually pull at a loose thread so that the dress would slowly unravel, leaving a naked Leigh in the window.

By now Leigh had been working for Lucian as a model for several months, and his concept of fashion was radically changing. He didn't see clothes as mere fashion items but as a way of changing the whole shape of the human body. Lucian used the naked, unadorned body as the subject matter for most of his paintings, and Leigh was fascinated by the way Lucian's figures sometimes had oversized feet because they were nearest to him when he painted them. Leigh became interested in perspective and decided to use his body as his main material and find as many interesting ways as he could to distort it and change people's perception of what the body is. He decided to drop all the fancy decoration on his clothes, all the sequins and all the glamour. While he was in Japan he found a brochure for a range of Transformer robots. He loved the strange shapes they made and the exaggerated limbs with massive feet. He used this as inspiration for his new look.

As soon as he was back from Japan, he set Lee the task of making a pair of boot covers for his platform trainers. He bought a large roll of gunmetal nylon and lined it with foam rubber sheeting to make a quilted jacket with enormous breasts built in. His ideas then got more ambitious: he decided that he wanted to make a jacket with sleeves made with a ball from the shoulder to the elbow and then a bell shape to the wrist. He set Lee challenges, which Lee really enjoyed. The next jacket they made was to be in beige nylon with completely spherical sleeves. Leigh used to go to a shop in the Pentonville Road that specialized in rubber and foam to buy great big blocks of foam rubber. He and Lee would carve away at these blocks to get exactly the shape that they wanted. The sleeves took ages to perfect, but in the end they were very successful. Leigh loved the idea of complete distortion and went on to make several other outfits with the foam. It was very good for travelling, too, because you could squash it into a suitcase and it would jump back into shape as soon as it was unpacked.

Just before this look, Leigh had been wearing LL Cool J-style hats that he had made out of netting. He made one with a net mohican down the middle, which he quite liked, so he decided to extend the look further. He made a hat with one-inch frills all over it that completely covered his face. He wore it to a Kinky Gerlinky party (a club night hosted by Michael and Gerlinde Kostiff), but when he saw the photographs afterwards he was very disappointed, because he realized that people could still see his eyes and mouth through it. He then decided to make the frills about six inches across, which made his head look like a massive pompom. People couldn't understand how he could see, but as the net was so close to his face he could see right through it, although his vision was somewhat blurred. These headdresses perfectly suited his new look and his new philosophy, moving the emphasis away from his face and making his head a simple ball.

The next big outfit Leigh and Lee made together was called 'Globe'. It consisted of a brown nylon top with a massive pregnant belly, straight, elbow-length sleeves and a high collar with a wide neck, out of which popped the netting-ball head. With it, Leigh wore a plain, knee-length brown skirt and huge brown half-globes on his feet. This outfit started out as a striped swimming costume; after three months of alterations, Leigh was finally happy with it.

Leigh then decided to completely change the shape of his legs. He wanted to make a boot that would disguise the fact that he had feet and ankles. He wanted it to go straight up from his toes to his knee. He and Lee carved away at the foam, but it was very difficult. Whenever Leigh walked the leg would crease. Finally, after several weeks of trying, he came up with something that seemed to work. Instead of going up to the knee, the boot went right to the top of the thigh. And to make things even more distorted, Leigh decided to wear this on one leg and to keep the other a normal shape. As the built-up leg had a platform trainer inside it, he had to make his other leg the same length by building up his platform stilettos so he could wear one on the other foot. Leigh loved the 'leg in plaster' look and stuck with it for a couple of years, incorporating it into several new outfits.

In 1993 Leigh was interviewed by Nilgün Yusuf for the *Sunday Times* magazine. He explained why he was no longer interested in fashion as such:

> My body is capable of innumerable shapes and forms. The idea of transforming oneself gives courage and vigour. It reduces the absurdity, you can do anything dressed like this. Things that used to embarrass me, like nudity and gender confusion, don't any more. I have used my discomfort to explore these areas. I don't even know where some of the ideas come from. I want to disturb, entertain and stimulate. It's more about silhouette alteration than restriction, though I do like that frisson of sexual danger. I don't practise S&M, but it interests me. I like to think that I reform rather than deform the body. In the past we became accustomed to strange shapes such as padded shoulders and crinolines.

He explained further to *HQ* magazine:

> It's not as though I have a formula for fear or merriment. When I make a costume I'm not thinking about how people are going to react. It's much more sculptural than that. The human form is something which I am totally obsessed by. I'm interested in a jarring aesthetic and the tension between contradictions – the idea that something can be frightening and heroic and pathetic all at the same time.

Leigh's costumes were certainly uncomfortable, but he thought that the pain was well worth the result. Although he wasn't interested in S&M as a sexual practice for himself, he was very interested in it when done by others. Nicola had begun to go to fetish clubs, and she persuaded Leigh to come with her. He thought that most of the people and most of the outfits were naff, but it still inspired him to design a fabulous all-in-one black PVC Lycra body suit. He had made the original prototype in white stretch satin: it had a round neck and short sleeves, and he wore it with a Madonna-style pony-tail with small plaits wrapped around it stuck to his head. He wore it once in New York, but decided it was 'too sixties', so he went to work with the black PVC. The outfit had one padded leg, padded hips, enormous pointed breasts, gloves attached to the arms and a black, tight-fitting hood over his face with long thin slits for eyes, all topped off with a long black ponytail. It was an incredibly strong look, but rather frightening. Nicola had to squeeze him into it, zip him up and then polish it with Mr Sheen.

Leigh's next look was inspired by home improvements. He had finally decided to buy a new toilet seat because the old one, made out of padded maroon vinyl, was all ripped. He had fitted the new seat and was wandering around the flat wearing the old one round his neck, pretending to Nicola that it was his new necklace. Suddenly it was a joke no longer and within a week he was out in London clubland with a brand-new look: he attached the seat to a long, Lycra tube dress, painted his face white and stuck lots of Rice Krispies on his head to look like excrement coming out of the toilet.

He used this look as an inspiration for costumes for Michael Clark's 1992 show. Lee Benjamin helped to make costumes for Michael for about a year. When the show was nearing, he and Leigh would work for three nights in a row without any proper sleep – just a couple of hours grabbed here and there. Lee often went without sleep as Leigh approached a deadline. It wasn't that either of them was lazy – they worked constantly – it was just that they set themselves such difficult challenges and Leigh was such a perfectionist he insisted on everything being perfect. He would think nothing of unpicking six hours' worth of sewing if he thought another centimetre off a seam would improve the hang of the garment.

The most complicated outfit he ever made looked like it was knocked up in a couple of hours, but in fact it took about three months. Leigh had found a picture of Audrey Hepburn in a simple, one-shouldered pink dress designed by Yves St Laurent that inspired him to design a similar look for himself. The material he chose was a very garish floral fabric that he had picked up in Shepherd's Bush Market for 99p per metre. The dress was very heavily corseted inside, with cast-iron bones that Leigh had found in New York. They were designed for orthopaedic patients and had no give in them at all, so they were absolute agony to wear. The dress was originally going to have a long skirt, but Leigh decided he wanted to wear the fat leg with it, so the skirt was designed to go just round that leg and to leave the other one free. In the end, the dress had one shoulder and one leg, on opposite sides of the body.

Even while making all these freaky clothes for himself, Leigh continued to make me lots of gorgeous, wearable creations. Sometimes I would go round to his house and he would just throw something at me saying 'Oh, I just knocked this up for you', and when I looked at it, it would be the most beautiful gown. Sometimes if I did an errand or a job for him he would make me something in return, or if he was particularly poor and I had some money I would pay him to make me something. He would refuse to take more than about £40 and often provided the material himself too. When his washing machine broke he couldn't afford a new one, so I bought him one out of my Janet Frazer catalogue and he made me a coat, five dresses and four tops in return. I would sometimes give him a rough idea of what I wanted, or sometimes he would just design it himself.

If I was going to a special party he would spend hours making me a fantastic outfit. I used to tell him he could just throw it together but he couldn't do it; everything had to be perfect. Once, Kinky Gerlinky had an international theme, so I decided I wanted a tartan dress for a Scottish look. I bought some cheap red tartan in Brick Lane, and when I went to pick the dress up a couple of days later I couldn't believe my eyes, it was so beautiful. It had leg-o'-mutton sleeves, a square, low-cut neck with a beautifully fitted bodice and the fullest skirt made up of two whole circles of fabric. He had also made an underskirt out of white taffeta that was just as big, and he had gone to the trouble of hemming it with red bias binding. To wear underneath it he had made me a fully boned corset with a beautiful cotton modesty frill at the top, attached to the main corset with tiny buttons so that I could remove it if I felt particularly daring.

He was not happy with just making the dress, but insisted on coming round to my house on the night of the party, lacing me into the corset – which I moaned about constantly as it hurt so much – doing my hair in a very elaborate style with about three hair pieces and even applying my make-up. It was worth it: everyone admired my dress, but most of them were more stunned by my massive bosoms, which were hoisted up so high they made a shelf under my chin that easily supported two glasses of wine and an empty ash tray. However much attention I got, I realized that I would always put comfort before fashion. It was the best feeling in the world, getting home and ripping that corset off. Leigh must have suffered so much in the name of style, but he didn't mind at all. When I asked him about it he said that the vodka soon dulled the pain and the flattering comments and attention made it all worthwhile.

As well as sewing me glamorous ball gowns, Leigh made me fashionable clothes for work. Whenever he rang me at the office, which was frequently, I had to describe what I was wearing. To make the conversation quicker we decided to name all the garments he made me. The Scottish dress was called Merry Queen of Scots (Merry for short); a blue, lacy, frothy dress was called Brook; a sensible pinstriped dress was Constance due to its constant stripe; a very plain burgundy dress was Margaret; a small blue flowery pinafore was Lobelia; and a massive orange Madras-check Country and Western dress was Clementine. I had a good friend at work, Graham Stevens, who used to go to ChaChas and Taboo and therefore knew Leigh. He absolutely loved the names of my dresses and used to run round work telling the other people which one I had on that day. So I used to be surprised when a very straight boy would come up to me and say 'Oh, I see you're wearing Martha today.'

Rifat Ozbek recognized Leigh's amazing talent and asked him to help him with his collections. 'I just wanted somebody from the outside who had a different idea of proportion, of body distortion, of how he thought, his mind, in my collection. I just wanted to have him around.' They travelled to Italy several times and Rifat was thrilled with Leigh's advice: 'He'd say, "If you're going to slit it high, slit it higher! If it's short, make it really short! If it's long put a train on it!'"

As ever, Leigh liked to take things to extremes. His designs, although never available to the general public, have influenced a generation of designers and I'm sure they will do so for many years to come as people catch up with his advanced vision.

8

At Home

Soon after meeting his new friends at ChaChas, Leigh became a fully-fledged Londoner. He took to drinking when he found that he could consume more than two pints and also started to experiment with drugs, but never on a major scale. At the beginning of 1982 he and Trojan moved to a squat that they shared with two glamorous black sisters, Debbie and Marulla, but they soon fell out with the girls and Leigh managed to rent a bedsit in a large house in Ladbroke Grove where the landlord let rooms exclusively to gay men. David Walls moved in, too, and Trojan moved to a flat on the Caledonian Road near Pentonville Prison.

There was a gay evangelical bus driver in the room next door to Leigh. He didn't really fit in with all the other occupants, who liked to think that they were a bit trendy. Leigh badly wanted his room as a studio, so he did his best to get rid of him. He found a way to get into his room and once or twice a week he would go in there and move everything around, but not take anything. He would play his music really loudly and make his slave of the time, Lorraine, come round at 3 a.m. to knock very loudly on the door and beg for drugs and syringes just to disturb his neighbour's sleep. None of this worked, so Leigh decided to take more drastic action. He persuaded David to go into the room with him and they laid the bus driver's clothes out on the bed in the shape of a man, then got out his Bible. As Leigh and David both came from religious backgrounds they were well versed in the Bible and knew where all the gay references were, so they underlined them all in red biro. This was the final straw for the man. He moved out and Leigh got his studio.

The house was divided into about ten flats and everyone knew each other. Most of the tenants were unemployed and so were at a bit of a loose end during the day. One of their favourite tricks was to pour buckets of water onto the passers-by below and then quickly duck back inside the window. One day Leigh saw a woman approaching with a very high bouffant hairdo. She was an ideal target, so he threw the water all over her, causing her hairstyle to collapse in a very dramatic fashion. Unfortunately, she was a friend of the landlord and she came sobbing into the house to tell him her tragic tale. Her husband had died a couple of days earlier and she was on her way back from the Town Hall where she had just registered his death. The landlord was furious, but when he accused Leigh, he denied all knowledge of the event. This turned into one of Leigh's favourite stories of the time.

Two boys from Portsmouth lived there, Simon and Stephen. Simon had managed to get a job in a classy antique glass shop in the King's Road, so he had to get up early and wear a smart suit for work. Leigh had a crush on him, so to cover this up he did his favourite trick and bossed him around as much as possible. One evening he invited Rachel for dinner and made Simon serve the meal naked. Leigh and another occupant, Kenny Miller, decided to play a terrible trick on Simon. They told him that they were going to cut his hair in the latest style and then treat it with a special conditioner that he had to leave on all night. Kenny got hold of the clippers and shaved 'FUCK' into the back of Simon's head. Leigh then came into the room with a huge bowl of some horrible mixture he had concocted of toothpaste, treacle, jam, flour and a small amount of hair dye. They rubbed this on Simon's hair and he then went to bed, as it was about 2 a.m. and he had to get up at 8 a.m.

Leigh was so impatient to see the result that he crept into Simon's room and put the clock forward about three hours. The alarm went off and Simon couldn't understand why he was so sleepy – it was the middle of winter, so he wasn't puzzled as to why it was still dark. Leigh and the others had been wandering around the house, staying up all night as they often did. Simon's hair was a gruesome, sticky mess, and Leigh kindly offered to wash it for him. Simon got ready for work and set off still unaware of what was written on the back of his head. He wondered why the buses were empty, why it hadn't started to get lighter and why everyone was staring at him. He soon realized why when he arrived at the glass shop and saw a nearby clock that said 7 a.m. When his boss finally arrived, he went mad about Simon's new hairstyle. Simon had to rush to the barber's and have the whole back shaved off.

Leigh regularly added to his dole money by shoplifting. He was a very keen collector of art books, and he and Rachel would often go to the Design Council bookshop in Haymarket wearing long, flappy coats he had made with lots of pockets, which were soon filled with several books that he had been coveting but couldn't afford. Another favourite trick was to shoplift from Mothercare in Oxford Street, because he could easily convert the goods into cash. He would make a small purchase and then stuff all his booty into the carrier bag, and then take it back for a refund with a tragic tale about his girlfriend's miscarriage.

After about eight months in Ladbroke Grove, David Walls moved into Trojan's flat in Islington. Leigh was homeless for a while and stayed round at Rachel's, then squatted in a council flat in Grimthorpe House in Percival Street, just off St John Street in Clerkenwell. It only had one bedroom and he used the front room as a workroom. Then, for some strange reason, David and Trojan moved in too. They all lived and slept in the same room, Trojan and Leigh sharing a double bed and David in the single. This was very claustrophobic, especially as none of them was working. Leigh used to spend his days cottaging just to get out of the house. His favourite haunts were in the Clerkenwell Road and in Exmouth Market, and he would rush home to fill the others in on his conquests.

They soon realized that they couldn't go on living in these cramped conditions, so Trojan decided to take drastic action. He poured some petrol through the letter-box, set fire to it, then dashed back into the flat to join the others waiting to be rescued. Leigh was very dubious about this plan, as it seemed a bit too dangerous, but once Trojan made up his mind to do something nothing would sway him. The fire brigade arrived and were rather surprised to find three strange young men sitting on the bed wearing long dresses with stars on the front. They always wore these around the house as they were so comfortable and had forgotten to change for the rescue, but they decided it would work in their favour as it would make their rescuers realize they were gay and add substance to their case of being persecuted by local queerbashers.

Trojan's plot worked and they were very quickly given a new flat in Stepney. In January 1984 Leigh, Trojan and David moved into their new flat in Ronald Street. It was on the eleventh floor of a fifteen-storey brown-brick block that had been built in the late sixties on a small estate off the Commercial Road. There were four flats on each floor, with two front doors facing each other on either side of the lift. There was a biggish hall inside the front door with all the other rooms leading off it. There were three bedrooms, a large lounge with fantastic views over the City and the Thames, a small balcony and a kitchen, bathroom and toilet.

Leigh was thrilled to get a proper flat at last, where his name was on the rent book. Ever since he had been in London he had longed to have a place he could call his own and decorate to his own taste.

The boys had a bedroom each, but David only lasted about six weeks before Leigh's and Trojan's teasing drove him mad and he left. He also found the acid they were taking difficult to deal with. He was becoming more spiritual and had decided to go to university to study divinity with the ultimate aim of becoming a priest. David realized that Leigh was doing his best to get him out because he wanted his bedroom for a workroom, and decided he should leave while they were still on speaking terms. Even then David realized that Leigh would be someone special. 'I knew he would never be satisfied with being an ordinary person. He wanted to be the Andy Warhol of London.'

Once David had gone Leigh turned his room into a workroom, and using their small amount of dole money the two of them started decorating. Trojan had far more interest in interior decoration than Leigh and he was the one who spurred Leigh into action. They were living in a very unsophisticated area and were delighted to find that the local DIY shop – Dee Jay Decor in Watney Market – sold incredibly tasteless seventies' wallpaper. Leigh described the shop in an article in *i-D* in 1984: 'They cater for the Paki sort of clientele, which suits our tastes as well. Some of the stuff they have is so gross that even the Pakis turn up their noses at it. I think they're very grateful when we go in there.' They decorated the lounge first, covering the walls in a dark *Star Trek* wallpaper, not that it gave him inspiration: 'I never liked science fiction when I was younger but I do now. *Star Trek* isn't bad but I watch TV for ideas for clothes and they always wear the same thing.' They covered the ceiling in a silvery paper with pictures of dolly birds wearing picture hats and put plain lino on the floor, which Leigh later painted with brightly coloured ovals. He acquired a brown corduroy and chrome settee that was very low slung, and Leigh loved to lie on it to watch the television, which had been painted to match the room. He also found some square turquoise vinyl chairs that had a space-age feel and went marvellously with the wallpaper.

Leigh was more extravagant when he decorated his bedroom: 'The wallpaper in my room is really strange, that sort of bubbly aluminium stuff, it's quite expensive and I didn't buy it at first, but because my room's the smallest in the flat – I felt it well worth it.' When he came into some money he bought some mirror tiles for his room. They had a gold squiggle pattern on them and he put them on opposite walls so that when you looked into them your image went on for infinity because they reflected each other. The bed, which was a double and a single bed put together, filled the whole room. Eventually he got round to having a platform made so that the bed was really high off the floor, with lots of room underneath for storage, but he never got any steps, so it required an athletic leap to get into. Gradually, as Leigh's wardrobe got bigger and bigger, his clothes crept onto a rail at the end of his room.

Trojan's room was painted in apricot gloss, which made a fine backdrop for the gallery of his paintings that he had hung all over the walls. After Trojan died, Leigh made his room into an office, and had shelves put up to store his enormous number of books. He loved reading and finding out things, so his book collection was very interesting. He had everything from novels by Joan Collins to the complete works of Beatrix Potter, which Lucian gave him, tons of dressmaking reference books, history books, biographies, art books – all in all they took up a whole wall of the room. He also had his desk and typewriter in there, and a bed-settee that he had bought when his mother and father came to stay for the first time.

The kitchen was yellow with black and white checked lino on the floor. When Leigh's mother came to stay she made some net curtains, which she proudly hung for him, but as soon as she had returned to Australia he ripped them down. There was a silver fridge that Leigh was always diving into. He had a typist's chair, and he used to wheel himself up to the fridge, open the door, root around and then just stuff his face with bits of cheese, slices of cold meat, cold baked beans and anything else that was in there, washing it all down with Diet Coke.

The bathroom was painted in orange gloss, which Leigh decided to brighten up with a wall-sized tropical mural that he bought from my Janet Frazer catalogue, paying for it in weekly instalments. It was always filthy in the bathroom because Leigh and Trojan washed their make-up off when they were drunk, so the grease paint would go all over the place. It was very hard to get off unless you really scrubbed at it, and both of them had better things to do. Leigh loved lying in the bath, and eventually all the steam made the mural peel off the wall, so it was replaced with one of Trojan's paintings.

They decorated the toilet with Indian-restaurant-style red flock wallpaper, but because they didn't use heavy-duty paste when they stuck it up, it came away from the walls. Leigh tried to stick it back on, but only bothered with the top bits, so it hung off the walls in rather forlorn banners. To add a touch of class there was a large picture of the Queen above the cistern.

The hall was painted in a greeny yellow and the back of the front door was covered in the same flock wallpaper as the toilet. By the front door there was a standard lamp with several coloured bulbs on it, none of which ever worked at the same time. Around this was wound a plastic blow-up snake. There was a large picture that Trojan had painted of the two of them on the wall. Leigh has a blue face and is sniffing poppers, while Trojan has Picasso-like make-up and a hook for a hand. He's smoking a cigarette, which Leigh really hated, as he detested smoking. (When Nicola used to stay around there a lot he used to hide her cigarettes. Eighteen months after he died, she found a packet hidden in one of his coat pockets.) The doorbell was fixed to a tape recorder that was supposed to play sex noises, but it wasn't very good, as Leigh explained. 'Every time someone pressed the bell and I heard all the gasping and moaning, I just thought it was Trojan having an asthma attack, so I never bothered to answer the door.'

One day someone else's Girocheque was delivered to their flat by mistake. This was a wonderful bonus for them, and Trojan swiftly cashed it and went off to the Disco Shop in the Edgware Road, where he bought several ultra-violet bulbs to give the flat an added nightclub feel.

The flat always had a special smell that never changed. It was a mixture of make-up, cats, material and wet washing. It was forever bedecked in rows of drying clothes, sometimes just socks and pants but often some exquisite garment that Leigh had ruined with make-up and had bunged into the washing machine in a (usually) futile attempt to get it clean.

Leigh was not keen on cleaning or tidying up, as he once explained to the *Evening Standard*. 'Whenever I'm feeling depressed or anything, the idea of cleaning to cheer myself up seems like such a cheap trick: stuff like that is so obvious, it wouldn't do any good.' However, if someone was coming round he would run about like a maniac shoving everything away and sweeping the floors.

Leigh's workroom was painted lilac and it housed his sewing machine and overlocker. Trojan had disguised the cutting table as a painting: a leg and foot hung from the top of it and it was hinged to the wall at the bottom, so you could unhook it and rest it on the leg to make the table. Around the walls were rails of fantastic costumes: a mixture of shiny sequins, bright satins, strange pieces of foam rubber and a sprinkling of fur and feathers. There were pictures and drawings on the wall that gave Leigh inspiration. A favourite was a small black and white photo of a native African woman with such a protruding bottom you could rest a plate of food on it. There were jars of sequins, buttons and bugle beads, reels and reels of thread and all the other paraphernalia needed by an avant-garde designer. I had painted a rather poor portrait of Leigh, which he put to use by banging nails into it and using it as a cotton reel holder.

Leigh loved the district he lived in, although he wished it was a bit nearer to the West End. He had everything he needed close to hand. At the bottom of the flats there was a small row of shops, which included an Indian take-away and Sancho's Pizza Parlour.

Leigh often popped down there if the fridge was empty and he was feeling peckish. A little further along Commercial Road was Watney Market, where Leigh did most of his shopping. There was a big Sainsbury's and a few vegetable stalls as well as Dee Jay Decor. He was frequently to be seen in Sainsbury's stocking up his larder with sliced wholemeal bread (Leigh was forever eating toast – in the time I knew him, he wore out at least four toasters) and various tins of beans, sweetcorn and tuna. His fridge usually had the same things in it – a tub of Flora, orange juice, a bottle of vodka, several cans of Diet Coke, a bottle of poppers, cheese and sliced chicken-roll for the cat.

Leigh had acquired the cat for his birthday. Baillie Walsh had rescued it from a homeless person and, as Leigh had been being particularly evil to him when they were on a trip to Los Angeles, he decided to punish him by giving him the cat. To make matters worse he put the cat in a big stereo box so that Leigh would think that was what he was being given. When Leigh opened the box his face was a picture. Baillie couldn't believe the effect it had. 'I have never seen him look so horrified. All the muscles in his face sagged and his face dropped about three feet!' But deep down Leigh was very kind-hearted and he soon loved the cat, which he named after his friend Angus Cook. He only got angry when the cat pissed on his fabric. To punish him, Leigh used to loosely wrap a piece of the wet fabric over the cat's nose, and it was hilarious to see Angus running backwards trying to escape the stench of his own urine. Leigh was very concerned when Angus became sexually frustrated, and phoned up my friend Graham, who worked in a pet shop, to see if it would be safe to tickle him with a cotton bud to ease the tension.

Angus was much better cared for than the two cats that Leigh and Trojan had owned years previously. Trojan didn't really like them, and it was rumoured that he had put one in a box on a tube line. He definitely dropped the other one off the balcony. The poor thing fell eleven floors to its death. Leigh was upset by this, as he loved animals. Not wanting Trojan to think he was a softy, he pretended he thought it was funny, but then locked himself in the workroom to have a quiet sob.

Brick Lane was about three-quarters of a mile down the road from Leigh's flat. In 1989 he told lifestyle magazine *Girl About Town* about his local area:

> There's a couple of sari shops which I often buy fabric from. One
> of the huge bonuses about this area is that there are lots of Indian
> and Pakistani people living here and I'm forever seeing the most
> fantastic colour combinations, saris and perhaps a synthetic
> jumper and some coloured shoes. And the children also wear
> really exquisite things as though they're dressed up for a party.
> It's always so colourful and it's so much inspiration to see them.

He loved the fabric shops, the Indian supermarkets and restaurants and the general feeling that you were in downtown Bangladesh and not downtown Stepney. He became very well-known to all the shop keepers as he hunted for unusual fabrics. They loved it when they saw him coming because they knew that he would buy the garish and tasteless fabric that no one else would want. There were also a lot of little factories down there willing to do tiny one-off jobs for him, such as buttonholing and pleating.

Leigh's favourite restaurant in Brick Lane was the Nazrul. It was very cheap with no fussy extras, and the food was served on Formica tables. There was no drinks licence but you were very welcome to bring your own alcohol. The food was delicious and two of you could have a feast for the princely sum of £10. After a visit there we often got into my car and drove round the block several times looking at all the prostitutes. Leigh's particular favourite looked about seventy, was as wide as she was tall and had no teeth. It was hard to imagine that she would be able to find anyone to have sex with if she paid them, let alone if they paid her. It was always the highlight of the evening if we saw her standing in her usual dark doorway on Commercial Street.

Leigh left the decor of the flat more or less as it was when he had first moved in, but as time went by he decided it (and he) needed a few improvements:

I Need Money For
Piano
Fridge with glass door
Settee/double bed
Answerphone
Rent (council)
Bookshelves
Mirrors
Clothing labels
Clothes production
Art and video acquisitions
Pierre Cardin shoes
Teeth
Plastic surgery
New mattress and duvet
Crockery
Dining table and chairs

Eventually Leigh acquired most of the things on the list, but for some of them he had to wait five or six years. Unfortunately, though, he never got round to having his teeth done or getting plastic surgery. He was forever trying to convince Les Child to have surgery and would spend many happy hours moulding Les's face into different shapes. He was so desperate for it to happen that he would offer to pay, but luckily for Les he never came up with the cash.

One of my old flatmates, Luke Branson, was a builder, and on one job he came across some massive mirrors about six foot square. Leigh decided to buy them off him and Luke put them up all around the sitting-room walls. Leigh also decided to make some curtains for the windows and to cover the walls that had no mirrors on them. He then collected all of Lucian's old paint rags, which were made of very high-quality cotton and were covered in smears of fleshy paint. He washed them, cut them into squares and made very beautiful patchwork curtains out of them.

Michael Clark gave Leigh a grand piano, which took pride of place in the middle of the room and at which Leigh would often sit to bash out a few bars of Chopin. A small trampoline doubled as a coffee table and a scratching post for Angus. It was originally a prop for a show Leigh did in New York, but he neglected to rehearse in the giant platform shoes he was wearing for the show and when he went on stage he immediately fell off it.

Eventually the whole flat turned into a massive workroom as Leigh's costumes grew ever bigger, and it was only thanks to Nicola, who sometimes tidied up, that you could see the floor at all.

9

Daytime

For most of the eighties, unless he had a big job to complete such as making clothes for one of Michael's ballets, Leigh's days followed more or less the same pattern: he would lie in bed until lunchtime, wearing a grubby old T-shirt and his tea cosy, which he said he'd found in a tip. It was a brilliantly knitted replica of a country cottage, with a little chimney at the top and flowers growing up the walls. He took it with him everywhere because his head felt the cold at night due to his baldness.

After Leigh had woken up, he'd pick up the phone and call several of his friends for very long chats, just gossiping and spreading rumours and lies. He loved talking to people on the phone, much more than face to face. When I first knew him he used to ring me up and make me laugh so much that on several occasions I thought that I might choke to death. We'd be on the phone about the slightest little thing. Maybe there was something on the television worth watching (we would sometimes watch an episode of *EastEnders* or *Brookside* on the phone together without exchanging a word but then carry on the conversation as soon as it had finished). Maybe we had just spoken to someone else on the phone and needed to pass on vital gossip, or perhaps we would discuss the night before's activities or make arrangements for the night ahead. When I first knew Leigh I didn't know anything of his past, so he had twenty-two years' worth of stories to tell me, and he could relate the most boring events in a way that would make you almost crack your ribs laughing.

Typically, Leigh would tell the most heinous lies. He once told me that Brad Branson, an American photographer who I knew in passing, had been on holiday in Ibiza, caught a terrible tropical disease and dropped dead. I was very shocked at this because it seemed such a strange thing to happen. A couple of weeks later, I was sitting in my little cashier's booth at Industria and suddenly Brad Branson came down the stairs. I nearly jumped out of my skin, screeching 'I thought you were dead.' I still don't know why I believed the story, because after ten years I should have realized what a liar Leigh was, but I didn't think that even he could make up stories that bad.

He was also very keen on telling me that various people had been raped in the back streets of Soho. He once told me that Christine Binnie (a member of the Neo Naturists, who gave naked performances in nightclubs in the early eighties) had been horribly attacked by a six-foot monster who had tied her up for twenty-four hours while he had his way with her in every position imaginable. Even I only believed that one for half an hour. But I was thrilled when he told me that Tallulah, a very large, kind, camp queen, had turned straight. According to Leigh, Tallulah had been having quiet nights in with the divorcee who lived in the flat opposite, and one night they had got rather drunk and ended up in bed together. In the morning they had been very shocked and agreed it was a one-off, but that very same night it happened again and now they were building a relationship. I was very happy with this new romance, because Tallulah didn't have much luck with the boys and I was thrilled that he had found happiness at last. A couple of times a week Leigh would fill me in with new details of how their love was blossoming, and when I eventually bumped into Tallulah I congratulated him on his newfound romance. I was devastated when he stared at me blankly because he had no idea what I was talking about.

When Leigh was asked by somebody on what occasions he lied, he replied, 'On what occasions do I breathe!' At least he was honest that once.

Because Leigh told such terrible lies, sometimes people didn't believe the truth. He once told Cerith that Les Child was working in the gay sauna in Covent Garden making sandwiches for the snack bar. Cerith couldn't believe that as talented a dancer as Les would be doing such a job. So when he bumped into Les several months later and asked him how things were going, he was completely gobsmacked when Les replied 'Fine, girl, I'm not making the sandwiches any more.'

Leigh was once asked for an article in a magazine what piece of dream furniture he would like best for his home, and was photographed (strangely enough by Brad Branson) with a vast sixteenth-century altar piece. 'This piece represents everything I like: grandeur, ritual, camp, death and drama. I think it would give me the incentive to behave very badly. Even mundane events like over-eating and bitchy phone calls would be fabulous with this piece of kitsch queening it up in the corner of my flat.'

He had many telephone friends who were always thrilled when the phone rang and Leigh was at the other end. He used to talk endlessly to Les Child, just winding him up, and after Leigh died

Les really missed those calls. 'It was gorg' just being on the phone, not talking, watching the same TV programme. He made me laugh so much.' Rifat Ozbek felt exactly the same. 'Leigh and I became close and started talking on the phone a lot. I used to have literally hour-long calls with Leigh. Forever. We used to talk for hours about everything: girlies, sex, all about what he did, what I used to do, from intimate sex to arts, to whatever, movies, this and that, people, gossip. And when we started working together then we'd have even more conversations because we'd talk about ideas. That's what I really miss, talking on the phone with Leigh.'

For about a year Leigh was very good friends with the former Alan Pellay, now known as Lanah. I had first seen her in *The Comic Strip Presents* on Channel Four. I thought she was fantastic. Leigh got to know Lanah and found that he had met his match in the world of sick, twisted minds. They were forever winding each other up. When Leigh was on the phone to Lanah she'd keep interrupting the conversation and talking to someone else, saying 'Just two lumps, darling, that's right put it there'. She'd then whisper to Leigh that she had a rather handsome young lover there. Leigh soon cottoned on to her tricks and would do the same thing himself, pretending that Michael Clark was round, or Boy George. Leigh realized that it had all got out of hand when ten minutes after finishing a call with Lanah in which he had pretended that practically everyone they knew was round at his flat, she turned up in a taxi frightened that she was missing out on something.

Leigh used to speak to John Maybury regularly too, but after a while he decided he preferred talking to his boyfriend Baillie Walsh. 'It used to drive me insane because they'd sit on the phone for hours and I'd be in the room listening to snippets, with Baillie roaring with laughter and I'd be calling out "What, what?" but they'd never let me know what was going on. Then after three hours Baillie would pass me on to Leigh, but he'd be all talked out so I would only get five minutes of chat.'

Leigh liked to keep his friends under control, and people fell in and out of his favour. He didn't really like people from different parts of his life mixing – perhaps he was afraid that they might gang up on him. While he kept them separate, he thought he had power over them. He once told Richard Torry what he used his friends for: Nicola was the one he could be himself with, I was the one he told everything to, Cerith was to have intellectual conversations with and so on. It was strange but it seemed to work for him – the only trouble was that he'd have to speak to so many people that his phone bill was about £600 a quarter (£2,000 to £2,500 in today's money).

Leigh also used the phone to play tricks. He would give you a message that someone wanted to speak to you urgently, usually about some job or other, and then, when you rang, it was someone completely different on the end of the phone. He was forever getting me to phone Paul Bernstock for some unknown reason. He discovered that years earlier David Holah had been indiscreet with someone, so he played the same trick on David, who was mortified to find his old lover on the other end of the phone when he was expecting someone else completely.

He was also very fond of dialling 174, which made your own phone ring. He had phones rigged up all over his flat so that he could chat wherever he was. When he was throwing a party for Trojan's nineteenth birthday, in the afternoon he kept sneaking into the workroom to dial 174 and would then come into the front room and answer the phone to say 'No, sorry, the party is private and you can't come.' He'd then look proudly at me and Trojan and say that it was Tony Hadley from Spandau Ballet, or Steve Strange, or Paul Bernstock. We completely believed him until he went too far and said it was Bryan Ferry ...

This party was about the only one that Leigh ever threw. I did the catering (sandwiches and little snacks from Marks & Spencer). Leigh bought some drink, but in those days everyone knew to bring a bottle. Trojan, Leigh and I started drinking the vodka far too early and by the time the guests started to arrive we were paralytically drunk. Several of the guests brought Trojan flowers for his birthday, and Leigh rushed about maniacally trying to find somewhere to put them all, ending up putting them in the bath. He left the taps running while he went to greet another guest (he always liked to make people welcome) but then got waylaid and starting chatting to someone else. Everyone was fairly drunk by the time we suddenly noticed that the flat was two inches deep in water, with flowers floating around on top. Nobody really minded and just sloshed around in the mess. By about 11.30 p.m., Trojan and I had passed out on the bed along with Judy Blame. Leigh soon joined us, and the party just went on around us for about another four hours.

The next morning the downstairs neighbours came to complain about the water that had been seeping into their flat overnight. They later made an official complaint to the council about Leigh having a sewing machine going all night, and he was almost evicted because they thought he was running a sweat shop on the premises. But when he showed the man from the council his press cuttings he just got a warning about working late at night.

When Leigh was wandering around the house he would usually just wear old underpants, an ancient T-shirt and a pair of down-at-heel clogs. If he knew you were coming round to visit, he might give you a surprise by putting on some ridiculous drag look or wearing an even more ridiculous wig than usual. Sometimes when he knew Nicola was coming round he would listen out for the lift, and when he heard it on its way he would dash out into the hall and lie down by the door so that Nicola and anyone else in the lift would get a terrible fright.

Leigh had a bit of a reputation in the area, especially as he had been seen on television so many times. Once I arrived at his flat early and Leigh wasn't home yet, so the woman opposite asked me in to wait. She was a very nice black woman, also called Sue, with three little children. She told me that when she had been allocated to Farrell House her neighbours had warned her against it, saying, 'It's where that weirdo lives, the great big one who goes around in women's clothes.' It didn't put her off, though, and she was pleased to find out anything she could about Leigh.

Once Leigh started working for Lucian his routine changed and he had to get up very early. He would leave Nicola in the flat embroidering or sewing some garment for him. When he returned home at about 5 p.m. he would fling off all his clothes except for his T-shirt and pants and pose in front of the mirrors. He would dance around, looking at his body, getting inspiration for how he could next use it for a costume. He would then jump into the bath and call for Nicola, and she would join him in the bathroom, maybe shaving his legs or his head. He loved to dip down and fill his mouth with the warm soapy water, which he then propelled towards Nicola, soaking her. It was here in the bathroom that they had their most chatty conversations.

Leigh's daytime attire was, in its own way, even more shocking than what he wore at night. In the mid-eighties he used to wear one of the jackets he had made himself, with shorts to show off his very shapely legs. Later on he gave up trying to be stylish and adopted, according to Boy George, 'A Benny Hill child molester look'. (Leigh's similarity to Benny Hill was a phenomenon, and when he was abroad people would shout 'Benny Hill' at him all the time.)

Leigh had a selection of wigs, which he often hacked about, trying to change the style. Most were short but he sometimes wore a longish blond one. They were usually a greyish or brownish kind of colour, and because Leigh had quite a big head they used to stretch and it was easy to spot the tell-tale strips of lacy elastic at the back. But he was convinced that they looked natural and got very offended if you dared to suggest otherwise. He was once walking down the street in Italy when he heard several transvestites shouting out *'Paluka, paluka'*. He didn't know what it meant, but soon discovered *parrucca* was Italian for wig, and from then on he was forever talking about his new palukas. His face had two knots in the dimples on his cheeks where he had threaded catgut through his piercings to keep them open, and he often caught people staring at him, totally engrossed, trying to work out what the knots were, though he convinced himself they were admiring his dimples.

He had two bought jackets that he used to wear. One was a navy Yohji Yamamoto number that Leigh had got cheap in Japan. It was made of beautiful fabric, but soon Leigh ripped it and managed to make it look like something out of 'Man at C & A'. His other jacket was a beige windcheater from Marks & Spencer, which is where Leigh bought most of the clothes that he didn't make himself. He would team one of the jackets with grey schoolboy trousers and usually some sort of chunky jumper with a T-shirt underneath. For shoes he wore clogs, cheap green trainers or an old pair of lace-ups, all scuffed and down at heel. Sometimes, just to ring the changes, he wore an old pair of green velour track trousers that he had made ten years earlier. They were so worn out between the legs, where his massive thighs had rubbed away the pile into a sheer net, that they were indecent.

When I asked him why he didn't get a more stylish daywear look, he said he was wearing it to entertain people like me: 'You know you get a buzz when you see a weirdo in the street and rush home to tell all your friends, well, I'm one of those weirdos, think how thrilled you'd be to see me if you didn't know me!'

It was frightening walking down the road with Leigh, because he would always call things out to passers-by. He said it was to entertain you, but it was really to cause as much embarrassment as he could, as well as to take the pressure off himself as an object of ridicule and pass it on to someone else. When he was young he hated embarrassment, but as he got older he realized what a strong emotion it was and revelled in it. He liked being embarrassed himself and loved causing embarrassment to other people. It was surprising that he didn't get more abuse in the street. Les Child remembers walking through New York with him. 'I was walking along with Leigh and we were approaching a big gang of workmen. I was thinking "Here we go, trouble", but they just got out of the way and it made me realize that with his bigness and freakiness, people just didn't understand him. He would freak them out. He'd walk down 42nd Street and Times Square and the bums would run a mile. They'd shout "Are you from the institution?" They were terrified of the girl, he could swish with confidence down there.'

Most days Leigh used to do some work at home, sewing clothes for a commission, for himself or for one of his friends. He would work very hard making sure that everything was up to his high standards. Up until Leigh found out he was ill, when he felt he couldn't waste time hanging about, he usually spent one day a week just relaxing, lying on the sofa watching rubbish on the television, dancing around the flat to his new favourite song or popping down to Sainsbury's for supplies. When Trojan lived there they used to do little things to amuse each other. One day Trojan was sitting on the sofa when Leigh came into the room dressed as Ilse Koch, a German concentration camp guard nicknamed 'the Red Witch' because she used to make lampshades out of dead prisoners' skin. He put a sheet of newspaper on the floor and then ran out again. That was enough to make Trojan dissolve into gales of laughter, but when Leigh ran back into the room, hitched up his skirt and defecated on the newspaper, Trojan became hysterical. On another occasion Leigh walked into the front room naked except for a handbag hanging on his erection. That was a quiet night in at Farrell House.

If he wasn't going to a nightclub, Leigh would love to go to the cinema. He didn't usually see just one film: as soon as the first one had finished he would rush round Leicester Square to find another that was about to start. He fuelled his film marathons with vast amounts of fast food. He would pop into Burger King for a Whopper, then stop at a kiosk for a slice of pizza, buy some sweets at the cinema and then go to Kentucky Fried Chicken on the way home. I was with him there once when he decided to take off his wig, strip off his top and look at his saggy chest, which he made look worse by hunching his back. It must have put the rest of the customers off their chicken breasts.

Leigh was very generous and if he had the money he would buy you your cinema tickets and snacks. Les found him very kind when they were on tour. 'He never thought twice about giving you money or paying for things, his big fat hand coming out with a wad of money.'

My sister Alison came to stay with me and we decided to go to see Paul McKenna, the hypnotist. Leigh was desperate to come, so we got him a ticket too. When Paul McKenna asked for volunteers to be hypnotized Leigh dashed up to the front, only to walk sadly back before he reached the stage. When we asked him why, he said that he had suddenly realized that he had a wig on and would have been humiliated if it had fallen off in front of all those people. Alison didn't know Leigh very well but was thrilled at his antics and his 'excited little schoolboy face'. Before the interval several people were hypnotized to do stupid things throughout the break, such as talk to imaginary dogs or pretend to be a wicked school teacher. They were then let loose on the audience. Most people sat in their seats, trying not to be involved, but Leigh got up and avidly followed them around, trying to see if he could catch them out, though in the end he had to admit that he thought it was genuine. After the show he wished that he had the power of hypnotism so that he could play even worse tricks on people.

Leigh was incredibly nosey, and if he came to your house or you left something of yours at his flat he would look through things to find whatever information he could. If you left your address book out he would add famous people's names with imaginary phone numbers. Les Child discovered this side of Leigh when they were on tour. He had written some postcards and left them in his bag, and when he came back to their room, Leigh was mocking him: 'So the scenery is gorgeous and it reminds you of Spain, does it?' Les knew that he wasn't the only one Leigh tormented. 'Once right in front of me he dived into someone's bag, rooting around.'

It was worse when Leigh did things to you without you realizing. One Mothering Sunday all my family had come round to my flat, and most of them had gone out so there was only me, my Mum, my sister and my nephew Guy. Everything was going well when suddenly my mother's face looked like she had sucked six lemons. My sister and I were asking her what was wrong and she was saying 'nothing, nothing', although it was obvious that something was. About three days later she phoned me up and said she really was very upset at what she had seen in my handbag. I couldn't imagine what it could be, so I dashed to find it. I opened the flap where I had written my name and address, only to find that Leigh had added two new words to my name, so it said 'Sue Tilley sucks cocks'. I was hysterical with laughter, which upset my mum more, as she didn't think it was very funny, but when I explained that Leigh had written it she didn't mind so much because she liked him and as she had seen him on the telly he was able to get away with that sort of behaviour. I told her she was no better than him for nosing through my things. She just said that I had better cross it out straight away 'or people would get the wrong idea'. When I told Leigh he was just thrilled that he had written cock in the plural.

If Leigh came to your house and saw something he didn't like he would throw it out of the window. I dreaded him coming round after Christmas as most of my presents would end up on the roof of the nursery outside my flat. If his own house had been tidier or more stylish I wouldn't have minded so much. He believed completely in his own taste and would not be swayed otherwise unless somebody he was particularly impressed with liked something, and then he would like it too. Sometimes on a Saturday we would wander round Heal's looking at settees and he would snootily say, 'My taste is so much more advanced than yours, just take my advice and buy what I say!' But as usual I didn't and bought exactly what I wanted to.

10

TV and Video

Leigh always longed to be on the television, and one of his main ambitions was to be on *Wogan*. He was forever phoning me up and saying he had been booked, but strangely enough it always fell through at the last minute.

His clothes were first shown on television in October 1983. It was an odd children's programme about pop and fashion. Leigh and BodyMap were both featured, along with Jay Aston from Bucks Fizz. Leigh was completely excited that he was going to be on television and kept phoning me to check that I was going to watch it. Luckily, it was on the same day that I got my first video recorder, so it was the first thing I ever recorded.

Leigh was a bit disappointed with the reality of television. He thought it would be all champagne and limos, but he and his models had to make their own way to the studio with the clothes screwed up in red, white and blue laundry bags. It was a very low-budget show with lots of hanging around. Leigh didn't perform himself, but used friends to model his starry robes. Jay Aston surpassed herself showing her designs to bemused students from St Martin's fashion department. She had designed some fabric with black and white stripes and called it 'Zebra Crossing'. She also modelled her new look, which consisted of wearing her school blazer inside out and tying her hair up with a tape measure.

Leigh came round afterwards to watch the video and was delighted at his first minute of fame. It was the only video I had, and I gradually filled it up with pop clips. I must have watched it about a hundred times as it was the only thing I had to play when friends came to see me before going out. There were hardly any pop programmes on then, and MTV wasn't available, so every time there was a bit of pop on the telly you had to record it to make your own compilation tape.

In 1984, after Leigh had made a name for himself by wearing clothes with the bottom cut out, he was invited on to *The Tube*, which everyone under the age of twenty-five watched on Friday evenings. Leigh was interviewed by Paula Yates. He was wearing a pink frilly outfit with a little pinny at the front and of course his big derrière sticking out the back. Unbeknown to him, two alternative comedians had been primed to come and attack him. He was so nervous that they made him look a complete fool, and the bum-showing fashion never did catch on, although it was revived ten years later by Alexander McQueen.

When Taboo became a big hit, a London regional programme called *South of Watford* decided to make a documentary about Leigh. He couldn't believe it: thirty minutes all about himself.

For about a week Leigh was followed around by a cameraman and a sound engineer. He was overjoyed when he found out the presenter was Hugh Laurie, who he had always fancied. He rang me up from his bedroom, whispering 'I can't believe he's lying on my settee, I think he fancies me.' I tried to convince him that Hugh Laurie was a happily married man, but he preferred to live in his fantasy world. The camera followed him to Taboo, to a fashion show and to various other venues. Leigh still had the slightly camp London nightclub voice that was very popular at this time: he spoke quite quickly and dragged out the last word of the sentence. It was a strange way to talk, but everyone did it. And there are a few casualties about who still do.

The first time the camera crew came to Leigh's house, they left their van downstairs with all the equipment in it. When they went to get the cameras, they found that the van had been broken into and everything stolen. Leigh was mortified, but was happy that Hugh had to come round again the next day when they had got new equipment, which they brought straight up to the flat this time. The show was quite a success, and led to Leigh being asked in his local Sainsbury's if he was 'the freak from the telly'.

Later that year, Leigh was invited on to *Pebble Mill at One* to discuss the London nightclub scene with Peter Stringfellow. *Pebble Mill* was an institution, one of the first daytime television shows aimed at bored housewives. Leigh was going to wear his drippy-head look and as I had helped him invent it he asked me to go along with him. He had wanted to put drips on his head for the occasion, but couldn't get them to stay on properly, so I suggested he mix the ink with the adhesive Copydex (I was very keen on Copydex as I loved the way you could make it look like a disgusting skin disease if you rubbed it onto your skin, left it to dry, and then half pulled it off).

As I lived near Euston Station, Leigh stayed the night at my flat, because we had an early start to Birmingham. The journey was pretty uneventful except that we were a bit pissed off to discover that Peter Stringfellow was travelling first class, but we later found out he had paid for his own ticket. We got a taxi to the Pebble Mill Studios, where we were shoved into a small dressing room. Leigh was still nervous of cameras, so he had brought along his usual crutch: a bottle of Vladivar vodka.

I helped Leigh to get ready. He had a fairly subdued outfit on – high-heeled men's shoes, knitted, white knee-high socks, a blue mini smock with a washed-out white T-shirt on underneath, then thick white foundation with the drips on top of his head. He was ready at about midday and the programme didn't start until 1 p.m., so he started guzzling the vodka. He started to have a panic attack, so to calm his nerves he blew in and out of a paper bag as doctors tell you to. He was soon cured, and then had a nose around the cupboards to see what he could nick. There wasn't much available, but an unplugged telephone soon found its way into his bag.

We were then ushered into the hospitality suite, where we met the other guests – the 'Power of Love' singer Jennifer Rush, and a man who had invented some sort of hovercraft/dinghy/lawnmower. We were very disappointed with the news that the usual presenter, Paul Coia, wasn't on that day, but were thrilled to discover that his stand-in was Magnus Magnusson, the Icelandic presenter of *Mastermind*. We were expecting him to be dressed in his usual serious tweeds, but the wardrobe department had given him a more relaxed daytime look of pink cotton slacks and a pink blouson jacket. His face was pink to match. He started moaning that if he'd known he was going to have to wear such a ridiculous outfit he wouldn't have agreed to do the job. Then he took one look at Leigh and shut up.

The programme was about to start, so I joined the audience of middle-aged Mothers' Union members. Leigh's piece was to be about halfway through, and he was going to be interviewed by a woman called Josephine, who was later to find fame as the mistress of the smooth television doctor Hilary Jones.

Leigh made his usual entrance, walking on stage and immediately falling over. There was a large gasp from the Mothers' Union and worried looks from Peter and Josephine. They didn't know that it was one of his usual tricks to get attention, so they got all flustered trying to pick him up. However, he settled into his chair and started singing the praises of Taboo. Peter Stringfellow joined in, saying it was great that the freaks had somewhere to go, and then started comparing himself to Leigh. So Leigh said he might be freaky, but he wasn't freaky enough to dare to wear Peter's hairstyle. Josephine then asked if she would get into Taboo. Leigh replied that sadly she would be 'turned away for her looks but might be admitted as a very minor celebrity'. The interview was soon over and I went back to the hospitality suite while Leigh got changed. I got stuck with Jennifer Rush, who asked if Leigh was my boyfriend and who did his make-up, because it was 'really cool'.

As it was still quite early, we thought we'd have a day out in Birmingham. We decided to go to the museum to see the Pre-Raphaelite paintings, which seemed a lovely way to spend an afternoon, but Leigh had other ideas. The Vladivar had now taken effect, and adrenalin was pumping round him from the excitement of his television appearance. We went into the museum, but it was not to be the nice quiet visit I had imagined. As an elderly warden walked past, Leigh shouted out 'See my friend, she really fancies you, she wants to give you a blow job.' I ran off mortified and tried to hide behind a pillar. Then I saw a nun approaching and knew he wouldn't be able to hold back. I was right: 'My friend wants to eat you out,' he bellowed at her. All the art lovers looked horrified, so I grabbed him by the arm and rushed him out of the museum before we were thrown out.

We then decided to have a rest, and sat on a bench in one of the few grassy squares in the town. I started shouting at Leigh, telling him to stop making a fool of me, so he decided to cheer me up by falling over again and again and again. All the office workers walking through the square stopped to look at him, so he whispered to me, 'They must have seen me on *Pebble Mill*.' I didn't know whether to laugh or cry and ended up doing both.

We then went for a wander. We soon got lost because we didn't know our way around, but we stumbled across a cinema showing the latest Arnie film, so we decided to go and see that. The cinema was really bizarre. It was deco style but very run down, and it had an overpowering odour of cat's urine. When we went into the grand auditorium, we discovered that the audience was us and three old women who could have come from Pebble Mill. We settled into our seats, then Leigh got up and came back clutching two Cornettos. We soon finished them and he disappeared again, returning with two more Cornettos once more.

The cinema was so old-fashioned there was a B movie, which was a very serious film about computer dating, but the computer looked like it had been made out of cardboard boxes. The incidental music was rather cheery, so to relieve the tedium of the film Leigh decided to strip off and waltz up the aisle of the cinema naked. I was mortified yet again, so Leigh put his clothes back on, disappeared, and then came back clutching another Cornetto to cheer me up. As soon as I had finished it he came back with another, which even I couldn't eat, so he threw it towards the old ladies.

The film finished around 6 p.m., so we carried on our exploration of Birmingham. As Leigh was hungry we went to a very empty burger bar. It seemed to have been styled on the roaring twenties, but the only thing roaring in there was the noise of the deep fat fryer. We soon finished our dinner and Leigh only fell off his chair once.

We still had a couple of hours to kill until the train home, so we wandered off again in search of more entertainment. We came across the Civic Hall, where to our joy they were showing an amateur production of *Hello Dolly*. We rushed to the box office only to find that the performance had just started. Leigh explained to the cashier that we had come all the way from London to see the show as we had read rave reviews. She seemed thrilled at this and told us that we were very lucky as there were a couple of seats left in the Upper Circle that we could have for a pound. We climbed about twenty flights of stairs and finally reached our destination, where there was row upon row of children with special needs, who we had to climb over to reach our seats. Once we sat down all we could see of the wonderful hammy actors was the tops of their heads. We could hardly hear what they were saying, so we got carried away inventing the rehearsals for the production, imagining that Dolly had to sleep with the director to get the part.

We had just decided that the male lead had definitely slept with the producer to get his part when it was the interval. We were desperate for a drink by now, so we had to climb all over the children again and down the stairs to reach the bar. But it was worth it to see the special Birmingham fashion look. It was like a seventies time warp, Crimplene and bouffants everywhere we looked. Everyone seemed to know each other, and they also seemed to think they knew us; they kept saying hello as if we were their neighbours or members of their church. They soon stopped when Leigh asked a respectable middle-aged man in a beige polyester leisure suit if he wanted to shag me. The bell went for the show to start again, so we made our way up the stairs and clambered over the children who were having to sit through this so-called entertainment. After twenty more minutes of being unable either to see or hear any action we decided we had better leave to catch the train back to London. We arrived home at about midnight, thoroughly exhausted but thrilled that we had managed to fit television, art, cinema, theatre and fine dining into one day!

In early 1988, Leigh got his dream job. He was asked to be the assistant on *Take the Blame*, a chat show on MTV hosted by Steve Blame. Steve had met Leigh years earlier at the Camden Palace and had even had a crush on him. This had resulted in a snog, which never went any further because Steve had been ejected from the Palace when his flatmate set fire to the newspapers that Philip Sallon had used to tie up his hair.

When I was offered the show, Leigh was the natural choice for my sidekick. Guests would be instantly shocked by Leigh's look, but often left impressed by his humour and his obvious kindness. On the show Leigh was hysterical, often coming to the studio without sleep from a heavy night out. He was always nervous, his outfits and make-up providing the security he needed to perform. But his sharp-witted delivery was always perfect, often cutting people dead in their tracks with one pointed comment. Dolph Lundgren, who described in depth how he maintained his physique by a strict work-out routine, was humiliated when Leigh told him that he preferred to work out 'in the library'. Other guests who were in the direct line of

Leigh's humour included Gary Glitter, who was asked how he managed to get such a great tan on the palms of his hands, and Nina Hagen, who after describing the time she had met God was flabbergasted when Leigh asked if God 'drove a car'.

MTV had only just started in Britain at this time and not many homes had cable or satellite, so the programme didn't get the audience it deserved. However, it was very popular abroad, and when I was on holiday in Portugal, I had some locals round the apartment when it was on and they couldn't believe that this freak was my best friend.

Leigh managed to get a few well-paid jobs in the media world. He was asked to take part in a Kodak campaign in Germany, but it wasn't a happy experience, and he felt he was treated very badly by the company. The best-paid job he ever did was for Pepe jeans. He had to do a week's filming, but it resulted in a long advert, of which he was the star, that was shown in cinemas up and down the country. He had to whisper 'Wears Pepe', which was their advertising slogan at the time. The advert was considered to be a bit of a breakthrough and got lots of media coverage, which pleased Leigh no end, as it brought stardom one step closer.

Baillie Walsh started going out with John Maybury after Trojan died, and was commissioned to make the video for Boy George's 'Generations of Love' in May 1990. Baillie loved sleaze: he set the video in and around a dirty cinema in the back streets of Soho, and chose many of his friends to play the parts of prostitutes and transvestites.

Leigh was employed as fashion stylist for the shoot, and he was thrilled to rummage round charity shops looking for the most common clothes he could find. He made me a purple satin mini dress, which I could just about bear to wear as I had recently returned from holiday and had very brown legs. He also bought me a disgusting marbled denim coat that was gathered at the knees. This was all set off with plastic white stilettos with bows at the back of the ankle and carefully scuffed heels. Leigh was thrilled to see me dressed like this, as he was always encouraging me to look stupid, but I usually managed to resist.

The other prostitutes were David Holah, Les Child, Princess Julia – who was furious when Leigh said she had to have a greasy face and caked it with Vaseline – Rachel Auburn, Boy George, Stevie Hughes and Leigh himself. He was not supposed to be in the video, but the urge to show off got too much, so he stuck on his merkin, his blond wig, his massive false breasts and a shortie T-shirt with 'Goodnight' printed on the front along with a picture of a teddy bear and joined the rest of us on Old Compton Street.

The video was being filmed from a window, so the passers-by couldn't see the cameras and thought we were real prostitutes. Leigh and I stood outside an off-licence, and we could have made a fortune. We were propositioned by about ten men, a couple of whom were even quite good-looking. They were thrilled with Leigh's massive bosom – for once my own huge cleavage wasn't the centre of attention. Later on, Leigh went round phone boxes sticking up phone numbers, and took to the job with gusto, but unfortunately what he took for a sexy smile resembled Benny Hill's mischievous grin.

Baillie later employed Leigh as art director when he made the video for Massive Attack's 'Unfinished Sympathy'. This involved a trip to Los Angeles in late 1990. The video was very unusual in the fact that it was shot in one long take. It involved Shara Nelson walking along downtown streets singing the song, passing various down and outs and white trailer trash. Leigh was not made to be an employee. He drove Baillie mad by trying to insist that Shara wear a really freaky wig for the video to cover up her earpiece wire. This was completely the wrong look, and Leigh started shouting at Baillie in front of the band. Baillie recalls, 'I was furious and in the end I had to tell him I was the director and he had to do what I said. Our relationship was never quite the same after that.'

When Leigh got home, he spent ages moaning about Baillie: 'Honestly Sue, I was so embarrassed. Baillie was walking down the street in a tight white vest, I mean, I couldn't believe it and then he was sucking up to all these film people, it made me sick.' I couldn't believe what I was hearing. Baillie was gorgeous, with a fantastic body and usually a golden tan; he must have fitted into the Los Angeles lifestyle much better than Leigh, with his grotty wig and tatty old day wear.

Leigh would never compromise himself by sucking up to people he didn't like in order to get work, which is probably why he never was on *Wogan*. He did eventually appear on *The Last Resort* with Jonathan Ross and on the *Joan Rivers Show*, where he became furious when he was harangued by the audience and one lone voice piped up to support him: 'Oh give the guy a break. He only thinks it's Halloween.' Leigh couldn't think of a greater insult.

11

Trips

Leigh loved to travel. He usually preferred to combine the holiday with some work to give the trip a purpose, but he was still happy just to go away to see somewhere different. He loved to explore new places and new cultures, and to broaden his knowledge of the world as much as possible. He didn't mind if it was Japan or Brighton, just as long as it involved a journey.

When he had been in London a couple of years and had made friends with Rachel, Trojan and David, they often went to Amsterdam for the weekend. During the day they would visit all the museums and galleries and at night they would go to the saunas and gay bars and enjoy the permissive side of Dutch culture. He also went to Berlin with Rachel, where they went to the Bauhaus and all the galleries.

In 1983, Susanne Bartsch discovered Leigh and Rachel, and she offered to take them to New York – Susanne had been championing young British designers since 1980 – but they had to pay their own fare and accommodation. As they were completely broke, this was a bit of a problem. They managed to scrape the fare together and then the *Face* magazine forwarded them a letter from a New Yorker called Amy, who was impressed by their work and invited them to stay any time. So the two of them stayed squashed into her small apartment in Manhattan. The fashion show was at the Roxy and was a big success, although Leigh got a bit jealous when Malcolm McLaren came up and congratulated Rachel while completely ignoring him. They had a great time and were taken out to dinner every night by different people. They met the designer John Badum, who took them to a tatty old shop that sold seventies platform shoes. Few people ever went in there as it was considered so un-hip, but Leigh snapped up several pairs and started a new trend in London.

My first trip to New York with Leigh was in spring 1984. Leigh had been asked to take part in a second fashion show organized by Susanne Bartsch. The show was to be held at the fashionable Limelight club, which was in a converted church. Trojan and I were desperate to go with Leigh because neither of us had been to America before, let alone New York. We took a flight the day before Leigh and Rachel. They had to leave as late as possible so that they could finish off their garments, because as usual they had left everything to the last minute.

Michael Clark decided to come too, with his new boyfriend Richard Habberley. Various other designers were on the Air India jumbo jet: Greg Davis, Richard Torry, Mignon Matthews, Judy Blame and John Richmond. We were thrilled with the plane, which was decked out like a cheap Indian restaurant with flock wallpaper and hostesses in saris. The windows were temple-shaped and there was even piped sitar music.

We soon made ourselves at home. I was sitting with Michael, Trojan, Richard Habberley and Judy Blame, while the others were further back. Greg Davis, who had long blond hair at this time, was

thrilled when the hostesses mistook him for Marilyn (the androgynous singer and friend of Boy George) and presented him with a
free bottle of champagne. Michael had bought a two-litre bottle of
Blue Label Smirnoff vodka in Duty Free, which we proceeded to
demolish, with the result that by the time we arrived in New York
we were paralytically drunk. Judy Blame was the furthest gone and
made a grand entrance into Arrivals by falling flat on his face. He
had five cases of his rubber jewelry to pick up from the carousel,
but was so drunk he could only find three. He had so much trouble
explaining to customs what these strange bits of twisted rubber
were that Michael had to do it for him. Judy had to go back the next
day to recover his lost cases.

Michael, Richard and I stayed at Charlie Atlas's apartment on
West 14th Street, in the Meatpacking District. It was a wonderful
place, with large rooms and high ceilings, centrally situated for
Greenwich Village and Chelsea. That night we got ready to go out,
but the last thing we could remember when we woke up at 5 a.m.
was sitting on the sofa at about 9.30 p.m. We were victims of jet
lag, which we had thought wouldn't affect us, as we were used to
keeping strange hours and staying up late. We couldn't believe
that we had fallen asleep fully clothed. We were wide awake now,
so we went up the street to a diner and ate meatballs and spaghetti.

Later that morning the rest of the party arrived: Leigh, Rachel,
Annie Le Paz (who had recently taken up designing as a change
from running clubs) and her posse. That night there was a fashion show in Macy's showing the best of British fashion. We went
along but it wasn't as exciting as we had expected, although it was
strange to be wandering around this great big department store
when it was closed. We went back to Charlie's to have a few drinks

before hitting the clubs, but unfortunately jet lag hit us again and we were asleep by 11 p.m.

The next day was the big show. We went along to the Limelight at about 3 p.m. to get ready, as the show was at 5.30 p.m. Leigh had a variety of models, all the misshapen ones who no one else wanted. I was wearing a blue face and a long, green velour coat with a bullseye effect on the front, over a red, blue and rust dress with a handkerchief hem and a silver star. I was also wearing a pair of the silver platform shoes that Leigh had had made for all the models at a small Greek shoemaker's in Camden Town. Everyone was also wearing the tall, sequinned hats that had become Leigh's trademark. Leigh and Trojan did everyone's make-up. Some models had blue faces, while others had the Picasso look that Trojan was so fond of, with the wonky mouth and extra nose. Some reporters were there from *Nationwide*, a British current affairs programme that was covering the British invasion of the American fashion market. Little did they know that hardly any of the designers had any production arranged, and were just using the occasion to show off their one-off designs. If anyone had ordered more than five of anything none of the designers could have coped. One reporter began interviewing me and was rather startled when I spoke with a woman's voice, as he had thought I was Leigh with my blue face. However, as Leigh was busy, he continued to interview me (my mother practically fell off her chair when she saw me on the television with my unusual make-up look).

Everyone was ready just in time and we paraded on the cat-walk that had been designed by Michael Kostiff. Apparently Andy Warhol was in the audience, but we never saw him (and he doesn't mention it in his diaries). The show was quite a success, but luckily for Leigh the orders didn't come flooding in – he wouldn't have known what to do if they had. The show was reviewed on the front page of the *New York Times*, who seemed more interested in the 'chunky models' than the clothes, which they dismissed as British eccentricity.

Before the show we had all been drinking vodka to give ourselves some Dutch courage, so when the show finished at 7 p.m. we were all rather restless and drunk, but there was nowhere to go as it was still early. Michael Clark was a bit bored, so he threw a pebble at one of the other models. Unfortunately, he missed her, and the stone smashed one of the stained-glass windows that had remained from the original church. This caused a terrible commotion, with all the Americans running around in panic to see who had done it. They thought it was a girl who was standing next to Michael, and despite her protestations, she was thrown out of the club. We quickly collected everything together and rushed back to Charlie's before they discovered that Michael was the true culprit. Leigh sat sobbing on the outside step because he felt that he would be blamed. Despite his own outrageousness and encouragement of all things shocking, he was still the well-brought-up boy from Sunshine, and he felt terrible that he was in some way responsible for the broken window. He cried for about an hour before we managed to calm him down. Yet again, we were so tired that we didn't manage to get out to a nightclub.

By the next day, however, we had recovered enough to hit the clubs with a vengeance. Annie Le Paz was staying in the Bowery, at the flat of the New York writer Kathy Acker, so we all met there and then went to the Roxy Roller Disco and on to Danceteria, which I had seen in the video for 'Into the Groove' by Madonna.

I was drinking Car Crashes, a debilitating cocktail consisting of vodka mixed with white wine, so everything soon became a haze of lifts, bars, dance floors and strange people, but I do remember bumping into Marco Pirroni from Adam and the Ants. Leigh, of course, was taking it all in his stride, having been to New York before. A strange young man called Cass, who had come in Annie Le Paz's party and was a bouncer back in England, decided he was in charge and kept telling us to behave as if we were 'representatives of our country'. Leigh did the exact opposite and went out of his way to jump on yet more chairs, spill more drinks and generally freak people out.

In the daytime we went sightseeing and shopping, hung out in the SoHo art galleries and Village bars. One day Leigh, Trojan, Richard Torry and I decided to go to the fair at Coney Island. It was a very old-fashioned place, stuck in a fifties time warp, so there were plenty of rides that weren't too frightening. Leigh and I jumped into a log canoe to go on the flume, but unfortunately our combined weight almost sank it, so I had to share with Richard instead. On the way out of the fair a thin old woman accosted Trojan. All she seemed able to say was 'V's, V's, I need V's' – at first we couldn't work out what she meant, but Trojan was over the moon when he realized she was asking if he had any Valium.

While in New York we discovered Dial-A-Drug, which was a service that delivered whatever drug you wanted straight to your door. It seemed a bit strange to Leigh and me, as we thought that the police would soon be on to it, but it seemed to work and Leigh got hold of some massive magic mushrooms.

We decided to go to Area, the most fashionable club in town, to meet John Badum. Trojan didn't come as he wanted to go to

St Mark's Baths in search of some sex. We took the mushrooms and ordered a cab to take us there. We were very impressed by Area, the decor of which was changed every month so that it always had a different theme. This was Bondage Month, so there were cages and bars everywhere. It was nothing like we had ever seen in England. The crowd were older than the London clubbers and were far more sophisticated. We were out of it on the mushrooms and had drunk copious amounts of vodka and Cran-Grape, which seemed to be the drink of the moment. Suddenly we saw a vision in silver come towards us, and realized that it was Gary Glitter. Leigh dropped to the floor and lay prostrate at his feet, shouting 'Gary, Gary, Gary, I love you.' I think he was glad to get the attention, because he wasn't well-known in America at the time.

We were feeling so ill and drunk we decided to go back to Charlie's, who luckily had gone away. Michael and Richard were there, as they hadn't wanted to go out. We drove them mad falling all over the flat screaming and shouting, and then Leigh threw up bright red sick all over the bathroom. The Cran-Grape obviously hadn't agreed with him. I've got fantastic photos of him with his head down the toilet, covered with what looks like entrails, but is really his own vomit. The shocking thing was that in the morning we crept into the bathroom dreading what we would find, but found it spotless. In my drunken state I had managed to clear the whole mess up, which I could never have done sober.

Leigh returned to New York many times after this trip, and became a major celebrity on the club scene.

Bronwyn came to stay with Leigh in the summer of 1984. It was her first trip out of Australia; she was very excited, and desperate to explore the English countryside. She hired a car, so we all decided to go to the Isle of Wight. We drove down to Portsmouth one lunch-time and luckily caught a ferry straight away. Bronwyn was thrilled, as she had never been on a boat before. When we arrived on the island we tried to find a bed and breakfast, but for some strange reason when confronted by a six-foot man wearing a red romper suit asking if there were any vacancies, they all claimed to be full. In the end Bronwyn and I thought we would have a better chance if we went and asked. We managed to get a family room at a rather severe guest house near Shanklin. We immediately christened it 'Mrs Shingles', as the landlady had told us in great detail about her latest attack of the nasty virus.

Bronwyn had brought everything with her: nightie, dressing gown, shampoo, conditioner and about three changes of clothes. Leigh, Trojan and I were still in Hard Times mode and all we had between us was a small bag of make-up. There were three beds in one room, so we slept there while Bronwyn had the small adjacent room. It was almost impossible to sleep because Leigh was winding Trojan up all night pretending to attack him.

In the morning we went down to breakfast in the large dining room, where a few other holidaymakers were eating cereals and toast. Leigh was still wearing his red romper suit, but the other guests tried to ignore this, politely mumbling 'good morning'. Leigh loved this old English custom and began loudly shouting 'morning' to anyone who came into the room. To entertain the other guests Leigh performed his usual trick of falling off his chair. The first time they all rushed to help him up, but by about the sixth time they sat in embarrassed silence, giving each other quizzical looks and not quite believing that this apparition was in their dining room on the sleepy Isle of Wight.

We decided to drive around the island, starting at Britain's first theme park, Blackgang Chine. We couldn't work out what the theme was, but it was very entertaining in its cheap, British, unsophisticated way. The most exciting thing about it was that big chunks of it fell into the sea each year. The first attraction we encountered consisted of models of various nursery-rhyme characters. These were behind a fence that Leigh jumped over in order to sit on top of one of the giant toadstools. He then entered a tableau representing the three pigs and hardly looked out of place as he held the little pig's hand.

The second attraction we reached was the maze, where we soon lost Bronwyn, and despite calling out her name we couldn't find her. I wanted to wait for her, but Leigh said he had seen her go on ahead, so we continued to explore the rest of the park, hoping to catch up with her. Trojan, meanwhile, spotted a boy who used to be in his class at school and was so mortified in case he was seen at such an unsophisticated resort we had to hide inside a glass-fibre mushroom until he had safely passed us by. I was getting more and more worried about Bronwyn, but Leigh assured me that she had gone on ahead, so we continued to enjoy the other attractions – the House That Jack Built, Dinosaur Land and the Cowboy Village. We then made our way back to the car park, and there was Bronwyn waiting by the car. She had been lost in the maze for hours and Leigh had just pretended that she had gone on ahead. I couldn't believe that someone could be so horrible to their own sister, but Bronwyn didn't seem to mind, so off we went to explore the beaches.

The next weekend Andrew Logan was holding an alternative art show at Henley-on-Thames, and as Bronwyn still had the hire car, Leigh persuaded her to drive us there. She made platefuls of sandwiches, which she covered in cling film and put on the back shelf of the car. We were flabbergasted by this, as it seemed so proper and organized. On the way we picked up Richard Torry and Rachel Auburn, who proceeded to give everyone speed, so the sandwiches were even more superfluous. We arrived at the show to find lots of people we knew there – the Neo Naturists and all of Andrew Logan's gang. The Pimm's tents were still there from the regatta, so we drank plenty of that along with the vodka that we had brought with us. Trojan got so drunk he stripped off his clothes, painted his body and jumped into the river, chased by Ula, Andrew's long-time friend. Poor old Bronwyn took it all in her stride, but must have thought that the English were a very strange race.

A few weekends later my parents held a Sunday afternoon party in their garden. As there was likely to be a lot of drink there, Leigh decided to come with me, yet again wearing his red romper suit. All my aunts and uncles were there, together with numerous cousins and some long-lost relations. They were all a bit flabbergasted by Leigh, who kept charging up and down the very slopey garden. He got drunker and drunker and kept giving my little brother, who was about eleven, big glasses of vodka, which he disguised with Malibu and pineapple. My mum thought it was over-excitement that caused him to collapse on his bed at about 6 p.m.

As Leigh guzzled even more vodka, he decided to entertain certain members of the family by waving his penis about, much to their surprise. It is an incident that has never been forgotten by most of them, but as Leigh was also very charming, they took a liking to him and were always pleased when they later saw him on television or in newspapers. My cousin Debbie and her boyfriend gave us a lift home in the back of their Mini, which was a tight squeeze.

Leigh passed out with his head on my lap, waking up every now and then to mutter some rubbish and wave his penis about.

Two years later Leigh had an opportunity to show his clothes at an exhibition and fashion show in Vienna. It was when his parents were visiting for the first time, so he asked them to come too. The Austrians were paying for Leigh's accommodation, as well as mine, as I was acting as his assistant. The event was being run by the U4 Disco, who asked if Leigh would host a Taboo night while he was there. He agreed, so they also paid for Jeffrey Hinton to come over in his capacity as DJ.

We set off from Gatwick. There was quite a large party on the plane: Wigan, who was covering the event for *i-D* magazine, and his girlfriend Kerry; Simon Witter, who had organized the event; Michiko Koshino, who was showing; Cindy, Rifat Ozbek's assistant, who was taking care of his show; and someone from the fashion house Joseph. We were also accompanied by a tall, black girl called Georgia who wore blue contact lenses and phenomenal amounts of make-up. She was appearing as a celebrity model along with her sister Janice, who was a bit younger and shorter than Georgia and who followed her about constantly clutching a tissue and sniffing.

When we arrived at the airport a coach picked us up and took us to the hotel. Then Leigh's father took it upon himself to sort out the accommodation, and to Leigh's great embarrassment suggested that the girls and boys separate out and the rooms be allotted that way. Everyone looked at Tom aghast. In the end I shared a large room with Leigh and Jeffrey. As soon as Leigh entered the room he insisted on rearranging all the furniture. The beds had wooden slats for bases, which weren't very firmly fixed. Every time one of us sat on the bed we broke another one. We didn't know what to do with these broken bits of wood, so we ended up hiding them in a shower down the corridor, leaving our mattresses balancing on about three slats each. Luckily, it wasn't a very high-class hotel.

The show was taking place in a deserted shopping mall above the U4 Disco. All the designers were given an empty shop where they were supposed to show their fashions for the week-long event. But Leigh couldn't be bothered to set up a display, and certainly didn't want to sit with it all day trying to sell things that he didn't have to sell. As much as they tried to persuade him, he refused, though the Austrians didn't seem too disappointed – they were just happy to have Leigh there.

On the first night we decided to go to a gay disco that Leigh had heard of called 'Why Not?'; I think 'Why?' would have been a more appropriate name. There were about three sad queens in there sipping half-pints of lager. Even though Leigh wasn't dressed up, he still had a twirl on the dance floor before we went home in search of food.

Each night of the exhibition there was a fashion show by a different designer. The Austrians provided a few models; the rest of the designers were expected to find their own. As Leigh was showing only menswear there were even fewer models available, so he roped in Wigan and Jeffrey. All the models were to have the white, drippy-head look. As much as he would have loved them to, even Leigh realized all these men would not be willing to shave their heads, so he provided rubber skullcaps to cover their hair. He stuck these on their heads, I covered them and their faces with white make-up, and then Leigh put the drips on and painted in the eyes and mouths. It was surreal looking at six miniature Leighs (especially knowing that one of them was the very ginger and very straight Wigan).

Most of Leigh's menswear consisted of short skirts and jackets teamed with knee-high socks. Leigh modelled his beautiful green jacket with angel wings, which was always one of my favourites. The models strutted their stuff on the catwalk to the cheers of the delighted Austrian crowd. Leigh's parents, meanwhile, watched with some pride, but also bemusement that their son could demand such adulation.

After the show we went to the disco downstairs, which was full of students. The two most popular bands were the Sex Pistols and the Cure. It was hilarious watching Wigan do his Wigan Casino-type dancing to 'God Save The Queen'. We got very drunk as they gave us free drinks tickets. Leigh ended up wetting the bed, as he often did if he was too drunk, so the next day I had to wash the sheet in the wash basin and hang it out of the window to dry.

The Taboo night was a bit of a flop as none of the Austrians had dressed up and it was a normal studenty crowd. Jeffrey was doing his best to whip up the crowd with his trash disco hits, but it really wasn't happening. Leigh ran out of drinks tickets, so he said he would pop across the road to our hotel room, where we had a stash of vodka. After about half an hour he still hadn't come back, so I went to look for him. He was rolling around on the floor just giggling to himself he was so drunk. He pulled me down on top of him and got his penis out. He kept waving it at me and touching me with it. He then grabbed the end and made his penis hole move in time to the squeaky voice he was talking in, pretending that his dick was speaking to me. We were laughing so much we didn't hear the door open, and there stood Georgia Hart and her sister, staring at us in complete disbelief. They always gave us funny looks whenever they bumped into us after that.

In February 1987 Leigh was invited to do a fashion show in Melbourne. He couldn't believe it. It would be the first time he had gone home in six and a half years, and coincidentally Michael Clark and Company would be there performing at the same time. He was excited but nervous. As the organizers couldn't afford to pay for an assistant he wasn't able to take many garments with him. Instead, he decided to use the costumes that he had made for Michael Clark and Company and use the dancers as models. He arrived after a nightmare flight, in which the plane kept stopping for refuelling, and things were made worse by his horrendous hangover. He wrote a very entertaining and poignant letter to me about his trip:

> My parents and Bronwyn were there to meet me and one of
> the organizers of the show, and the following day Michael
> and the Company arrived. It was so weird being back.
> Everything seemed so bright and wide. None of the placement
> of anything seemed right. Slowly over the next few days things
> came into range and my memory of how things were laid out
> became sync-ed with the way they really were. I was suffering
> from fatigue and jet lag chronically. There were photo sessions
> and interviews set up for every day. I kept waking up in the
> middle of the night and not being able to get back to sleep.
> The only things that seemed as they should were Michael and
> the Company. It was so gorgeous seeing Mike and Dave and
> Les Child.

The show was beset with problems from the start. Michael's promoters wouldn't allow his company to perform or to lend any costumes from the show, but at the last minute they reluctantly agreed as long as Michael didn't feature any of the dance sequences from his show. Leigh was fed up with the whole business by now, so Michael volunteered to choreograph a fifteen-minute show. Leigh's mother was exceedingly excited and at 2 p.m. on Valentine's Day she proudly led a large crowd of her friends and relatives to join the audience at Melbourne Town Hall. Leigh finished the letter:

> I gave Michael a free hand and told him to do whatever he felt like. Michael thought it would be wise to include all the sex sequences from the show. The audience saw Michael wearing the apron and rubber dildo, then David licking and sucking it. There was nudity from nearly all the girls and Les Child, David and me were as camp as Christmas.
>
> What was planned by my mother to be the *piece de resistance* of a triumphant home-coming turned out to be the most mortifying experience of her life. She was seated in the Town Hall of Melbourne surrounded by all her friends and relatives and had to endure the most self-indulgent and sick show she's ever likely to see. Which explains why I'm typing a ten thousand word essay in my bedroom while she's crying her heart out. But to take a page out of your book – I'm a twenty-five-year-old figure and what my parents think is their business and what I do is mine. Guilt trip, get out that window.

Years later Leigh's mother was upset by an article in an Australian paper describing Leigh's antics. She had tearfully phoned him and asked why he couldn't be like normal people. Leigh hated his mother being upset, so he asked me to phone her and tell her that he was quite kind-hearted really. While I was on the phone she mentioned the show. 'Do you know what, Sue? Even after all these

years, if some of my old friends who were at that show see me coming they cross over to the other side of the street.'

When I spoke to his father a couple of years after Leigh had died,
he was more philosophical about the whole business.

> Well I suppose that it was terrible in that we didn't have any
> idea of what was going to happen and looking back on it when
> we heard that he was coming back to perform, my immediate
> thoughts were, well who is going to watch him. Evelyn asked
> some of her girlfriends to go along and from that day to this, I
> think they were quite shocked and didn't speak to us because
> of it. OK, it didn't please us but again I also think we could
> see there was talent in what they were trying to do. The shock
> tactic and things of that nature. Some of the audience were
> normal people but I still maintain that there were a lot of
> artistic people who went to see the group, they were interested
> in that nightclubby type of activity and they seemed to enjoy it.
> A lot of them were thrilled by the show but a lot of the, as we say
> in inverted commas, ordinary people were shocked by it.

After a couple of days Evelyn had forgiven her son because she
was so happy to have him home, and despite the fact what he did
wasn't really to her liking, at least there were pictures of him in
the newspaper. He told the *Herald*: 'My parents find what I do very
peculiar, mainly because I have so much attention. Seeing me in a
magazine somehow makes the whole thing more real for them and
gives them a kind of reason for what I do. I think they'd find it harder
to cope with if I was living in their own suburban neighbourhood.'

In September 1990, Cerith and Angus rented out a very large
house belonging to the Astor family in Trebetherick in Cornwall.

Cerith was doing a project on tractors and there had been a magnificent display at the Royal Cornish Show. It was typical of their extravagance to rent an eight-bedroomed place just for the two of them. To make it more worthwhile they invited Leigh to stay with them, and he decided to ask me so that I could drive him down. I went to pick him up from outside Lucian's house one Sunday afternoon. I had to park a few doors away from the house because Leigh didn't want him to know that he had told me where he lived. I had bought a few snacks for the journey and by the time we had reached the M4, which was about three miles away, Leigh had devoured all of them with his typical greed.

We arrived at about 7 p.m. and found that Lucian's daughter Esther was there with her friend Janet. They had just been sightseeing in Tintagel, where King Arthur was supposed to have lived. The house was designed for a huge family so we rattled about in all the space. The lounge was like something you would find in an old people's home, with about twenty high-backed vinyl chairs. Leigh and I slept in a very cosy room with incredibly comfortable beds.

Angus had recently taken to cooking in a big way and had brought bags of provisions from Neal's Yard with him. The larder was full of bags of pulses and dried apricots. He made everything from scratch and was forever trying new recipes – you would suddenly be presented with a batch of scones that he had just popped into the oven. On our first day he decided he was going to make pea soup, but he had to have fresh peas. As he wanted about ten pounds of peas, he decided it would be cheaper to buy them wholesale, so he phoned around all the wholesalers in Cornwall until he found one willing to sell one box of peas. Leigh, Cerith and I were sent off to buy them. The wholesaler was about thirty miles away on a deserted industrial estate, but we managed to buy our peas. We were quite near Port Isaac, a very picturesque fishing village well known for the fact that you can only park there at certain times because the car park is on the beach and half the time it's under water. You have to drive down a very steep incline to reach the town centre, and it was school lunch hour as we drove very slowly down, Leigh wolf-whistling at every schoolboy he saw, all of whom he thought were 'gorgeous'.

Of course by now Leigh was hungry, so we went to a pub for crab salad. He then found a fudge shop and bought some fudge in a crumpled paper bag, which he proceeded to offer to every schoolboy he saw. Not surprisingly they all ignored him, as he looked like a child molester in his blond wig and beige windcheater. We bought some fresh herbs from an old lady's garden and some scallops from the fishermen on the shore. Leigh then started crawling around the fishing nets, sniffing them like a dog just to entertain us, much to the dismay of the car-park attendant, who was urging us to move our car as the tide was about to come in.

Back at the house, Angus was waiting anxiously for the peas, which we had to shell while he pottered in the kitchen. For some reason known only to himself, Leigh had brought with him a massive, shocking-pink tutu-like dress made from at least 100 metres of tulle. He decided to put it on and wander across the golf course to the beach. It was an unbelievable sight, the garishness of the pink against the earthy, subdued colours of the countryside. Cerith captured it on film and the faces of the golfers and ramblers are truly marvellous: they must have thought that they were hallucinating when they saw this gigantic pink vision approaching them. Leigh then decided to paddle in the sea, dragging the extraordinary robe behind him.

When Janet and Esther returned from their sightseeing and Leigh returned from the beach, Angus triumphantly served up the soup. We couldn't stop laughing, since we had travelled sixty miles to buy the peas then spent hours shelling them, and there was only one meagre bowl each. But that one bowl was truly delicious.

Next morning the girls returned to London and we decided to drive along the coast to St Ives to visit the Barbara Hepworth Sculpture Garden. This is next to the studio where she was burnt to death after accidentally setting fire to her bed with a lighted cigarette. Her holey sculptures are dotted around some beautiful plants and shrubs. It was all a bit tame for Leigh, so he decided to do his own art performance: he quickly pulled down his trousers and stuck his bum through one of the holes in the sculpture. The other rather staid visitors, of course, studiously ignored him.

The next stop was Penzance, where Angus had tracked down a gay bar by phoning Gay Switchboard. Sadly we arrived too late (the opening hours were 10 a.m. to 5 p.m.), so we were unable to savour the delights of Cornish gay life. Well, Cerith and Angus weren't, but as usual Leigh managed to get a taste of it. He went into the public lavatories while we waited outside for him. As he didn't come out straight away, we could imagine what was going on. Our fears were confirmed when a rather burly chap dressed in denim came out, wiping his mouth. He was closely followed by Leigh, who had a very self-satisfied look on his face.

The next day we walked to the beach. The way was marked by little bits of shocking-pink net stuck to all the thistles. At this point Cerith, Angus and Leigh were thinking of starting a band, so they did some pretend band shots on the beach, jumping up in the air and on top of each other, but then Leigh got distracted by a giant stranded jellyfish and chased us all over the beach with it. He was like a little kid who had found the most disgusting thing, the way he was poking and prodding it. He kept throwing it about until it eventually fell to bits.

As Leigh had already missed one day working at Lucian's we returned to London that night, chuckling all the way, thinking about Angus's soup and playing singing games to pass the time.

Leigh's last holiday was on the Greek islands with Richard Torry in September 1994. It was the first proper holiday he had had in a warm place for about ten years. They took a flight to Athens and then took a ferry to the nearest island. Richard had wanted the holiday to give them a chance to write lyrics together, and had bought Leigh lots of new note books to give him inspiration, but Leigh was intent on seeing as much as he could, and as soon as they reached one island he wanted to go on to the next. Richard remembers: 'He was manic to see everything, it was almost as if he had a death wish all the time we were there, he had to dive off the highest cliffs and ride his motor bike round the sharpest bends as fast as he could. I couldn't keep up because I wasn't so heavy so my bike wasn't so grounded.'

Leigh insisted on going to smart restaurants all the time, and wasn't happy with the cheap local cafés. He loved the food, as he wrote to me on a postcard: 'Crete 26. 9. 94, Met some nice Cretans the other day. Greek men love fat whores – so you'd do very well. Octopus for lunch, Fish souvlaki for dinner … and for breakfast. Wish you were here, love Leigh.'

At first Leigh wouldn't go in the sun because he didn't want to get a tan, which would change his appearance and make life difficult for Lucian, but in the end he gave in, sunbathing in the nude so that at least he wouldn't have any white bits. He spent most of the holiday composing two postcards to Lucian because he wanted them to be just right.

Towards the end of the holiday Richard had left Leigh diving off some very high cliffs, from which he then disappeared. Richard was very worried, and after waiting for some time decided to return to the taverna where they were staying. He found Leigh marching around in a mad panic. He thought that £100 and his Walkman had been stolen from his rucksack. He was convinced that it was the lovely couple who owned the inn. He went and accused them and told them that he was going to report them to the police. This was completely out of character for him, and Richard tried to dissuade him. Then Leigh looked in another pocket in his rucksack and found the stolen property. He felt utterly embarrassed and couldn't face the couple, so he made Richard do a flit with him, leaving the money they owed on the bed.

When he got home this was the first thing that Leigh told me about. 'I'm really worried, Sue. I think this illness is sending me mad. How could I do such a thing? Normally I just wouldn't care, I'd have never considered going to the police, but the fact that I couldn't find my own things – it's a sign.' Leigh at last really began to think about the virus he had known that he had for almost six years now, and he felt sure that his health would begin to deteriorate soon.

12

Dance

Michael Clark was brought up on a small farm in Scotland. When he was four, he begged to learn Scottish dancing. His mother, Bessie, sent him to classes and he soon picked it up, showing such an aptitude that his teacher suggested he learn ballet, which he proceeded to do despite the taunts from other boys at school. He auditioned for the Royal Ballet School in Richmond Park and came to London when he was thirteen to train to be a ballet dancer. Michael outshone all the other pupils, but couldn't keep his rebellious and experimental nature under control. Glue was found in his locker, and if he hadn't been given the leading role in the end-of-term performance, he would have been expelled. Instead, he was sent to live with a teacher who could keep an eye on him. On leaving he joined the Ballet Rambert, where he excelled, but found that no one was making the kind of work he wanted to see, let alone dance. This is why he began making his own work. He became choreographer-in-residence at the Riverside Studios in Hammersmith, where he was given a free hand to produce his own work.

Michael did not live the normal, disciplined life of a dancer, but spent most of his free time drinking, smoking, taking drugs and hanging out in London's more alternative nightclubs. 'If I hadn't lived that life I wouldn't have felt so inspired. It was living that made me want to dance. I had only known dance before. It made me feel free enough to jump about like that, people in clubs thought it weird that I really could dance, like if I kicked my leg high in the air, like the incident outside the Pink Panther, it was part of my nature.' He met Leigh in a nightclub and was immediately attracted to this large, painted person. They became the best of friends and had complete mutual respect for each other. Michael was determined to work with Leigh not only because he respected his talent, but also because he enjoyed his company. 'He was charismatic and had an amazing presence, we egged each other on. It was like he was daring me, we both had similar ideas and worked off each other.'

Leigh was delighted to design costumes for Michael's work. The first piece he designed for was *Flippin 'eck Oh Thweet Mythtery of Life* in 1983.

The costumes Leigh designed initially reflected what he was wearing at the time. On one occasion he put the dancers in star tops with no armpits (for extra movement and freshness), hot pants, striped tights and wedged platform shoes. The dancers found them hard work, yet thrilling and comfortable to wear. It was the start of an important collaboration and Leigh continued to work with Michael for the next ten years.

An earlier piece really put Leigh and Michael on the map. Leigh had been wearing bottomless outfits for a while and decided to make them for the dancers in *New Puritan*, which was performed in 1984. They were made out of stretch rib jersey, as Lycra was prohibitively expensive then. As it was, Leigh made hardly any money – he was so determined to make the outfits absolutely perfect that he ended up putting his own money into the costumes.

The press went crazy about this shocking new dancer who exposed his own and his Company's bottoms to the audience. It was hardly anything really: just a hole cut out of a pair of tights so you could see the bum crack, and Leigh couldn't see what the fuss was about. 'Most people missed the point of the costumes. All they talked about was the fact that they were bottomless. They didn't mention how the cut of the outfits added to the performance.' Despite the outraged press coverage about the bottomless outfits, Michael was soon being hailed as the most exciting young dancer and choreographer in the world.

In 1985 Michael received a commission to choreograph a ballet for the Paris Opera, under the director Rudolf Nureyev. Rudolf continually chased Michael, and was always trying to lift up his kilt and feel his packet. Michael ignored his advances and got on with his work, asking Leigh to design the costumes, which he was thrilled to do. At last he would be working in Paris, and at somewhere far more glamorous than the Burger King on the Champs-Elysées. They were treated very well, put up in a great hotel and every day they were issued with a generous amount of spending money to pay for their meals and other incidentals. Michael recalls: 'We had to pinch ourselves, we couldn't believe it.' Leigh made all the costumes himself instead of using the array of dressmakers made available to him. He travelled to and fro across the Channel, taking bags of new garments with him. (Of course there was the added bonus of seeing well-built men in tights, which sent Leigh into fits of giggles.) The ballet and the costumes were debuted to great acclaim at the Pompidou Centre.

Charlie Atlas, who had been friends with Michael since they had worked together in New York, decided to make a film of Michael's work. It was a 'day in the life'-type documentary. Charlie combined all aspects of Michael's life to make this innovative work, which was shot in the spring of 1985 and shown as part of the 'Dance on Four' season in 1986. The film starts with a dream that Michael is having: he is dancing with his friends, who are covered in grey grease paint to give them a blurry, dream-like quality. The Neo Naturists are doing one of their shows and Cerith is wrapping his head in cling film. Leigh, Trojan and I are marching up and down eating turkey legs and bananas while watching *Young Doctors* on the television.

Next, Michael wakes up and starts rehearsing with Matthew Hawkins, Les Child, Ellen Von Schulenberg, Julie Hood and Gaby Agis, all of whom regularly worked together. They do a very lively and energetic dance to 'Shout' by Lulu, then go their separate ways around the streets of London. Michael and Gaby go to shoot a film within a film, which is being directed in an ironically pretentious way by Cerith.

The film then cuts to Leigh's flat, where he, Trojan and Rachel are preparing for a night out. It is a very bitchy scene, with them all picking on each other and forever changing their clothes. Leigh's voice is hilarious – it is at its most camp and he drags the end of his sentences for what seems like several minutes. Michael arrives and they bitch over his outfit. He then goes for a hot date with a boyfriend. The date was filmed in Leigh's mirrored bedroom with a boy Michael had met in Glasgow. Michael was unable to use his own bedroom because at this time he was living at my flat, and the boy concerned had written a letter to Michael saying he could never return there as it was so untidy. Sadly, neither Michael nor I was blessed with housekeeping skills.

Then Michael goes on to a nightclub, where he meets up with all the freaks of London. We see an eclectic mix of fussy clothes, ridiculous hairstyles and too much make-up, but that's how things were then. The club was meant to be in the West End, but it was really the Clarendon in Hammersmith. Michael had filled it with his friends, who certainly lived up to expectations by getting roaring drunk, sniffing poppers, smashing a mirror in the toilets and stealing the make-up lady's make-up. Jeffrey Hinton was the DJ and Princess Julia and I recreated our heavy rock band The Curse by strumming cardboard guitars. The Neo Naturists were shaking away in the corner. Scarlett, Jallé, Louise Neel, Fat Tony and Mel O'Brien were propping up the bar as usual. Leigh, Trojan and Rachel were sitting around the edge sniffing poppers.

Everyone was meant to learn a synchronized dance and perform it together. Most people joined in half-heartedly, but not Leigh: he had made Michael teach it to him a few days earlier and he was step perfect. When everyone else was mucking about he went off into a corner to rehearse on his own, and for years later he used to do it, just to check that he could still remember it.

Michael arrives home alone as dawn breaks, and gets into bed after dancing to Elvis Presley's 'Are You Lonesome Tonight'. A typical day in the life of Michael Clark.

Leigh continued to design costumes for Michael Clark and Company, including for *Our Caca phoney H* and *No Fire Escape in Hell*, for which he was awarded a Bessie for the best costumes in a ballet performed in New York. He was beginning to get onto the stage – it was almost as if he was testing the water. During *Our Caca phoney H* he would stand in the wings pissed, whooping and hollering his approval; then, at the end of *New Puritan*, Michael would insist that Leigh and Trojan join in the conga. He loved these extraordinary creatures and he wanted to introduce them to the world.

Leigh finally joined the company as a performer in 1987. He had a variety of roles: acting as a flying teapot; playing Chopin on the piano; taking part in an East End pub-style singsong. Leigh saw this as a natural progression. 'It appeals to the theatrical in me that's been there all along ... I get more pleasure out of being on stage than I ever did from people looking at my clothes.' Obviously he was not ballet trained, but he was an excellent dancer and he was willing to put in the hours to make what he did as perfect as possible. Despite his large size, he was very agile, and had tremendous strength and suppleness. He was also a quick and willing learner, which Michael particularly appreciated: 'I didn't try to control Leigh, but at the same time he was so determined to get the movement exactly as I wanted it.' Michael adored Leigh's wild, abandoned dances on the dance floors of London nightclubs: 'I would have loved to have captured that spirit and bottled it.' He found that untrained dancers still had a certain spirit that 'proper' dancers had lost in their rigorous training.

By now Michael was going out with David Holah, who had also been designing clothes for one of his ballets under his BodyMap label. He had also joined the Company, but as he was small and slender he did not stick out as a non-dancer as much as Leigh. At first Leigh and David were wary of each other, but they couldn't help but become friends. They had seen each other around nightclubs for years, but David had never bothered to get to know Leigh as he was 'too freaky' for his taste. But once they started to tour together it all changed: 'It was a treat to share a dressing room with Leigh, it was a sanctuary, he was a gorg' person. I felt comforted by his presence, he liked my relationship with Michael. He thought I kept him on the straight and narrow.'

Leigh was very excited about going on his first tour in late 1987 and was thrilled to be involved in such an inspiring project. He told a local newspaper, 'This is going to sound silly because I'm in it, but I really think this new show is the best thing that Michael's ever done, it's still visually stunning but in a lot of ways more serious – and as a non-dancer I can say that there's a lot of pure dancing that's quite breathtaking.'

During the tour Leigh and David made the company into a family. They would go off to the local market and make soup for everyone to share. But being on long tours becomes boring after a while, and Leigh soon had to invent a few tricks to entertain himself. Yugoslavia was particularly tiresome, as there wasn't much to do. Leigh and Michael plotted a particularly cruel trick to play on Les. For two days they defecated on a tray and saved it all up. During the show, Les had to take a baby piano out of the big piano and open it up. Leigh and Michael put all their shit into the little piano then carefully put it back into the big piano, liberally spraying the area with perfume to cover the foul stench. Throughout the performance they were waiting for the special moment when Les would open the piano; when he did his eyes exploded in horror, but he carried on like a true professional until he was scheduled to leave stage, when he dashed into the wings and threw up.

Flying also got to be a bore, so on one flight Leigh decided to make some mischief. He wrote a note supposedly from a very handsome man sitting a few seats behind Ellen Von Schulenberg and then asked the air hostess to give it to her. Ellen's face broke into a broad beam as she read the note declaring an attraction for her. Throughout the flight, to the delight of the others, she kept turning round and making cow eyes at the handsome traveller. When they disembarked she couldn't understand how a man who had written such an ardent note could ignore her despite her continually staring at him.

There were often long delays at airports, and on one of these occasions Leigh decided to entertain everyone. He fell onto the floor and began to really shake, as if he were having some sort of fit, making sure that his wig fell off. It rather backfired on him, though, when a group of very concerned nuns rushed over to bless him.

Although Leigh was accepted by the other dancers in the company, the critics had a problem with him, as Michael remembers. 'I think that the critics thought Leigh was a bad influence and he was leading me astray. If it wasn't for all the shocking costumes I might be able to settle down. One critic said, "Cut out the gimmicks and dance", so we made this part of the performance. The Neo Naturists chanted it during the show, "Cut out the gimmicks, cut out the gimmicks." Of course I cared what they said, but I knew beforehand what the response would be. The dance world is a very predictable and dull place.'

Les Child loved working with Leigh and admired his dancing. 'She was so aware of her body and as she got older and did more performances she used to shock me with the awareness of the body. He had those very feminine hands and those brilliantly arched feet. It just worked, that big woman, I loved to see her work.' Les usually shared a room with Leigh, which was an experience in itself:

Me and Leigh were sharing a room and we were reading each other. Leigh was so interested in the whole blackness thing and

culture. Things he'd never experienced before. I think the way
I was black, gay and came out with all that parlare speak. He
really provoked me one time when we were in Yugoslavia. If
you left your bag in a room when he was alone he would grab it
and go through it to find out more about you. Your personals,
he would go right through them, and anything you told him,
sisterly in confidence, which he was brilliant at wheedling out
of you. He'd try to get your deepest thoughts and secrets, and
it would be filed in the head. To make light of and trivialize,
to spread around to other people. 'Girl, I told you that in
fucking confidence.'

Leigh used to drive Les to the limit: on one occasion he went
downstairs and found the rest of the company in fits of laughter.
Leigh was parading around in Les's clothes, which he had somehow
managed to squeeze himself into, and was swishing and talking
exactly like him.

Michael took no notice of the critics and tended to do the exact
opposite of what they wanted. They merely provoked him into more
and more outrageous performances. Leigh, of course, revelled in
this, as he loved to take things to the limit. His designs for Michael
became more extreme: he had the dancers wearing clear plastic
corsets attached to toilet seat rims as a collar with the lid standing
behind the head like a halo. But it is the costumes that he never
quite got round to making that Michael liked best. They spent
many happy hours talking about designs for the future. A particular
favourite of Michael's was a costume based on a nun's habit.

Michael was asked to do a benefit for Sadler's Wells at the Royal
Opera House in Covent Garden. He put together a performance
that involved about fifteen different people: his usual company

plus Charlie Atlas, the Neo Naturists, and the model Lizzie Tear playing organ in the background. Les played a fairy who danced around waking all the others up. Everyone was very keen to get on and didn't realize that the ballet before them was in three acts, so Leigh and friends kept leaping onto the stage too soon, then having to scuttle back into the wings as the previous show continued. Leigh encouraged the Company to do their best by telling them that the Queen Mother was in the audience, and encouraged the Royal Ballet dancers by offering them amyl nitrate.

Once the show was over, the Neo Naturists swooped on the wardrobe department and dressed up in the most outrageous clothes they could find, ripping them and covering them in body paint in the process. When it came to the final curtain, Dame Peggy Ashcroft was giving a speech and as she gestured towards the line up behind her, her mouth dropped, because instead of the stars of the show – who she was expecting to see – the whole front row was made up of Michael's very drunk Company dressed in a strange assortment of ragged garments.

In 1987, *Pure Pre-Scenes* was debuted in Brighton. Leigh didn't have much to do after the first couple of acts, when he had to dress up as a teapot and play the piano. Cerith also helped out, and his duties were over by the second act too. For the final act Michael recruited about fifteen local dance students to make up the numbers for a visually stunning crescendo of dancers. On the second night, Leigh noticed that one of the boxes overlooking the stage was empty, and came up with what he thought was a great idea that Michael would really like. All the dancers had received several good-luck bouquets, and Leigh persuaded Cerith to help him take them from the dressing rooms.

The idea was that we were going to sneak them up to the
box and when it came to the curtain calls we would shower
the company with flowers. We were giggling already, on
our hands and knees with all these wet bouquets of flowers.
When it comes to the end of the show, we could hear all this
applause, the curtain goes up, we throw these flowers, we're
hurling, hurling flowers, laughing hysterically, when we realize
it is the students who have taken their bow first. Michael is
absolutely furious, especially as one of the largest bouquets
fell on someone's head, which made the audience laugh, and
he didn't speak to us for the rest of the evening. Then when I
arrived home in London I opened my suitcase and found three
beautiful white sheets and two towels which Leigh had pinched
from the hotel and hidden in my bag.

Leigh did his last shows with Michael in 1992. They went to Japan
in January with Michael Clark's *Modern Masterpiece*, which was
later shortened to *mmm*. Michael's mother, Bessie, was part of the
show, and acted giving birth to Michael on stage. Leigh was fond
of Bessie: he was forever styling her hair and holding her hand as
they walked down the road together. Lee Benjamin, Leigh's sewing
assistant, also went to be in charge of wardrobe. Lee didn't really
want to go, as he was spending so much time away from home, but
by various cunning means Leigh managed to persuade him. Leigh
was still obsessed by him at this time, and thought the more they
went away together the more likely it was that romance would blos-
som. One day, when they were travelling on the bullet train from
Tokyo to Osaka, Lee got up to go to the toilet. When he got back
Michael was looking at him very strangely, and kept saying things
like 'I'm surprised you can sit down, it must be really painful.' Lee

couldn't work out why Michael was showing such an interest in his health until he blurted out, 'I hear Leigh double fisted you last night!' Lee was mortified at this complete fabrication; even Leigh was a bit ashamed to have been found out, and quickly dashed to the toilet himself.

The hotel was air conditioned, and as a result all the windows were screwed shut. The company wanted some fresh air, and Lee was called upon to open the windows because he had been brought up in the rough East End and had all the lock-breaking skills required. Later that night there was a terrible rumbling and the hotel began to shake. Michael thought it was because they had left the windows open, but it was in fact an earthquake. The whole Company ran and hid in Michael's mum's room, although she was the most frightened of them all.

Things went very well. Leigh sent me a postcard from Tokyo: 'I'm having a wonderful time. So glad to be back in Japan. Lots of work to do on the show before we open on the 29th. But the mood of the company is extremely good.'

The Company then went on a tour of Great Britain. Leigh sent me postcards from several of the towns where they performed:

> 9.5.92 'Brighton. Isn't it rich, aren't we a pair. Me here, at last on the ground, you in mid air. But where are the clowns? There ought to be clowns. Don't bother they're here.'
> 17.5.92 'Cambridge is so lovely – too lovely – so perfect – princess perfect. Where is the real world? – Where is the dirt? I like violence too much to live here.'
> 24.5.92 'Sheffield is the dullest and most hogly town I've ever been in. But there's a swimming pool at the hotel and the theatre's very modern, so not too bad.'

6.6.92 'Glasgow. We've had great audiences here – they
don't just clap – they stomp their feet as well! They don't just
throw flowers – they throw money also! They don't just want
one's autograph – they want to have full sex with one too!
It's been marvellous.'

Another stop off on the tour was Nottingham, where Leigh was
visited by Cerith and Angus. There was no rehearsal in the afternoon, so as usual Leigh made the most of his time and decided to
explore the town with his two friends. They found a deconsecrated
church that had been turned into the Nottingham Lace Museum.
There was a little tea shop inside, so the three of them sat down
for a snack. Leigh was wearing old trousers, a gingham shirt over
a heavy-metal black T-shirt, and a wig that had been spotted by
the teenage girls behind the counter, who were doing their best
to stifle their giggles. Leigh decided to make it really worth their
while, so he went back to the counter and accidentally on purpose
caught his watch strap on his wig so it fell off completely. Angus
and Cerith practically fell out of their chairs they were laughing so
much. 'The girls couldn't believe what was happening: they were
prostrate on the floor just laughing. And then he walked away
pretending he hadn't done it, and putting the thing back on and
looking really embarrassed and acting it up like it was a huge, huge
mistake. Everyone was beside themselves. On leaving the church
we were so weakened by laughing we were practically crying, but
then Leigh found a dusty model of the church hidden in a corner,
which he decided to carry out under his arm. He threw it on the
floor and started kicking it along the ground, then picked it up
again and walked into a charity shop and dumped it on the shelf
next to the books.'

Leigh kindly decided to buy Cerith a coat from the shop for £12, which he wore for years. 'We then went to the charity shop next door and there were two really old ladies working there. He turned to Angus and myself literally a foot from the counter where these two old ladies were working and said "Let's get out of here, this place stinks of piss!" The old women were absolutely mortified and we just stomped out in hysterics.'

In June 1990, the show had its London run at an old disused potato warehouse in King's Cross. By now Michael's drug habit had become an addiction and he was using methadone, a heroin substitute. Leigh was very concerned about this, because although he loved the idea of drugs and all the paraphernalia linked with them, he had never actually injected himself nor taken them on a regular basis, more often pretending he had taken them just for effect, because in reality they didn't agree with him. It really upset him to see Michael destroy himself and his talent with these drugs. Although he joked about it, saying that a refrigerated lorry parked outside the warehouse contained 'Michael's methadone supply for the night', he was actually deeply concerned. By this time Leigh knew that he had only a limited time to live and there was nothing he could do about it, and he was trying to achieve as much as he could in that short time. But Michael, who had his whole life in front of him, didn't seem to value it, and wasn't using his fantastic talent to the full. Of course, Leigh didn't tell Michael about his HIV status, and the fact that he was repressing this secret made the situation seem much worse.

By now Leigh had been working for Lucian for a couple of years, which had greatly improved his confidence and made him want to achieve things on his own. At the same time, Lucian didn't like

Leigh working for Michael, because when he went away on tour he wasn't available to sit and it put Lucian's work on hold.

However much Michael said they were a team and worked with each other, it was still Michael Clark and Company, not Leigh Bowery and Company. Leigh felt that he wasn't being given enough to do as a performer and a divide began to grow between them. Things came to a head when Leigh designed a costume with 'A CUNT' written on the front – he wanted to shock people, but also make them challenge their own inhibitions. He knew that this word was one that most people had a problem with, and he wanted to force them to look at it. He thought that Michael would think it was a fantastic idea, and was greatly shocked when Michael asked him not to use it because it was going too far. He had thought they were partners in crime, trying to shake the establishment, and now Michael had let him down. For the first time, he felt that instead of working *with* Michael he was working *for* him. Leigh ended up in tears, crouched in an alley behind the warehouse. Every time he thought of the unfairness of Michael refusing to use the 'C' word, he broke down again.

Finally, Leigh wrote a note to Michael and popped it through his letter-box. It said that as much as Leigh loved Michael, and loved working with him, he couldn't continue with the show. Michael had to use all his charm to coerce Leigh into finishing the tour. He did, but things weren't the same. The first night in King's Cross was all right, but by the second night everything was getting out of control. Michael felt that he couldn't carry on. 'I couldn't work. I felt paralysed. I was on methadone. Leigh was encouraging me to take more to make me feel better and mum was trying to stop me. I was green, I was so sick. Leigh said I stunk of it, it was coming out of me, he said I should stay on it the rest of my life, but that night at King's Cross, I felt I couldn't continue. It was always methadone I craved, not smack, I only took that if I couldn't get methadone. It was mad.'

Michael managed to do the show and finish the run, but it was to be the last time that he and Leigh worked together. Michael last saw Leigh when he performed *O* at the Brixton Academy in 1994. By now Michael's addiction was so bad he was falling asleep on stage and having to be prodded awake by stage hands.

13

Performance

Leigh was once asked if he was a performer, and replied, 'every time I go out, it turns into a performance'. It seemed a natural progression that he should do 'performances' that were advertised in advance and for which he sometimes even got paid.

His first-ever advertised performance was with Trojan in 1984 at the Hail Mary club night, which took place in the crypt of a church near Great Portland Street. On this particular occasion it was being run by the Neo Naturist crowd, a group of 'new hippies' usually including Christine Binnie and her sister Jennifer, and Grayson Perry, a gifted potter who had an alter-ego called Claire. Various other people came and joined the show at different times. They were usually naked, but decorated themselves with carefully applied body paint.

There was no stage, so Leigh and Trojan's show took place in a little side cloister. They had their 'Paki in Outer Space' look on, Leigh with a blue face. They both stripped naked, in the process of which Leigh managed to catch one of his recently pierced nipples so blood began to trickle down his chest. He then put on a white doctor's coat and fiddled around with various syringes, pretending to stick them into Trojan. Trojan threw some lighter fuel onto the floor and set it on fire, while Leigh pissed into a glass, which he gave to Trojan to drink. Trojan managed to empty half the glass and then used the rest to douse the flames. The crowd looked on in stunned silence, but gave a massive round of applause at the end.

Leigh and Trojan both starred in the arty films made by Cerith Wyn Evans and John Maybury. They had first been spotted wearing Leigh's 'Paki in Outer Space' look at the Bell, a dingy Sunday nightclub at a pub in King's Cross. Cerith found Leigh a very willing subject, and gave him free rein to be himself – Cerith just wanted his image for the film. Leigh and Trojan turned up fully attired with blue and red faces at 11 a.m., Leigh clutching a bag of accessories and make-up for touching-up purposes. Leigh had gold Sanskrit script on his face that he had copied off a box from the greengrocer's. Cerith wondered what it meant, and was overjoyed to discover that it said 'Fresh satsumas from Nepal'.

Cerith started filming, and then gave Leigh and Trojan a monitor to use as if it were a mirror. Towards the end of the afternoon they began to get a bit bored – this was still the early eighties and Leigh was not as inventive as he later became – so he and Trojan just had a pretend fight to relieve the tedium, with Leigh trying to pull out Trojan's nose ring. Cerith used Leigh in many of his films, the last being *Degrees of Blindness*, which won several awards in Geneva and Holland and was shown on Channel Four. Cerith was thrilled when Leigh was asked by a newspaper, in a review of 1989, to name his favourite film of the year and replied *Degrees of Blindness*.

Just before Christmas 1984, Princess Julia and I were due to perform as The Curse, our very amateur cabaret act, at a sauna party held in Old Street by Laurence Malice, who later went on to run the all-night gay rave Trade. Julia was to play the Virgin Mary and I was going to be one of the Three Kings. We went round to Leigh's to record some music, which consisted of Christmas carols and Christmas hits, scratched together on a tape. Julia had not begun her DJ career at this point, so I tried to make the tape. Predictably, it was awful, as I had no musical talent whatsoever, and was just scraping the records in any old manner around the turntable. We also wanted to borrow some costumes. Leigh got rather excited as he dressed us and decided to join us as another king, while Trojan opted to appear as the little baby Jesus.

Off we trooped to the sauna, only to discover that we had to perform in a dressing room and the only tape machine available was a £20 job from Dixons with a dodgy lead. But it didn't matter to us, and we made our little tableau. Trojan was too drunk to take part, so Mark Vaultier played the part of the baby. It was almost impossible to hear the tape machine, so we led the audience in rousing choruses of 'Away in a Manger' and Wham's 'Last Christmas', which was number one at the time. Julia did a seasonal rendition of 'Like a Virgin'. To our surprise, instead of being booed off, more and more people came and joined in, and we had a lively singsong for about two hours.

Through working with Michael Clark, Leigh met Mark E. Smith of The Fall. Mark wanted to branch out from pop music and had written a play that was to be performed at the Riverside Studios in September 1986. It was called *Hey Luciano* and was about a corrupt Pope in Renaissance Italy. Leigh was to play a crooked Vatican cardinal who was also a Chicago mobster. Cerith was a rock guitarist and trade union official. Leigh did Cerith's make-up, changing it on a daily basis: sometimes Leigh painted bark on his face, but Cerith's favourite was when he painted it like a jigsaw. The play was not a great success, and the performers soon got a bit bored. There was a massive rider in the contract allowing the performers a bottle of vodka each per day and Leigh, Cerith and Michael took full advantage of this; they were often completely pissed by the second act. Leigh would ad lib outrageously. On one occasion, much to the consternation of the crew, he marched onto the stage singing 'Lemon tree is very pretty, but the fruit of the lemon is impossible to eat.' The three of them would drunkenly walk through the Hammersmith subways in order to catch the tube home. One night there was a very tired old homeless woman curled up in a corner. Michael shouted out to her 'Cheer up, love!' She looked pathetically up at Michael and replied 'Sometimes I do.' This made Leigh roar with laughter.

In the late eighties a new club opened at the Fridge in Brixton. The Daisy Chain was a very successful mixed gay night run every Tuesday by Jimmy Trindy. According to Rifat Ozbek, Leigh attended every week: 'The Daisy Chain was a great period for Leigh. It was the best club then. He was there every Tuesday night. All I did was wait for him to arrive. We were all on ecstasy and everything. Every week I thought he couldn't possibly surpass himself. Every week he did! I never saw him looking weak or in a look that didn't work. Whatever he did it was absolutely amazing. I used to dance around him. He used to sparkle. I loved his sparkle period. Nicola had to sequin everything, and do all the beading. He was like a disco goddess in the middle of the dance floor, half-vogueing, running around like mad.'

He was so much the spirit of the club that Jimmy asked him to do a performance for an anniversary party. He was dressed in a sequinned cloak, and he flew onto the stage down a hidden wire to 'Ride on Time' by Black Box, which was one of his favourite songs. He then joined comedy drag queen Lily Savage on stage for a quick dance.

Later the following year, Leigh was asked to perform a show at the Daisy Chain for an AIDS benefit. He agreed with some reluctance, as he wasn't really interested in gay politics: 'It seems so dreary and depressing. You have to locate yourself as some kind of victim and I've never wanted to do that.' What he did wasn't quite what the organizers had in mind, although they should have guessed it would be something shocking from his own performance manifesto: 'I try to have as much sex, violence and gore as possible in the shows – pee drinking, vomiting, enemas and fake blood. It's a formula which always seems to please.' He decided to train himself to squirt a fountain of water out of his bottom. He practised endlessly, filling his bottom with water using an enema and then walking around his flat seeing how long he could hold it in; he would then see how far he could squirt it. He became quite proficient, and decided he was ready to inflict it upon the general public.

Leigh dressed in his look of the moment: a tight, beaded corset that made him look as if he had a massive bosom, a beaded headdress and a merkin to cover his private parts. He wanted to make a grand entrance, so he roped Baillie in to carry him on his shoulders. He then made a very long cloak to cover the two of them, so he looked about twelve feet tall. He filled his bottom in the dressing room and off they went to start the show. Baillie sunk to the ground and Leigh clambered off his back. He danced around and then bent down on the floor with his butt in the air. He proceeded to squirt, but it all went terribly wrong. His corset had started sticking into him, with the result that he lost control, and a nasty stinking brown mess spurted out of his bottom and onto the audience seated below, who were all sitting at beautifully decorated round tables. There was mass panic, with the first couple of rows scrambling to get out of the line of fire. Unfortunately, Lynne Franks didn't get away fast enough. But Leigh kept his cool and clambered back onto Baillie's shoulders, who now had a disgusting stench to put up with, along with the revolting mess all over his clothes. Leigh described it as 'a real stinker of a show'.

Jimmy Trindy was flabbergasted. 'It was the most shocking cabaret I have ever seen in my whole life.' There was a huge furore about this disgusting act, especially as some of the water almost landed on Susan Carrington, who owned the club with her partner Andrew Czezowski. She was completely appalled, especially when Lambeth Council heard about it and tried to close the club down. Because it was an AIDS benefit, some people thought the act was particularly tasteless, but Leigh wasn't having any of it, and also explained his feelings about the illness (although nobody was aware he had it himself at this time): 'If you've got AIDS it doesn't mean you've lost your sense of humour, does it? I didn't want to make concessions just because people were ill or dying. I was quite pleased with the hostile reaction. If anything I want to make reactions stronger. If I have to ask, "Is this idea too sick?" I know I'm on the right track.'

Lady Bunny, a New York drag artist, was backstage, and was probably the only person who wasn't completely appalled. 'I loved to see the rewards of the inner workings of an artist of Leigh's stature.' She added a tribute to Leigh to her drag show after his death: she would lift up her skirt and pretend she was going to poop, but just fart instead, being far too ladylike to go all the way.

Leigh added fuel to the fire by writing to the gay press, expressing horror at the foul act and signing the letters from horrified lesbians. He was delighted when they were published, thinking himself very Ortonesque. As a result of the show he was not asked to appear in the Gay Pride Parade that year, not that he had any wish to anyway.

Leigh went on to cause even more controversy with his next show. It took place at the opening of Smact, a supposedly S & M club that was held in Industria in Hanover Street. Leigh had teamed up with Barbara, a twisted, tortured lesbian who later committed suicide. They both dressed up as Nazi doctors sporting Nazi arm bands, Leigh wearing a very severe shirt and skirt with a massive upholstered bosom. Berkeley, the club host, lay down on a stretcher and the two doctors castrated a dildo that took the place of his penis. Fake blood and shit sprinkled the audience. The shit was really dog food that Leigh had quickly purchased at an all-night supermarket just before the show because the original had been pinched from the club's fridge. Berkeley then gave the dildo a blow job and, to finish off, Leigh pushed it up the patient's arse. The operation was greeted with very tepid applause. Leigh went down to the club the following week, but when the lesbian DJs saw him they turned off the music and refused to play any more records until he had left the club.

Leigh couldn't believe their reaction, and was hurt that they called him racist. 'After all,' he said, 'I didn't show the Nazis in a kind light.' Leigh was far from being a racist – he was fascinated by different cultures and one of the reasons he loved London was because, compared to the sterile WASP culture of Australia, it was a melting pot of different races, religions and colours.

Every trip to a nightclub, whether he was paid or not, began to become a performance for Leigh. Michael Kostiff remembers, 'If Leigh was where you were, you always knew you were at the right place, as he always brightened everything up and wouldn't go anywhere naff.' He would always home in on celebrities and act as if he had always known them. I went to a *Daily Star* pop party at Stringfellows with him once, though unfortunately on the way in I fell down the stairs, badly spraining my ankle and landing on top of a Page Three girl wearing a gold puffball dress. Leigh pulled me around the club, introducing me to Bill Roache, better known as *Coronation Street*'s Ken Barlow, and his wife, who both looked horrified to meet us, and various other, minor celebrities, such as Chris Quinten, who was also in *Coronation Street*.

One Monday night in 1989 Charlie Atlas went with Leigh to Bang at Busby's. Leigh, who was wearing a merkin, a massive sequinned bra, a bugle-beaded headdress and platforms, was in a great mood as he left the club to walk down Charing Cross Road to Heaven. He started doing high kicks and going to and fro across the street, using the car headlights as spotlights. 'Cars were honking and beeping and swerving to miss me. I was having a fantastic time.' He was in his element showing off to all these stunned people. Suddenly a couple of coppers stopped him: 'That's very funny, you're under arrest.' Leigh thought they were joking and started the old routine: 'Don't you know who I am?' Unfortunately, they didn't, and he was taken along to the police station, with Charlie following behind in a taxi as he wasn't allowed in the car. At the police station they put Leigh into an interview room where they tried to get him to remove his headdress, which he professed was impossible. Gradually more and more policemen came into the room to look at the freak – the duty sergeant had called in all the men off the beat to take a look at him, and as soon as they had had their fun they let him go without charge.

In 1992, Leigh was asked to do a performance at Kinky Gerlinky, a club that was held erratically at the Empire in Leicester Square but had originally started at Legends in Burlington Street. It was run by Michael and Gerlinde Kostiff and it was supposed to give all their friends the chance to dress up, preferably in drag. Men who didn't usually bother loved the opportunity to strut their stuff, and would spend hours getting ready, practising make-up techniques and working out what made the best bosoms – socks or balloons filled with water, depending on the look they wanted to achieve. It became incredibly popular and transferred to the larger premises of the Empire, which was usually a tacky tourist disco. Leigh had been inspired by the portrayal of Michael Clark's mother giving birth to him on stage and wanted to do something similar. He was also madly in love with Divine, so he decided to combine his two enthusiasms and recreate the scene in *Female Trouble* where Dawn Davenport gives birth to her daughter, Taffy. Leigh came waddling onto the stage in a massive striped dress, wearing a headscarf and miming to the soundtrack of the film. He lay on a table with his legs in the air and there was a sudden movement between his legs. Suddenly a head burst out of the flesh-coloured gusset of his tights, followed by a wriggling body covered in a bloody placenta. 'Divine' then bit the umbilical cord that attached her to her child, which she picked up and carried off the stage to the rapturous applause of the shell-shocked audience.

This was the first performance of an act that was to be repeated many times, though it would evolve slightly each time. The Divine angle was soon dropped and Leigh changed the look for his performance at the New York drag festival Wigstock. The act was reported in the local gay paper:

Wigstock '93 gave Leigh a warm reception and in return Leigh delighted the crowd. He came out wearing a dark green, floral printed, velvet knee-length skirt with matching jacket, looking larger than life. Rather than wear make-up he had on a nylon face-mask that zipped up the back with three holes in front, two for the eyes and one for the mouth. Eye make-up and lipstick on the mask are permanent so there is no need for reapplying or worrying about eyelashes peeling off. Nicola, his long-suffering assistant, was strapped to his body under his outfit in a cloth harness. She was covered with red body paint and KY Jelly and wrapped with a string of sausages. She was curled in an embryo position with her feet up by Leigh's shoulders and her head in his smelly, sweaty crotch. At the end of his number he shocked the crowd by pulling up his skirt and giving birth to Nicola, who popped out of his Velcro womb while his arms and legs flailed in the air, all the time belting out an amazing on-key rendition of the Beatles' song 'All You Need Is Love'.

Leigh's good friend Lady Bunny also performed at the show. 'Even Leigh was taken aback by the size and wildness of the event. The show was filmed for a cinema movie and the director was thrilled with Leigh's performance: "That'll sell more tickets."'

The next day they performed the show again at Jackie '60, a very trendy club, but to ring the changes Leigh sang 'Eleanor

Rigby'. I imagined that it must be hell for Nicola to hang in this position for so long, but she actually found it 'quite comforting'. When she got up her face was bright red from being upside down so long.

Leigh's shows were taken far more seriously abroad than in England. He was completely revered in New York and Japan. Most of Europe thought he was fantastic and he was often asked to perform in nightclubs in Paris, Madrid and Amsterdam. Sometimes he didn't even have to do anything except turn up at the nightclub. He was flown over, put up in a hotel, given a couple of hundred pounds and several free drinks. The promoters advertised that he would be there and knew that would guarantee a full club, as people could be sure that if Leigh was in attendance anything could happen, and they loved to admire his new looks. Leigh always sent me postcards from wherever he went. I got two from Italy when he was paid to be there: 'Beautiful sunny Rome. How I love the balmy days, the hot sexy nights, the thrill of the shows and the glamour of a city that looks like a film set. Thank you for your card from Malta. I ate Dolphin steak here … delicious.' The other one was shorter. 'Turin, 27.10.91 Hello, the Italians were gagging – me too considering what they paid me. 8.3.1. Leigh.' (8.3.1. was a ridiculous phrase that we had picked up from a television programme about couples who were madly in love: a plain woman said she whispered it across crowded rooms whenever she was separated from her husband. It means eight letters, three words, one meaning – I Love You.)

Leigh performed several more times in New York, with varied success. On one occasion Lee Benjamin went with him, but the show didn't go as planned.

Leigh had taken a small round trampoline over with him
and he was going to jump up and down on this during a
performance at the Limelight. He was wearing the toilet
seat look and was so drunk he kept falling off the trampoline,
especially as he hadn't practised in his platforms. He had
asked the promoters to supply a jig saw, and his intention
was to cut round the trampoline so that he fell through the
stage, rather like something in Tom and Jerry. However, the
management got wind of this, and when he went on stage
the only thing there was an electric drill, so he had to rush
round the stage randomly making holes in the floorboards
instead. The audience didn't get this at all and just stared
at him askance.

He did a show that went as planned at the Red Zone, but the audience felt very short changed when it only lasted two minutes. He
came on stage fully dressed up and then Charlie and Pearl came
on dressed as beauticians and threw eggs at him.

When he was asked to perform at a club in Holland, Leigh
thought that he was only expected to turn up and be himself, but
when he got there he realized that they wanted a proper show. He
had nothing planned, so he had to improvise. He arranged to get
a huge paper hoop made, from behind which he would vogue, and
then jump through it. Charlie was watching from the wings as he
got onto the stage. 'He was standing behind this hoop giving his
all, looking very pleased with himself as he vogued and danced
making all these exciting shapes, the only trouble was he didn't
realize that the light was in front of him instead of behind, so the
audience couldn't see anything. So when he crashed through the
paper they thought that was the show.'

He was asked to the Roxy in Amsterdam to perform at a party to celebrate Queen Beatrix's birthday, although she would not be in attendance. He wore an outfit that he and Lee had spent months perfecting. He had devised a special method of having a mouth permanently full of vomit. There was a contraption inside his hat full of vegetable soup, which was meant to go down a transparent plastic tube through the piercing in Leigh's cheek and into his mouth. But when it came to the big moment the tube wouldn't go through the hole because it was too thick, so Leigh just stuck it to the side of his mouth – as he was wearing a Lycra face mask it was still practically invisible. The backdrop of the stage was a huge painting of the birthday girl's face. MC Kinky had been on before and had slid out of her nostril. Leigh leapt out of her mouth and started dancing to 'Everybody' by K-Klass. The vomit was meant to pour out of his mouth in an endless stream, but sadly chunks of vegetable kept blocking the tube, so in the end he ripped off his hat and let the soup pour down his face and all over his new out-fit – much to the despair of Lee, who had put so many hard hours into its creation.

However, Leigh managed to clean up the one-legged, one-shouldered outfit, and he wore it for some filming in New York with Charlie Atlas. The top hat was attached to a Lycra face mask so it just perched at a strange angle on the top of his head. The film involved Leigh walking around the city early in the morning, mix-ing with all the commuters going to work. The passers-by stared at him in amazement. One shouted out 'Mrs Peanut Head', which made Charlie crease up laughing because there is a well-known advertising character in America called Mr Peanut Head who wears a jaunty top hat, so after that the look was always named after him.

In the middle of 1993 Leigh was asked to do some 'proper' act-ing. Stewart Laing and Gerard MacArthur had discovered a script for a play entitled *The Homosexual*, which had been written in the 1970s by the French-Argentinian playwright Copi, and were very keen to work with Leigh. Stewart had seen Leigh do the birth show at the Tunnel Club in Glasgow and was completely knocked out by him. Leigh had known Gerard MacArthur for about ten years and he was pleased to be asked to appear in the play. Naturally, the title appealed to him, but he was unsure whether to do it or not. There wasn't much money involved, and it would mean taking a break from Lucian, which would infuriate the artist as he was in the middle of painting. It would also mean staying in Scotland, but on the other hand it was a challenge and a chance to try something new. The subject matter was the main attraction: 'It's got all the things I really like. You know: abortions, infanticide, a whole range of scatological things. It's funny and sort of grotesque.'

Leigh was never one to miss an opportunity, so he decided to do it. He had to spend about three weeks in Scotland for rehearsals, which he wasn't looking forward to, because there was no budget for fancy hotels and he would have to live in student accommoda-tion. The day he arrived he phoned me, screaming with excitement: 'The boys I'm staying with are so gorgeous, they're so handsome, so clever and so well read. What more could I want?'

Leigh played Madam Garbo, a 'normal' woman with a sewn-on penis. Madam Garbo wore a brown leather suit trimmed with fur that was squeezed over Leigh's heavily corsetted body. Lee Benjamin made the suit using twelve complete hides that Leigh had managed to get hold of. For his first entrance, Leigh wore an amazing fox-fur coat that was made up of about thirty-five skins.

(That year *Elle* magazine rang Leigh up for their Christmas issue and asked him what his favourite garment was, and he replied that it was this fox-fur coat. A while later they phoned him back and asked if he could say something else as they had a no-fur policy. He responded, 'Well, I have a no censorship policy, so goodbye', and slammed the phone down.) The outfit was topped off with a blond wig, a cream wimple and a large fur hat. The make-up was very extreme – large maroon lips and black eyes.

There were two other main characters in the play, Mrs Simpson and her daughter Irena, who were both of very confused sexuality and seemed to have had various sex changes throughout their lives. Mrs Simpson was played by Adrian Howells, who had been acting for a long while. He was very camp and very 'actor-ish', which greatly amused Leigh. He would entertain Leigh for hours by acting out make-believe conversations in the back of a cab between Dora Bryan, Su Pollard and Rex Harrison. He would also tell Leigh old theatrical terms, such as 'Page the Drapes', which means draw the curtains. In return Adrian loved hearing Leigh's camp expressions, such as 'Sit down and take the weight off your slingbacks' and 'Oh, Queenious, Girl', and all the tales of his cottaging. Although Adrian was over thirty, he had never really had any sort of sex life. Leigh found this unbelievable, and when they were doing the play in London he decided to take Adrian under his wing and introduce him to the delights of Russell Square. After a performance he took him along, gave him a guided tour, and said 'I'll leave you on your own now, and I'll be back in twenty minutes.'

He actually came back in five minutes, saying he'd already had two encounters. Adrian still hadn't had any luck, so Leigh went off again. Adrian finally saw someone he liked the look of: 'He was a burly sort of bloke in a puffa jacket. We made contact and without touching we masturbated in front of each other. I was thrilled that I had finally done some sort of sexual act, but Leigh was very derisory that this was all that I could manage and I've never dared go back since.'

Irena was played by Ivan Cartwright, who Leigh already knew, because as well as being an actor he worked at the Fridge. Gerard and Stewart had originally thought that maybe Adrian and Leigh wouldn't hit it off, but in fact they got on very well and ganged up on Ivan, who Adrian constantly mimicked, not that Ivan really seemed to mind. Ivan was a bit of a moaner and constantly held up rehearsals by saying things should be changed. Before rehearsals began they were a bit worried about how Leigh would behave, but he was fantastically professional. Even after rehearsals were over he would ask Adrian to come back to where he was staying so they could go over their lines again. Leigh had changed greatly from when he was in *Hey Luciano* and wouldn't have dreamt of improvising or getting things wrong as he realized that it would throw the other actors out of sync.

The play was set in Siberia, and the only other parts were two Russian officers played by Ricardo and Max, who were straight (though at different times Leigh had crushes on them both). It was Max's flat where Leigh was staying and he used to rather hold court, impressing the boys with tales of his life in London.

The play opened in Glasgow to good reviews and then had a short run in Manchester as part of the Queer Up North festival. The company were then asked to perform in London. *The Wasp Factory* by Iain Banks was showing at Bagley's warehouse in King's Cross, and it finished quite early, so *The Homosexual* was to be performed afterwards, at about 10 p.m. Leigh was thrilled about this, as it meant that all his friends could come and see him.

The play opened on 9 November to a full house. Although the other actors were really good, it was Leigh who stole the show. He gave his all to the part of Madam Garbo. Every line was greeted with gales of laughter, and he was so charismatic it was hard to take your eyes off him. The play was only about three-quarters of an hour long and was action-packed, so there was no chance to get bored. Leigh really wanted it to be successful, so he did everything he could to improve it. He got Nicola in to help with dressing, and would arrive two hours early just so he could do the others' make-up to his own satisfaction. Gerard was doing the ticket box, but for some unknown reason Leigh thought he would frighten the customers away, so he asked me to do it instead.

After each performance he would phone Adrian to discuss the good bits and the not so good bits, to see what they could do to make it better. One night lots of things had gone wrong, so Adrian had started to improvise to try to cover up. Leigh told him that it hadn't really worked, and Adrian didn't really mind – he was just amazed at Leigh's eye and how he knew exactly what was best to do.

The play ran for two weeks, and while some of the nights weren't very busy this was probably due to the lateness of the performance and the fact that King's Cross was rather out of the way. Lucian came with his friend Frank Auerbach and thought it was marvellous, and his daughter Bella came twice, bringing different people with her the second time. RuPaul came out of drag, which was a thrill for the whole cast. (Three years later Adrian still wasn't sure if he had really come or if it was one of Leigh's lies, but I was able to reassure him that I had seen him with my own eyes.) The last night was completely packed, as the word had finally got out about how entertaining the show was.

Leigh gained even more confidence by doing this show and realized that he really had to get something of his own off the ground. He knew that if he became an actor he would still be performing other people's material and would be at the mercy of directors, so he really had to do something where he could be in complete control.

14

Art

'I always say that I stay clear from art as much as I possibly can. I say this because most art has such hoity-toity connotations and appeals to really boring middle-class people. I don't want my stuff to do that. To be truthful though, I do think of it as art.' So Leigh told an Italian magazine in 1985. 'I think that when I'm dressed up I reach more people than a painting in a gallery. When Trojan and I have gone to openings of exhibitions we've gotten twice as much interest as the paintings. We wear it all the time as well. It's not for show.'

Whatever Leigh may have said, he couldn't help being interested in art. He had always been very creative, and when he first came to London he often visited the Tate and the National Gallery to see the paintings that he had only seen in books in Australia. As well as being interested in classical art he was particularly obsessed with the Viennese Actionists, a group of people who carried out very extreme art performances in the sixties. The leader of the group, Rudolph Schwartzkogler, was reputed to have committed suicide during a performance by hacking off his own penis. This is what Leigh and Trojan aspired to, but even they were not prepared to be that extreme.

Leigh had soon become involved with arty people, such as Cerith Wyn Evans and John Maybury, and often appeared in their films. He encouraged Trojan to become a painter and Trojan soon had an exhibition in Japan that Leigh told him how to hang and generally tried to run for him. When Trojan was interviewed by an art magazine about his work, Leigh constantly interrupted and told Trojan what his answers should be. 'You want your pictures to be shown in the biggest gallery in the world. Trojan and I are very different. I don't want middle-class sorts of people looking at my clothes. I want people who understand clothes. Trojan wants all the ordinary people to come and he just wants to stand back. When you see Trojan beside his painting it means a certain thing as well because he looks a certain way.' Trojan tried to interrupt to say how he felt, but Leigh wouldn't let him. 'Oh, come on, when you had that exhibition in Tokyo you were pestering me for days for something to wear. You were worried about how you would look beside your paintings.'

Whether Leigh wanted other people to see him as art or not, they soon did. A card manufacturer called Clive Ross saw Leigh compèring an Alternative Miss World Competition at the Piccadilly Theatre and thought that his image would look fantastic on a card. 'I got such a buzz from seeing him, and as I owned a greetings card company I wanted to use him on a card. He was so ahead of his time.' He arranged for an American photographer called Johnny Rozsa, who Leigh was quite fond of, to take the photographs. Clive designed the cards and made some of the costumes, but he wanted Leigh's input, so Leigh did all the make-up. He had a spotty face for a get-well card and was dressed as a birthday cake and a Christmas pudding for seasonal cards. The

cards were sold in Clive's shop in Beak Street and were promi-
nently displayed in the window.

One day the art dealer Anthony d'Offay was walking past the
shop with Lorcan O'Neill (who later became a director at the d'Offay
Gallery before opening his own gallery in Rome). Anthony thought
that the photos were fabulous and sent Lorcan to investigate this
strange being. They went to see him perform with Michael Clark
at Sadler's Wells and afterwards attended a talk given by Michael,
Leigh and BodyMap about the clothes. Anthony felt that this was
a real turning point in art and youth culture.

> Everyone talks about London now as one of the most exciting
> places. If you look at moments when things change, I think
> Michael and Leigh were very important. I felt at Sadler's
> Wells that it was an amazing coming together of art, dance
> and fashion. Shortly after that you had the situation where
> young people didn't feel that they had to go to the Courtauld
> to find out about art. Before that they thought that it was
> rather a closed door and you had to be intellectual or read
> a lot of art magazines before you could get an inkling of
> what it was about. That all changed and I think that one
> of the factors which helped it change was Michael, the
> crossing of the boundaries. Michael had horrible music and
> dreadful clothes but it came together to make very beautiful,
> excruciating performances and the idea of having people who
> were not so perfect in it. It was to do with a different idea of
> what could be beautiful, it was to do with acceptance.

A little while later the gallery held a party for artist duo Gilbert &
George at a nightclub called Paramount City. It was a rather dry

affair and the establishment were finding it hard to let their hair down. Suddenly, Leigh, Michael and the BodyMap crew arrived, and hearts leapt as they showed everyone how to enjoy themselves. This reinforced Anthony's impression of Leigh.

I tried to think what was it that changed one's feelings about things, why he was so important, the thing that I decided whether right or wrong was this: I felt that what Leigh did was to be a very bright shiny mirror to reflect very clearly one's conscious and unconscious thoughts. I have an interest in Hinduism and a salient feature of this is that the Gods had all sorts of sides and the Gods were in a bad mood and in a good mood, Gods facing the front and Gods facing the back, Gods that are half human and half animal, the whole range, 360 degrees of human emotion and human thought are possible, nothing is excluded so our total human experience is mirrored in this pantheon of Gods.

And I felt that Leigh was like that and served the same purpose. You couldn't say that any way in which he presented himself was totally positive or totally negative or totally masculine or totally feminine, there were different aspects. He allowed you to have total freedom. His presence allowed you to be yourself in a totally extraordinary cathartic releasing way and just as those Hindu deities whichever four you took would change into another four, whatever it was, Leigh's presence allowed you to grow into the person you really were and face your real feelings at that moment.

He allowed you to feel real. When I said he was a shiny mirror what I meant was he allowed you to see yourself in this strange shape that he took and that for me that was his genius. He was clearly someone who was totally unique, remarkable

TOP Leigh and Michael Clark, 1988.

ABOVE Boy George and Leigh in the background at
Boy George's 'Generation of Love' video shoot, 1990.

OPPOSITE ABOVE Leigh, Cerith Wyn Evans and Angus Cook
on a boat crossing the River Camel from Rock to Padstow,
Cornwall, September 1990.

OPPOSITE BELOW Leigh, Cerith Wyn Evans and Angus Cook:
'Magpie Schmagpie' jump for joy on Trebetherick Beach, 1990.

ABOVE Leigh, Angus Cook and Cerith Wyn Evans
in Barbara Hepworth's Sculpture Garden, 1990.

Leigh posing for Lucien Freud in his studio, 1992.

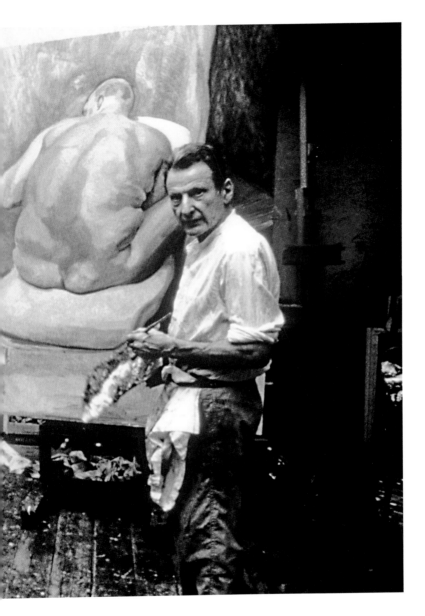

OPPOSITE ABOVE Leigh with his parents.

OPPOSITE BELOW Leigh and Sue in Sue's flat before Kinky Gerlinky, 1993.

ABOVE Wedding day, 13 May 1994.
From left to right: Cerith, Nicola, Leigh and Christine Bateman.

TOP Johnnie Shand Kydd and staff installing Lucian Freud's monumental portrait of Leigh at The Fine Art Society on Bond Street for Leigh's memorial, January 1995.

ABOVE As well as a huge image on the front of Sydney's Museum of Contemporary Art, there were posters all over the city's buses for Leigh's retrospective, January 2004.

and unlike anyone else, that since he had this factor of holding this very, very clear mirror up to people to see themselves but they didn't become Leigh or want to be Leigh, you looked at him and saw yourself. It's a very curious thing that part of yourself was in Leigh. He unlocked a key in you, you would see this shiny mirror, it was an amazing thing and I thought that would be an interesting thing to invite him to do something at the gallery.

The show was arranged for October 1988. Leigh would perform daily for a week between the hours of 4 and 6 p.m. Lorcan was put in charge of the arrangements. As a token of his appreciation for what Leigh was doing for the gallery he gave Leigh a copy of a Van Gogh flower painting that he had found in a market. Leigh thought that this was the gallery's way of checking up on him and was convinced that there was a bug in the picture, so he hung it outside the front door so that they wouldn't know what he was up to. Lorcan could never work out why on earth he thought this and put it down to his warped mind.

Leigh decided he would like to perform behind a one-way mirror. He didn't need to see the people, but they needed to see him. He told Ian Parker from the Independent his feelings about the show.

The intention has always been to provoke and the attraction of settling into a gallery lies both in the presence of a fresh audience (I don't like always going to places where I know everybody) and in becoming a new kind of object. Sitting behind glass will be different from standing in the street. Even though I will feel vulnerable. I won't feel nearly so vulnerable. If I'm on the pavement, I end up feeling like a stand-up comic, people say things and I'll be snapping back at them, with the tired old cliché one liners. Underneath all this, there is something else. You see something very human and something very non-human at the same time, they don't really merge. They're pulling against each other ... There'll be people I know from the clubs who'll think I'm out of my depth, taking myself more seriously than I ought ... But there's also a certain levity, a self-mocking part to the whole thing. And in the end if people are laughing at me, that's fine: I invented the joke.

There was a simple set, just Leigh and a chaise-longue. In the gallery he had the sound of traffic playing and each day a different smell was wafted around – one day banana, the next marshmallow. Every day Leigh wore another one of his looks. He would lie on the chaise-longue and then maybe prowl around or do some high kicks or keep a pose for ten minutes, depending on what sort of mood he was in. The performance and the costumes were described in *Artscribe International*:

> It was fashion slowed down, collapsed into performance, the designer making clothes for himself that became more and more obsessive, with bizarre new connections across the body. On the first day a green suit with tangerine spots was complemented by make-up of the same pattern. On the next, extremes of colour and identity clashed – long black hair, green skin, fur coat, scarlet clothes and enormous jewellery. Eliminating effect, Bowery presented a paradigm of beauty: a disco-ball crash helmet complementing a delicate light blue frock or a lurid green bodice and feather tutu matched with a paint dripped head. The last costume – a fur cape which also covered the head with small openings for eyes and

mouth – was simpler than some of the previous offerings, and the spotlight playing across the fur hood was analogous to Bowery's own position: a camouflaged dissimulator, within the media but totally inexplicable to them.

The show was a great success. Plenty of people stayed the full two hours and returned every day. It was the first time that many of the 'club' people had been into an art gallery, and it showed them what exciting places they can be. Cerith Wyn Evans filmed every performance and on one occasion took along his great friend Lucian Freud. It was this occasion that inspired Lucian to ask Leigh to sit for him: he was very impressed, deciding that he would like to meet this strange figure and maybe even paint him. He had seen Leigh twice previously when he had walked past him in the street: 'I noticed his legs and his feet. He was wearing clogs and his calves went right down to his feet, almost avoiding the whole business of ankles all together.' Then Angus Cook had taken Lucian to Taboo, where he introduced him to Leigh.

It always took Lucian a long time to get round to doing something, and as his work was so important to him, he had to deliberate for a long time on what he was going to do next. So it wasn't until about a year later that he took Leigh to lunch. Leigh described the meeting to *Modern Painters*:

Our first meeting took place over lunch at Harry's Bar. I dressed in colours from Lucian's palette – grey-brown trousers and jumper, and a man's short mouse-coloured wig. I was hoping he would ask me to sit for a picture and I wanted to please him. I was nervous and Lucian is always nervous. Lunch was tense and enjoyable. We talked about a show I'd done that week in Amsterdam which climaxed in my squirting an enema at the audience. I described my costume and dance. Lucian finally brought up the idea of painting me. I told him I loved the idea. He hadn't spooked my wig so I asked him if he wanted me to wear it in the picture or not. I hoped I might go on to declare some of my other physical irregularities. He said 'Oh, we can decide later', and closed the subject.

What Leigh did not tell the interviewer was that when he arrived at the bar they weren't going to let him in because he wasn't wearing a jacket, but they compromised and lent him a waiter's jacket that was two sizes too small. Leigh continued:

I had slightly incorrectly assumed that it would be a naked portrait, because the male models that he'd worked from before who were gay were always painted naked. Lucian, however, had thought that I would be reluctant to pose without my regular crutch of make-up and costume. I showed up at the crack of dawn. I immediately began to peel. Lucian wasn't quite expecting me to, but he just got on with it, took up some charcoal and began to sketch.

Leigh's life was to radically change from this moment on. He would learn an enormous amount and found that working for Lucian would give him great credibility in the art world.

At first he didn't tell Nicola where he was going every morning. She had been nagging him to get a job because she thought he needed to do something more with his life. So to explain his early-morning absences he told her that he had got a job in a stables mucking out the horses. She didn't really believe him, but she couldn't think where else he might be going. When he told her what he was really doing she was a bit disappointed, as he said he wouldn't be able to go out at night any more – he'd have to be in bed by 9.30 p.m. in order to get up so early. He kept that up for a couple of weeks, but he soon realized he could go to Lucian's still drunk and have a sleep when he got there.

Lucian Freud thought that Leigh was 'perfectly beautiful'. He loved the colour of his skin and the abundance of his flesh, but most of all he loved his brain. During their thousands of hours together they would discuss everything under the sun. They would learn from each other. Leigh soaked up everything Lucian told him like a sponge and Lucian loved the way Leigh's mind worked. Leigh told the *Australian Herald* what he thought of Lucian:

> I love the psychological aspect of his work – in fact I sometimes felt as if I'd been undergoing psychoanalysis with him – and because he is an artist who has always worked in the figurative idiom he has given me lots of ideas. His work is full of tension. Like me, he is interested in the underbelly of things. There are parts of myself that I hadn't really thought about before that I really like now and other parts that I'd felt uncomfortable about that I quite like now as well.

Lucian thought that Leigh had 'Gigantic modesty and an enormous presence, very good manners and an exceptional awareness.' He liked the way he would bustle around the room rearranging the heaters and, unbeknown to Lucian, when he was out of the room Leigh would add bits to the paintings – only tiny brush strokes, but it made him feel that he had contributed even more to these great works of art.

Lucian liked Leigh so much he introduced him to all his friends. When he took him to Bindy Lambton's house she was so taken with him she sat 'toying with his hand' for several minutes. Leigh loved mixing with these aristocratic folk and started getting even more snobbish. All his friends noticed the change in his voice. He started to speak in a very 'proper' manner and became very authoritative, looking down on people he felt 'weren't intellectual enough'. Sometimes his voice became so posh he could almost be mistaken for Brian Sewell.

The first picture Lucian did of Leigh was called *Leigh Bowery (seated)*. Bruce Bernard, an old friend of Lucian's and respected art writer and photographer, described the painting in his book about Lucian's work:

> The first picture from their collaboration is one of the most remarkable images of a naked human being ever put on canvas. Bowery, posing as a huge insouciant Lord of Misrule, lounges provocatively on his unworthy neat little throne, and seems to be questioning the artist about his conduct of the whole enterprise, while Freud refuses to be daunted by his not entirely mock-imperious sitter. It is a reckless conception meticulously executed and Freud cannot but tell the home truths about the folds of fat and flesh, the naked dull colour and transparency of a white man's skin as well as Bowery's basic if heroic lumpishness.

Their days would follow the same pattern. Leigh would arrive at about 7 a.m., depending on the time of year. They would have some breakfast and discuss what had happened since they had last seen each other. They would then start work, stopping every forty-five minutes or thereabouts so that Leigh could have a stretch, read the papers and play with Lucian's whippet Pluto. There would be interruptions when the papers arrived, or the postman or the fishmonger or the butcher. Quite often Lucian would take Leigh to Clarke's in Kensington Church Street for morning tea. Lucian managed to shock even Leigh one morning. He always took Pluto into the shop even though dogs weren't really allowed. One day the whippet was sniffing around the bread when a woman said it was disgraceful that a dog should be allowed to do such a thing. Lucian took great offence and told her to mind her own business. She threatened to report him to the police, so Lucian kicked her, aiming at her bottom. He was upset that he missed: 'Unfortunately I kicked too high and only managed to get her handbag.' She was livid and tried to get him banned from the shop, but as he was such a respected and regular customer the shop chose to ignore her.

Leigh loved the fact that Lucian did exactly what he pleased and didn't much care for convention. 'Lucian has put things in perspective. I feel much more confident. He never had money and always did what he wanted, which sets a precedent for doing what gives you pleasure, even if it is unconventional.'

Sometimes Lucian would cook lunch, which would probably be a salad, some sort of small bird, such as woodcock, or some roasted meat, and cake or Häagen-Dazs ice cream. Or else he would take Leigh to the River Café, which he loved. Leigh couldn't believe the prices, but he thought that the food was delicious and loved spotting stars such as Princess Margaret and Joan Collins. Eating with Lucian changed his attitude to food: he realized that it was worth spending money on the best ingredients and that processed food really wasn't worth eating. He didn't eat any less, just food of a much higher quality.

They would drive there in Lucian's Bentley, which would terrify even Leigh. Lucian thought he was king of the road: however much he was in the wrong, he would always blame the other driver. Leigh would engage him in banal conversation just to keep Lucian's mind off the road, which strangely enough made for a much safer journey. One day Cerith joined them for lunch. He had a party piece that he was fond of performing, which involved imitating Linda Blair in *The Exorcist*. Leigh loved this and asked Cerith to do it for Lucian. What Cerith didn't realize as he gurgled out 'Your mother sucks cocks in hell' was that there was a waitress standing right behind him who practically dropped her notebook with shock. Leigh was roaring with laughter, and practically doubled up when Lucian chipped in 'I'm sorry, I missed that, could you do it again?'

To try and make me jealous Leigh would continually lie about how many times he was taken to the 'River'. Sometimes he would say that he had gone there for lunch and dinner as well as going to Clarke's for morning coffee. Lucian used to be fascinated by Leigh's lies. He thought that they 'weren't told viciously but were designed to confuse'. He quoted the well-known saying 'What is a lie but the truth in make-believe.'

Leigh would tell Lucian about all his friends and in return Lucian would tell Leigh about all the people he had met. Leigh loved the stories about Picasso, Judy Garland, Cecil Beaton and Greta Garbo. Lucian would quote poetry to Leigh and sing him old music-hall songs. Leigh echoed the sentiments that he had said to Dolph Lundgren years earlier when he told him he should go to the library rather than the gym. Lucian hated make-up and suggested that libraries should be renamed – 'Beauty Parlours'. Leigh thought that Lucian was the most fantastic and brilliant person he had ever met; he couldn't stop talking about him, and all his friends became experts on the life and loves of Lucian Freud. But this was good for Lucian: his paintings of Leigh brought his work to the attention of a different, younger crowd and helped to establish him further as the greatest living figurative painter.

Lucian had a special pass that enabled him to go round the National Gallery whenever he wanted to, even in the middle of the night. He decided, as a treat, to take Leigh there to see some of Goya's *Majas* and a couple of Velázquezes. He arranged to meet Leigh in Trafalgar Square at about midnight. He was flabbergasted when Leigh turned up on a pair of roller skates, but it only made him admire his original thinking more.

Leigh often pinched the pound coins that Lucian used to leave lying around the studio as he didn't really like loose change and preferred to pay for everything with £50 notes. Leigh used to say that Lucian left them there on purpose for him to have as he felt embarrassed giving them to him! As he got away with taking the coins for so long he decided to be more daring. All around the studio there were old and unfinished paintings, and Leigh decided to nick a couple. He found a tiny one of Angus Cook that he sneaked out under his coat along with an unfinished head of a woman. He went round to Cerith and Angus's flat in Bloomsbury to show off his booty. They couldn't believe that he had done it, and to make it all the more shocking, he started kicking the picture of Angus around the flat in a punkish manner. Angus couldn't decide if it was him he was kicking around or Lucian. Leigh had only taken the paintings as an act of bravado, and once he got them home he didn't really know what to do with them, so he hid them behind a mirror and forgot about them, although he would sometimes brag to his friends about his 'hidden masterpieces'.

Lucian painted several more big pictures of Leigh: one where he was lying on the floor with his leg up on the bed and a very impressive one of Leigh's back, sitting on a chair on a beautiful red carpet. The first time these pictures were exhibited in Britain was at the massive Lucian show at the Whitechapel Gallery, which opened in October 1993. It was their most well-attended show and got a huge amount of press coverage. It was then that Leigh almost became a household name. It was impossible to pick up a quality newspaper or magazine without seeing his naked body. He loved the attention, and was even happier when the show went to Madrid and New York and received the same kind of press there. One picture did not transfer to New York though. *Parts of Leigh Bowery*, a close up of Leigh's genital region that had been cut down from a larger painting, was considered far too shocking for the prudish New Yorkers. Leigh loved it as it made his dick look gigantic. It is now on the wall in the hall of art dealer Jay Jopling.

Leigh decided he wanted me to work for Lucian too. He used to say to me, 'Why do you waste your time in that Jobcentre? You're much brighter than that', and he thought that working for Lucian would broaden my horizons as it had his, so he decided to convince Lucian that he should paint me. Lucian began to like the idea and decided he wanted to meet me. He knew all my business anyway, as Leigh told him everything during their many sittings. We arranged to meet at the River Café one Saturday lunchtime. Leigh gave me so many instructions – he told me what to wear, what to say, not to wear any make-up. Anyway I ignored all his advice and that's probably why it took Lucian another year to decide to use me. Leigh had warned me that Lucian was very scary, so I was petrified about this lunch. Cerith and Angus were coming too, and then Lucian's daughter, the novelist Susie Boyt, turned up. As it turned out, Lucian was hilarious and kept telling stupid jokes. The one that sticks in my memory was something to do with a whale masturbating, which he made all the more interesting by doing all the actions.

I wasn't quite what Lucian had thought I would be. He had imagined that I would be rather doleful and cowlike, but, according to Leigh, he was surprised that I seemed so fidgety and interested in my surroundings. He decided not to use me then, but took me on about a year later. In the meantime he had started painting Nicola, who was much more his type.

He decided to paint a picture of Leigh and Nicola lying on a bed together, which he called *And The Bridegroom* after a poem about an unconsummated marriage by Housman: this was before Leigh and Nicola had even thought of getting married, so it was a very prophetic name. Leigh had a different name for the picture: *A Fag and his Hag*. It is a beautiful painting and one of Lucian's stylish. Nicola loved the opportunity to spend time with Leigh every day and is very happy that there is a painting of them together.

Lucian also started a picture with Leigh, Cerith and Nicola. But Cerith couldn't bear to give up so much time to sitting, especially since he was in a standing pose, which is very tiring. So the picture was changed and it was decided that I should lie naked at the front, while Nicola sat in a chair sequinning and Leigh lay naked on the bed. I was very nervous on my first day, so Leigh came round to call for me. It was to be a night picture, so he arrived at about 5.30 p.m.

He made me strip off in my lounge first so I would be used to it when I arrived. I think he only wanted to do it to give himself the opportunity to laugh at my fat stomach.

He again warned me how frightening Lucian was and how I was not to speak unless I was spoken to. We drove there and clambered up the many flights of stairs. Lucian seemed very friendly and had prepared dinner for us. He always used very fresh ingredients, but served them in a weird style. There were never any potatoes and if there was fish or meat you would have the vegetables afterwards. We spent many happy hours shelling peas and broad beans. Pudding was usually a delicious cake from Cullens or, more often, Clarke's. On my second day, as we climbed the stairs, the smell of garlic got stronger and stronger. I was horrified when Lucian proudly removed four enormous heads of garlic from the oven. They were the size of oranges. I didn't dare say I wouldn't be able to eat it, so just I picked at it delicately with my fork, wondering how on earth I was going to dispose of it. Luckily I was saved by Leigh, who was brave enough to say that he thought that maybe it was a bit too strong.

On my first day I was instructed to lie on the floorboards in the most uncomfortable position. I didn't think that I could complain, so I suffered in silence. I got colder and colder as a draught blew from the open balcony door right onto me. It was all right for the others – Nicola had a woolly dressing gown on and Leigh was lying on a blanketed bed. I couldn't stand it any longer and asked Lucian if he could possibly close the door as I was freezing. He happily did so, but on the way home Leigh was furious with me, saying how dare I ask such a thing. Luckily, Leigh was soon dropped from the picture because he was going to do the play in Scotland, and his place was taken by Pluto. It was much easier when Leigh wasn't there because I could say what I liked without him sticking his nose in, but he still managed to have goes at me when Lucian discussed me with him while he was sitting for other paintings. I didn't take any notice, though; I was never scared of Lucian and just treated him like any other person (although of course he wasn't).

Lucian continued to work with Leigh right up until the time he went into hospital. He had just finished a mammoth portrait, *Leigh under the Skylight*, and had a couple of tiny pictures on the go that he managed to finish after Leigh's death. Leigh had started to think that maybe he should stop working for Lucian and spend more time working on his own projects, but he didn't want to, as he told Richard Torry: 'I know I should stop but I can't, I just get so much inspiration from Lucian.'

The summer after Leigh died, there was a show of Lucian's and Francis Bacon's work at Fondation Maeght in the south of France. I went to the opening with three of Lucian's daughters, Bella, Ib and Susie. When I walked into the massive gallery perched in the hills I couldn't really believe that there were two huge paintings of me hanging on the walls. There was a little picture of Leigh in between them. I immediately started crying, thinking that it was because of Leigh that I was here in this fantastic place; then I started laughing through my tears, thinking about how bitter he would be that there was only one small picture of him.

In 1992, Cerith was working at the Architectural Association in Bedford Square. He taught the foundation-year students and he really wanted to make it exciting for them, so he decided to get Leigh in to teach once a week for a term. On Leigh's first day he met him in the cafeteria. Leigh was wearing an old jumper and Farah slacks, a wig and a sprinkling of day make-up. When he stood up, he seemed to tower over Cerith, who was normally at least two inches taller than Leigh. Cerith was a bit puzzled by this, as Leigh only appeared to be wearing a pair of trainers, but on closer inspection Cerith realized that he was wearing a pair of four-inch stilettos, tucked inside the trainers and hidden underneath his trousers. Cerith couldn't believe that he managed to walk around like this, jumping on buses and running up and down stairs.

Leigh was a big hit with the students. He had a very clear and interesting way of explaining things, and on his first day taught them how to make a glove pattern, making it seem easy even though it's very complicated. He then tasked them with making an outfit in the style of their favourite building. By the end of the first lesson he had learnt all their names by heart. His particular favourite student was a girl called Dana who always arrived for class with her work in a Chanel carrier bag instead of the usual black portfolio. Leigh and Cerith arranged a fashion show so the students could show off their work. They managed to hire some small red and gold seats and set everything up with a catwalk. The principal of the college came, and there is a fabulous picture of him shaking Leigh's hand – Leigh is wearing his special costume for the evening, the toilet seat look. The show was a great success. Dana surpassed herself and came as the Taj Mahal, with a huge onion-shaped dome on her head and rows of glittering Perspex running down her front to represent the lake.

Leigh was always very impressed with Cerith's knowledge of the art world. He used to say to me, 'Cerith knows all the young British artists, every single one of them, he knows even more than me!' Damien Hirst had first seen Leigh at the Anthony d'Offay

Gallery when he worked there as a picture hanger, but he had never spoken to him. In the summer of 1993 Damien and his fellow artist Angus Fairhurst were performing at the Fête Worse Than Death in Hoxton Square. This was a big art event organized by Joshua Compston where artists had performances and showed their work. Angus and Damien were going to do spin paintings and sell them for a pound each, and to add to the entertainment value they decided to dress up as clowns.

Cerith suggested that they get Leigh to do their make-up, and Damien was very impressed when he turned up with a massive bag of accessories: 'He did us up right and proper, including our bits.' They'd got a bit carried away as they got drunker and decided to get their genitals painted as an added extra. Leigh was only too happy to oblige and quickly phoned me up. 'I can't believe it, I'm painting the dicks of the two most gorgeous straight boys.' He painted Damien's a bright fluorescent pink, and went to town with Angus's: 'Yellow bollocks with red spots, the shaft was bright red with a blue helmet, which was rather strange as I'm not circumcised.' They were a bit dubious at first, as Damien explained: 'We were nervous about doing the clown thing anyway, it takes a while when you get dressed up, you get the gear on but you still feel like yourself and you don't realize that you look like a fucking clown, but you gradually become a clown, and the genitals were a good ice breaker.'

They loved their new look so much they stopped doing the paintings and started charging 50p to have a look at their knackers. Joshua got rather annoyed as they were making too much money. They put on a competition where the maker of the best spin painting would be taken out to dinner by them. There was no artistic talent involved; they just chose the prettiest girl. They decided to take her to Green Street the following Thursday, still dressed in their clown costumes. They booked Leigh to do the make-up again as he was so brilliant. While waiting for the girl to arrive for dinner, they decided to make a video of themselves telling the most disgusting jokes they could think of. This was right up Leigh's street and the video is punctuated by him chortling in the background. Not to be left out, he told them his favourite joke: 'This bloke leaves home in the morning and looks up to the roof of his house. He reels in disgust as he sees that it's covered in shit, spunk, used sanitary napkins, phlegm, sewage, old condoms and tons of other repulsive things pouring down the walls of the house. As he leaves for work he shakes his head. "Why, oh why … do I do this!!!"'

Damien biked Leigh one of his spot paintings to thank him for his contribution. This joined the picture Angus Fairhurst had already given him for repairing his coat lining, and with Lucian's etchings and a picture by Cerith he now had quite an art collection. At the next Fête Worse Than Death in 1994, Leigh was to be the star performer with his band Minty.

As time went by, Leigh began to regard his performances in a nightclub as 'art' rather than mere entertainment. In April 1994 he was invited by Anna Tilroe to do a piece for an art festival in Holland held at Fort Asperen. This was to be his most ambitious piece to date and would involve him smashing through a piece of plate glass. There was a slight hitch, though, as they couldn't get a piece of sugar glass big enough, so they had to use the real thing. The organizers rigged up some electronics so it would shatter just before Leigh touched it, giving the illusion that he had smashed through it.

Leigh had been very inspired by Fakir Musafar, an American, whose life story he had read in a book, *The Modern Primitives*. Fakir had first discovered the joys of pain when he was a child by clipping clothes pegs to various parts of his body. In a tribute to him, Leigh had put clothes pegs on both of his nipples and along the length of his penis. He was then suspended upside down wearing only the pegs, a pair of black stockings and massive patent platforms. It was mid-afternoon and broad daylight. As he hung he could see crowds of young children and old people in wheelchairs. Richard Torry was naked except for some well-placed balloons and was strumming on his electric guitar. Nicola came round the audience spraying air freshener, dressed in the most exquisite tutu that Pearl had made. Leigh started singing, which isn't easy upside down:

This is like a dream
This is so unreal
I can't believe it's true
It's so beautiful
There is so much we can do
It's incredible
I can't believe it, I can't believe it
I feel so released
Oh, my God, it's a fabulous feeling
It's so gorgeous
This is so intense
I can't believe it, It's surreal
We can do anything
Anything is possible
Anything in the world
Yes, yes, nothing is Taboo
Total Pleasure.

Then the big moment came. Leigh hurled himself at the piece of glass and hit it the very second the electronics went off. He was showered with shards of glass, causing multiple lacerations.

He was hurriedly helped down and ran to the dressing room, leaving a trail of blood behind him. Charlie Atlas was there helping out. Leigh looked at him, shrugged, and said, 'That's the cheapest publicity gimmick I've ever done!'

15

Music

Leigh had studied music from a very early age, but by the time he came to England fashion had taken over as his main interest. He stopped playing the piano for a while – though he had reached Grade 8 – because he had no access to a musical instrument. He still loved music, though, and listening to it played a big part in his life. It wasn't until 1986 that he came across a piano at a friend's. He had gone round to visit John Maybury and Trojan one morning. They had been up all night and were completely off their faces. They suddenly heard beautiful Chopin piano music wafting around the flat. John thought that he was hallucinating, but when he investigated he discovered Leigh playing this gorgeous music. Leigh was bored by the drugged-up company, so he had gone nosing round the flat in his normal manner and had come across their poor, neglected piano. He decided to test himself to see if he could still play, and was delighted to find that he could.

Sometimes Leigh thought that forming a band would be a good way to find fame and fortune. He originally had plans to form a band with Richard Torry, Judy Blame and John Richmond back in 1984. They wrote one song but didn't really know what to do after that, and they were all too busy with their fashion careers to make a commitment, so the idea never got off the ground. Much later on, he talked about starting a band with Cerith and Angus. It was to be called Magpie, Schmagpie, but they never got beyond the stage of planning the group's publicity photos and discussing what they would do when they were famous.

In August 1992 Leigh achieved one of his lifelong ambitions, which was to appear on *Top of the Pops*. He was acting as a backing dancer for Felix, who was performing his club hit 'Don't You Want Me'. Malcolm Duffy had been involved in the production and he arranged for Leigh and Nicola to appear. They were dancing on podiums, waving their arms about in a rave fashion. Leigh had his face covered by a material mask and was wearing one fat leg, with a stiletto shoe on the other. He looked like nothing that had ever been seen on *Top of the Pops* before and the next day when I went into work all the other staff were discussing the 'freak on the telly'.

This appearance spurred Leigh into action, and he decided that pop stardom was the only way forward. He had made friends with Stella Stein, who had been on the London club scene for a while, although he was a few years younger than Leigh. His real name was Stephen Brogan and during the day he worked with mentally disadvantaged adults in a residential hostel. Leigh liked him because he was rather outrageous and loved to show off in nightclubs and bars. He was forever jumping onto the bar at Industria; the bouncers were always scared that he would chop off his hands on the overhead fans, as he waved his arms straight out in a kind of double Nazi salute but with the palms turned face out. He was recruited to the band along with another stalwart of the London club scene, Sheila Tequila.

Sheila came from a wealthy family who were rather worried that their son always stayed at home. When he discovered drag his mother was so thrilled he had a hobby that would take him out of the house that she encouraged him in every way, even converting the attic to make room for his large collection of vintage costumes. He had been doing a drag act for quite a while, not of the normal 'I Am What I Am' variety, but rather more eccentric, with him and his sidekick Donald Urquhart dressing up as fat old ladies or as Little Bo Peep. Sheila had a very weird and warped sense of humour, which Leigh loved, as well as a very strange sense of reality.

The three of them called their little group the Quality Street Wrappers. They rehearsed at Leigh's house. Leigh acted like a schoolmistress and treated the other two as naughty school children. He made and designed all the costumes: the first ones were mushroom and pale-pink mini dresses with square necks and medieval-type sleeves. Their first show was at the Iceni club in Mayfair. They sang the Donna Summer classic 'Enough Is Enough' to a live piano accompaniment. For the finale they stripped off naked and then walked around the club to receive the congratulations of all their friends. The management, however, was not happy with this, and asked them to put their gowns back on.

In order to achieve musical credibility, Leigh decided that the Quality Street Wrappers should sing live instead of miming. The second song that they chose to cover was 'Walk This Way', which was originally recorded by Run-D.M.C. and Aerosmith. Leigh rehearsed endlessly, demanding that every step was right and that they learnt how to throw the microphones to each other so that there was an element of juggling involved. Leigh designed new costumes for the band, big net petticoats with a tartan taffeta dress on top (a scrap of this material is featured in Lucian Freud's painting entitled *Leigh in a Taffeta Skirt*). They had their genitals strapped between their legs, so it looked like they didn't have any, and wore long black stockings and three belts wrapped around different parts of their torsos. They then teetered on top of two-foot-high platform boots that Leigh had had specially made at the Little Shoe Box in the Holloway Road. The look was completed with minstrel-style black faces with the main features highlighted in white.

I was round at Leigh's once when they were rehearsing. Leigh gave his all, but the other two were very half-hearted, although they said they were trying their best. When they had gone Leigh asked me what I thought and if they might get chart success. He was devastated when I replied that I didn't think the record-buying public were quite ready for three freaks on platforms doing second-rate covers of songs. It made me realize that Leigh really was removed from reality. He was so far ahead of the general public in what he accepted as normal he couldn't see that his semi-naked, blackface-wearing, genital-less band might cause a bit of a problem. He didn't talk to me for two days, and when he finally did, he said I was the one with the warped view and why shouldn't they be number one in the charts.

Their next performance was at the Fridge in December 1992. Stella played Leigh at his own game and told him that various record companies had been phoning up the Fridge and were sending their talent scouts along. Leigh took this lie very seriously, and told the others to put on a really great show. Just before they were due to go on stage, Sheila felt the need for a bowel movement, and as there wasn't much time before curtain up she squatted behind an artificial bush on stage and did her business. Leigh and Stella were hidden high above the stage and slid down thirty-foot poles to start their act, while Sheila lay at the bottom pretending she had fallen off. At the end of the night they got up on the stage and started showing off. A very drunk guy joined them; Sheila pulled him to the ground and started fellating him while Leigh sat on his face. To entertain the audience further, Sheila went and retrieved her poop from behind the bush and liberally covered the comatose man with it.

They were booked to perform three shows on New Year's Eve. Leigh made them rehearse endlessly for weeks beforehand. He used to bribe them to stay at his house longer by forever feeding them and promising them treats such as cherry pie. Still, he couldn't make them do what he wanted all the time, because they had strong personalities of their own – neither Stella nor Sheila had the slave mentality, so he had to think of other ploys to keep them hard at work.

He used to make them special toasted sandwiches that had about twenty different fillings. He once offered Stella a sandwich that was filled with tartar sauce, blue stilton, tomatoes, lettuce, watercress, gherkins, onion, Marmite, cheese, peanut butter and strawberry jam. 'Oh Stella, it's quite extreme but do try it, you'll get used to it.' Stella was not allowed into the kitchen, but sometimes he would sneak in and find Leigh unable to talk as his mouth was so stuffed with gherkins or some other delicacy.

During the day of New Year's Eve Leigh made the band rehearse for hours, with the result that Sheila and Stella were so late getting to the first gig at the Café de Paris they missed midnight. Leigh had to do the countdown, so he managed to get himself there on time. He had made them swear on their mothers' lives that they wouldn't drink any alcohol, so they were furious when they arrived at the dressing room and found that he had drunk half a bottle of vodka. He tried to deny it and said it was Nicola, but they could smell it on his breath. Nevertheless, the show went quite well, and they set off to walk to the Iceni for the Sign of the Times party, which was gig number two.

It was a ghastly walk, as the streets were thronging with drunken revellers who gave the three freaks mouthfuls of abuse. When they arrived at the club there was a huge argument as tempers were frayed. Part of the act involved making a human pyramid, but they just couldn't get it right and kept toppling over. At the fifth attempt Stella refused to try again as he had hurt his hip in the previous fall.

Back in the dressing room Leigh started shouting at them both, blaming Sheila for everything, and Sheila started waving his clenched fist in Leigh's face. Leigh stormed out of the dressing room, saying if that was their attitude he was going home and they could forget about the third gig at Heaven. Sheila and Stella decided to go home too, but thought that they should wait ten minutes to give Leigh time to get out of the club so they wouldn't have to speak to him. When they opened the door to leave they found Leigh crouched down listening at the keyhole checking that they weren't plotting against him.

This made them laugh so much they patched things up and went back to the Café de Paris to carry on the New Year partying. Their next gig was in Paris and was very successful – so successful, in fact, that Leigh really thought that showbiz stardom was just around the corner.

They were next booked to play at the opening night of Sex, a club at the Café de Paris. By now they had changed their name to

Raw Sewage, having decided that the Quality Street Wrappers was a rather twee name hardly likely to shock anyone. Leigh took them to an Asian shop where he had seen some orange anoraks that he thought would be good in the act. The bus was rather full, so they all got separated. Suddenly Leigh turned round and shouted out to Stella, who was sitting about four seats behind him, 'I say, Stella, how are your blackheads?' In the shop he carried on showing off and when he finally paid for the jackets he ensured that his wig slipped back four inches, much to the astonishment of the poor sales assistant. He took the jackets home, where he decided that they would look much more stylish upside down, and appliquéd 'Raw Sewage' on the back.

Leigh was furious that Sex had advertised them under their old name, but thought that the jackets might let everyone know of their new title. By now he had made the show a bit arty. They still started with 'Walk This Way', but the next number involved Nicola and Christine Bateman dressing up as nurses and injecting neat vodka into the group's bottoms (all except Stella, who had a phobia about needles, that is). They then rushed backstage and filled their mouths with vegetable soup, which they vomited all over the audience while singing 'Mickey', the old Toni Basil hit. Before the show, Leigh had phoned Stella constantly at home and work to check that he knew the routines, but on the night he was the one who forgot them, he was so nervous.

On 7 March 1993 Stella achieved one of her ambitions: playing live on-stage at the Black Cap, North London's premier drag venue. Raw Sewage were booked to play at an AIDS benefit. I don't think that the regular customers knew what to make of them; they were more used to tired old queens belting out versions of Shirley Bassey numbers.

To get more publicity, they decided to make a video, and despite knowing at least ten video directors Sheila had the bright idea of getting the video made at the Trocadero in Piccadilly Circus. There was a unit there that allowed you to either mime to a well-known record or to bring your own tape for them to video you against one of the many moving backdrops that they had on offer. They all got ready at Stella's flat in Swiss Cottage and then called a cab to take them into town. It was about 6.30 p.m. on a Saturday evening, but luckily it was winter, so it was dark, and they didn't frighten too many people. However, when they arrived they discovered that they would have to queue up for about half an hour, and they soon had a crowd around them wondering what they were going to do. The video worked quite well, except that according to Sheila 'We looked like something from *Planet of the Apes* rather than a sophisticated pop act.'

There was a performance in Brighton where they were booked by Yvette to appear at a club called Wild Fruit and were put into a grotty gay hotel. The show was pretty appalling, so afterwards they got very drunk, and Sheila and Leigh started fighting in the club. Sheila threw champagne over Leigh and in return he slapped Sheila round the face with a patent-leather-gloved hand. But they made up and went back to the hotel. 'Leigh was a monster and started trying to get off with me, so I sent him back to sleep with Nicola, who I always thought was Madge Allsop to his Dame Edna. I was still angry with him, so I did a big poop, and as I was still wearing my gloves from the show I picked it up and threw it at Leigh's door. It landed on the number and then slid down, it was horrible.' In the morning Sheila got up quite early, and as he left his room with his suitcase he saw two elderly cleaners trying to clear up the mess.

As they tried to hold their noses they moaned to each other, 'Who on earth could have done this, it's disgusting.' Sheila replied, 'Oh, I don't know, standards have certainly dropped, haven't they!'

It all turned sour at the Love Ball in Amsterdam. Leigh was still taking the band very seriously – he knew he was ill and was determined to make his mark before he died, and still thought that Raw Sewage would be his passport to international success. He thought that they would get a lot of press coverage from the Amsterdam show and they should put on a really great performance. The show was slightly delayed, so Sheila and Stella, not being aware of Leigh's shortage of time, decided to devour a bottle of vodka between them. They were on the verge of passing out when they were due to go on, and the show was a complete shambles. Leigh was trying very hard to be the star of the show: he was adding extra unrehearsed movements and doing difficult impromptu steps, with the result that he fell off his massive platforms, breaking them (and nearly his ankle) in the process. He also dropped his microphone. When he couldn't get up, he beckoned to a stage hand to bring the mic to him, and, true professional that he was, carried on singing from his crumpled-up position on the floor.

The atmosphere in the dressing room was terrible. Leigh refused to speak to Sheila and Stella, but there was another show to do the next day. Leigh got up really early and somehow found a cobbler to repair his boots. The show that night was fine, but they didn't even speak to each other on the plane home, and Leigh refused to speak to either of them for the next three weeks.

They made up, because Leigh still thought the project was worth pursuing. He stayed up for three nights to make Stella a new dress for his birthday, which he proudly took round there on the day. There were a few more shows in London, and the Festival of Erotica in Bologna, which went quite well. It went so well, in fact, that they were asked to appear on a Jonathan Ross-type of show on Italian television – on the condition that they didn't strip naked, as it was a live show. Of course, they ignored this, and the audience didn't know whether to laugh or scream in horror as they ripped their clothes off. They were on such a high afterwards that they went cruising in the local square and, very surprisingly, as they still had their black and white minstrel faces on, they did very well. Sheila was somewhat surprised when one man she was servicing compared her to Anita Ekberg in *La Dolce Vita*. She had no money for the taxi home, so she gave another hunky Italian a blow job in return for the fare and a bottle of Fanta.

Leigh was asked to perform with his group at the opening of a new club in London called Freak, which was to be held at the Astoria. It was a massively hyped-up affair – Jeff Stryker, the well-hung American porn star, was to make an appearance, and he was coming to London a few days earlier to get extra publicity. Jeff's manhood was so massive it had been used as the mould for a particularly impressive and lifelike dildo with realistic moving balls. Leigh was asked to drive with him in broad daylight along Old Compton Street in an open-top limo handing out flyers for the club. The money was good, but Leigh couldn't bring himself to do it, telling the organizers that it was 'too tacky'. However, he agreed to go round nightclubs with Jeff handing out flyers. A limousine was booked and it came to pick Leigh up at Farrell House. Leigh was amazed when Jeff himself rang the intercom asking if he could use the toilet. Leigh was in a terrible fluster as his flat was such a pigsty, and in the few minutes it took Jeff to come up eleven floors in the lift he dashed around shoving the mess into more tidy piles. He phoned me up, beside himself, saying 'I can hardly believe it, Jeff Stryker is in my toilet. Shall I get my Jeff dildo out and ask him to autograph it?'

The opening was the next day, and Leigh had really been getting on Sheila and Stella's nerves. He had told them there was no guest list, but when they went to the Astoria in the afternoon to check that they had the right microphones they saw Leigh's faxed guest list in the office. This was the last straw, and they decided that they weren't going to turn up. They got dressed in their leathers and went cruising instead. By now, Leigh had realized that the whole thing was going to be a complete debacle, so he didn't turn up either. He later told the others that he had done the birth show with Nicola and it had gone down a storm, but they found out from the gay papers of his non-appearance. This was the end of the road for Raw Sewage.

A few weeks later, Leigh and Stella bumped into each other cruising in Russell Square. Leigh was wearing his usual wig and anorak. He lost his temper with Stella, who remembers it as like 'Joan Crawford talking to Christina'. Leigh gave him a mouthful of abuse while all the other cruisers were staring at them agog: 'Stella, listen, without me you are going nowhere, I gave you the chance of stardom and you blew it. Without me you are nothing.' Stella giggled, turned away and marched off to find some action.

Leigh was still determined to get on in the music business, so when his old friend Richard Torry called him up to see if he'd like to join him in a musical partnership he jumped at the chance. Richard had given up a successful career as a knitwear designer in Japan to make music. He had previously been in a band called Un

Homme et Une Femme with a girl called Louise, but they had just split up. He enjoyed Leigh's company and got very excited by his performances, so he thought that they might work well together. Leigh went to Richard's flat in Old Compton Street most afternoons after sitting for Lucian. He didn't tell anyone what they were doing, and swore Richard to secrecy.

Richard's original idea was to have an electronic duo, rather in the style of the Pet Shop Boys. He knew how the music business worked now and had useful contacts. Leigh was very keen to learn all the electronics, but not so keen on the singing. Richard had to encourage him, so he would get out his acoustic guitar and they would find an old song book and Richard would play while Leigh sang along. A particular favourite of Leigh's was the '59th Bridge Street Song' by Simon & Garfunkel, but he preferred to feel groovy at his own flat, because there was more room to dance around staring at himself in the mirrors as he did so, whereas Richard's flat was rather cramped.

They would spend much more time talking about the aesthetics of the band than getting down to actually making music. Leigh made Richard go to art exhibitions with him. 'He particularly liked the work of the Wilson Twins and Sarah Lucas. He wanted the band to be like her work, unpretentious and crappy but brilliant at the same time.'

Leigh loved going to Richard's flat because it looked over Old Compton Street, the heart of gay London. His favourite pastime was to stare out of the window looking for people he knew. When he saw them he would shout out enough information so they knew that he was shouting at them, then would dive back inside the window before they saw him. He ambushed M.C. Kinky, Jean Paul Gaultier, and his old friend from *The Homosexual*, Gerard MacArthur, who was just teased with 'Wanker, wanker!' When they went on the tube to exhibitions Richard used to get terribly embarrassed by Leigh's personal art performances. 'The ticket collector got on and wanted to inspect our tickets. He started staring at Leigh's face piercings and asked him what they were. Leigh hid his head and acted like he was completely mental and couldn't understand English. The ticket man looked at me and said "Poor thing, what is the matter with your friend?"'

Paul Hitchman, Richard's old manager, volunteered to manage this new group. He arranged for Dave Ball, who used to be one half of Soft Cell, to produce their first record, an ode to S&M called 'Love and Pain'. But he suddenly had a big hit on his hands with his new group The Grid, and he didn't have time until later to do a remix. So Richard and Leigh recorded the demo on their own, but they decided it had too many lyrics and changed it into 'Useless Man', the lyrics of which were inspired by a Pepsi advert:

Boot licking, Piss drinking,
Finger frigging, Tit tweaking,
Love biting, Arse licking,
Shit stabbing, Mother fucking,
Spunk loving, Ball busting,
Cock sucking, Fist fucking,
Lip smacking, Thirst quenching,
Cool living, Ever giving.
Useless man.

A week after they had recorded the demo, a very enthusiastic club promoter called Matthew Glammore asked them to perform at his club Smashing, but he wanted a live band. Years previously, Matthew had gone around the clubs in full freaky make-up with a teapot on his head and had often been mistaken for Leigh. Leigh was dead against having a live band. He had no rock history – he hadn't listened to rock music as a teenager and since he had been in London he had really only listened to various forms of dance music. But Richard persuaded him and in a week they put together a band. Danielle was on bass, a Japanese boy called Honalulu on sampler, Trevor Sharpe from Miranda Sex Garden was on drums and Matthew Glammore himself on keyboards. They had about three rehearsals and then were ready to play at Smashing.

The gig started with Leigh singing 'Useless Man' while Nicola was hanging round his neck, and then he gave birth to her. This was a different, straight crowd, and they hadn't seen Leigh's act before, so they were thrilled. Leigh then stripped off and I had to jump onto the stage so my bosoms bounced about while Leigh sang the David Bowie classic 'Ashes to Ashes'. I had to scoop up his clothes in the manner of Steve Strange in the new romantic video for this great pop hit. Sheila Tequila then came on wearing a pantomime bird outfit and sang a duet of 'Orville's Song' with Leigh, which was usually performed by Keith Harris and his green duck.

The show was a great success, and Leigh decided he loved rock music after all. He went out and spent about £200 on all the latest CDs: Pulp, Elastica, Blur, Nine Inch Nails and Suede. He particularly liked the rock business of tuning up and doing the soundcheck.

They decided to call the band Minty. Leigh told Alix Sharkey in the Independent why he liked the name: 'It's an old theatrical term for someone who's very off-hand. I like it because it's such a fragrant word.' Danielle left the band because she found Leigh very hard to deal with, and her place was taken by Matt Fisher, a hardened, long-haired rocker who shared a flat with M.C. Kinky. The band was a strange mix of people. Trevor was a long-red-haired, straight transvestite who was fond of wearing slinky ladies' briefs and stockings. Richard Torry was tall and thin with several facial piercings, and he often appeared on stage wearing only a pair of ladies' ten-denier tights.

Several more gigs were arranged, and Minty got quite a following from the straight, *NME*-reading indie crowd. Boy George saw them several times, and told Leigh that it was like having your thoughts put into words. He, like Anthony d'Offay, recognized Leigh's knack of making people realize their own potential. 'I told Leigh that he'd make a great pop star, he said "thank you" in that very snooty voice of his and looked down his nose at me.' Although Leigh acted cool in front of George, he was really thrilled with his encouragement, and he began to think that this time he really would make it.

As Leigh got more confident he put more filth into the band. He pretended to rim Richard, secretly smearing chocolate mousse around his mouth. After he had given birth to Nicola he made her drink his piss and then he vomited into her mouth. Even though it was only vegetable soup and apple juice, to the audience, it looked real.

The band were invited to perform on a Welsh chat show, where members of the audience gave their opinions on various topics. This episode was devoted to Modern Art. The audience were discussing the usual hoary old chestnuts, such as the bricks in the Tate, when Leigh came on to do the birth show while the band played around him dressed in blue leotards. The audience were horrified:

'It's hard to shock me but that's the biggest load of pony I've seen on the telly for years.'

'I think this man is a sick pervert, making a mockery of someone giving birth, it's disgusting.'

'I wouldn't let my children see it.'

Leigh came on to join the audience, dressed in a massive, floor-length, sequinned floral gown, with a matching face mask and a purple German helmet on his head. He was asked if he thought his act was shocking. He replied in his poshest and most conde-scending voice:

> I certainly hope to stimulate people and if they are shocked that's fine as well. I've been very interested that in this conversation so far, everyone seems to focus on figuring out how you can make a living from it, how much it costs and how much it's going to sell for. People seem more interested in the money it's worth rather than the quality and I think that this is because the audience is such a dreary and unimaginative crowd and they find making money so completely difficult that artists who have imagination and ideas and actually stimulate people and fetch great prices through their work make them jealous, as it is something that these people could never achieve.

Minty played their best-ever gig at the Fête Worse Than Death in the summer of 1994. It was a lovely warm evening, and they were being watched by an artistic, appreciative crowd, so everything went well. Leigh had made a big, fun-fur smiley face with 'Minty' written on it. There were slits where the eyes were and I had to poke my bosoms through these all the time the band were play-ing. It was difficult to keep my concentration, as members of the audience kept leaping up to grab my breasts. Leigh had a lot of difficulty getting up onto the stage – he could hardly see, he had Nicola hanging round his neck, he was wearing eight-inch platforms and then had to climb up about ten steps. He almost fell over, but just managed to steady himself. Once he had done the birth bit of the show, he stripped off to reveal an old pair of baggy red underpants. He had streaked his body with reddish-brown grease paint and he looked his most vibrant and sparkling as he leapt about on stage, unhindered by any constricting costumes. It was almost as if he had finally come to terms with himself, saying 'Hey, look at me, I am a normal person inside all this dressing up.'

Everything was going well, with a record ready to be released in early 1995, and then the band were asked to do a two-week residency at the Freedom Café in Wardour Street. Leigh wasn't sure about it at first, as the space seemed rather small, but he agreed as he thought that it would be good discipline for the band and give them a chance to perfect their performance.

Leigh designed the lighting and decided the show should open with Venetian blinds in front of the stage instead of curtains; these could be opened gradually, and with lighting behind them it would be a very exciting effect. I was given the task of finding the cheapest blinds in London, which happened to be at IKEA. So one Saturday afternoon Leigh and I set off. He usually hated places like that, but he thoroughly enjoyed his trip there. We sat in the cafeteria eating fish and chips while Leigh ruminated on the lives of the other customers. 'He must be a divorced dad who's brought his son here for a weekend treat. They're two disgusting fags who have just moved in together. Oh my God, lesbians shopping for kitchen utensils.' He started telling me again how worried he was about his health.

'I've got a terrible headache that I can't get rid of and I keep feeling sick, I expect it's just flu, I hope it goes away by Thursday.'

The show opened on Thursday 24 November and was supposed to go on until 3 December. Most of the tickets had sold out for the whole run and the first night was so crowded that journalists, record company scouts and punters had to be turned away. The show was a great success, despite Leigh feeling no better; it was impossible to tell from his performance how weak he was feeling. The sound was incredibly loud due to the low ceiling, and poor Lucian Freud sat in the middle of the crowd with his hands over his ears until he could stand it no longer and had to leave.

The next day Leigh phoned me at work. 'I can't believe it. The show's been cancelled. Westminster Council said it's too disgusting what with all the shit and vomit and if Freedom carry on they will get their licence taken away. To be honest though I'm relieved. I feel so dreadful I don't think I could have carried on. Perhaps now I'll have time to get better.'

16

Hospital

On Monday 28 November 1994, I got home from work to find a message on my answering machine from Leigh asking me to call him. He had been feeling so ill over the last couple of days that I had nagged him to go to the clinic to see what was wrong. I phoned him straight away. He had been to the hospital and they had done various tests on him and then sent him home. He felt relieved that he had gone, thinking that it wasn't really anything serious. He was to go back for the results in a couple of days.

I felt much happier, too, because I had been very worried about him. I started making a vegetable chilli for tea. I must have been more upset than I thought, because I spilt about half a tin of chilli powder into it and was busy trying to rectify my mistake by dropping raw potatoes into the fiery mess when the phone rang. It was Leigh in a state of panic. The hospital had just phoned him and told him that they had completed some of the tests and it looked like he had some type of meningitis. They wanted him to go to the hospital straight away and to book into the Charles Bell ward, dedicated to HIV/AIDS patients. I arranged to pick him up and drive him there. I left my ruined chilli on the stove and to the astonishment of my brother, Chris, who was living with me at the time, dashed out of the house.

Since Leigh had been diagnosed as HIV positive in 1988 he had been attending hospital regularly for check-ups. He had originally gone to St Mary's, but in about 1991 he decided that he didn't like it there and wanted to transfer to the Middlesex Hospital. He didn't really know how to go about it, so he went to the Genito Urinary Medicine clinic to explain his symptoms and ask for a test. The doctor he saw was very sympathetic and counselled him before giving him the test and asking him to return in a week for the results. Leigh felt a bit guilty about having to put the doctor through the stress of telling him he was HIV positive when he already knew, and for a couple of days beforehand he practised how he would react when the doctor told him. He half hoped that the test would come up negative, but he was realistic enough to accept that this was most unlikely.

The clinic arranged for Leigh to have counselling, which he thoroughly enjoyed. He used to frighten the psychologist by saying that he worked for Sigmund Freud's grandson and he would argue with everything she said. He had told the counsellor that I was the only person who knew he was HIV positive, so she suggested I go along too, but as much as he tried to persuade me I couldn't face it. He often used to say he didn't know why he had told me, because I was so useless, but I did my best and I think he appreciated my down-to-earth attitude and lack of histrionics. The fact that I knew the terrible secret kept our relationship on an even keel: he could never be too horrible to me, because he needed someone to confide in when things got too much. When my flatmate Vaughn Toulouse had become ill, Leigh said that it was practice for me for when it happened to him. He came to see Vaughn in the hospital a couple of times, which took great courage, because it was the first time he saw close up what would probably happen to him. He came to Vaughn's funeral just to give me support, which was incredibly kind and brave of him, but he didn't feel up to coming to the party afterwards, so went to the cinema to see three films and sobbed uncontrollably through all of them.

Leigh had decided that he didn't want anyone else to know about his illness. He thought that if people knew they would treat him differently. He knew that he did this himself – if he knew that someone had been diagnosed HIV positive, he would try not to upset them and would excuse them for any strange behaviour, as most people would do. He hated the thought of people feeling sorry for him and excusing his outrageous performances by thinking that they were a release of his anger against the AIDS virus. He wanted to be accepted as himself and not as a person with AIDS.

As I drove to Leigh's, memories flooded back of how I had driven Vaughn to hospital the first time he had become ill. It is a completely horrible feeling, just how I imagine you would feel if someone close to you had just been given the death sentence. When I arrived at Leigh's he was surprisingly calm. He was mainly worried about what he was going to tell Nicola, because she didn't know what was wrong with him. But she knew that he was ill, and had been begging him to go to the doctor's, so he thought she would be pleased that he had taken her advice. She was coming round to the flat that night, as she did most nights of the week. He left her a note telling her not to worry, that he had gone to the hospital and would probably be back home tomorrow, but he would ring her in the morning. He was glad that she would be staying as she would be able to feed Angus the cat.

We got into my car and I had to describe the ward to Leigh. I had visited it several weeks earlier to see a friend, Owen Williams, who had recently died. It was a typical hospital ward, with several alcoves, each with about six beds in them. There were a couple of single rooms at the end. I did not tell him about the air of despondency hanging over the place. However hard the nurses tried to be cheery, there was no getting away from the fact that all the people in this ward were going to die sooner rather than later. There was no hope of recovery or a miracle cure for any of them.

Leigh still managed to make a few jokes on the way to the hospital. He said he was pleased that at least he knew what was wrong with him, and was pretty confident that he would soon be cured of the meningitis. He realized that this illness would change his status from someone who was HIV positive to someone with AIDS, but as nobody knew he was ill, and he still had no intention of telling them, this wouldn't really matter.

We arrived at Middlesex Hospital and made our way to the ward. We went to the desk and they asked us to wait in the television room while they arranged for the doctor to book Leigh in. Leigh gave his name as John Waters. He had given this name when he had first attended the clinic because he didn't want anyone to recognize his real name. He chose his false one in honour of one of his heroes, the producer and director of the fantastic Divine movies. He was also pleased to discover that Lucian often used the pseudonym Louis Waters, feeling that this made them somehow closer.

We sat in the horribly depressing television room and I think this was the first time that Leigh realized the implications of his illness. There was a very skinny man sitting in the room trying to eat some pasta from a Tupperware box but obviously finding it hard going. He kept coughing and spluttering and then looking at the television, which wasn't working properly. He picked up his box and shuffled out of the room. Leigh buried his head in his hands and there was a terrible, intense atmosphere in the room, as if there was too much electricity or not enough air. Everything seemed to buzz. Neither of us knew what to say, so we sat there in silence until the nurse came to tell us that the doctor was ready.

Leigh was given a bed and the doctor came over and asked him lots of questions. He enquired about his symptoms, how long he had been diagnosed, where he lived, what his lifestyle was. Leigh nominated me as his next of kin because I was still the only one that knew. When the doctor asked Leigh what floor he lived on, Leigh looked really concerned, as if the doctor was insinuating that he should live on the ground floor. He had really pulled himself together by now and told the doctor firmly that he did not intend that this disease would change his living arrangements or lifestyle at all. When asked what his job was, he replied 'performance artist'. This rather raised the eyebrows of the doctor, who had already been looking quizzically at Leigh's pierced face. The doctor then went off to sort out some medicine. Leigh immediately asked me if I thought the doctor was gay and did I fancy him!

Leigh lay down on the bed and said he had something to tell me. I immediately guessed what it was and told him that I knew he was married to Nicola (her sister had let the cat out of the bag a couple of months earlier). He said it was the only secret he had kept from me. He couldn't believe that I had known and not said anything. I had wanted to prove that I could keep a secret, and had found it funny that I knew something he thought I didn't know, especially when he had asked me to marry him (in jest) the previous week. I had wanted to call him a bigamist but had managed to keep my mouth shut, which is a very difficult thing for me to do. I asked him why he had done it. He told me he knew that he was eventually going to die and he wanted Nicola to take over the tenancy of his flat. He also wanted to make sure that she would be there to look after him if he got ill. This, of course, was probably only a quarter of the reason, as he had told everyone a different story. Only Leigh knew the truth.

The doctor came back and said that the medicine Leigh would have to take was very toxic, so he had to get the pharmacist to mix it up. He explained the treatment and said he thought that Leigh would be in the hospital for at least a week. Leigh was very worried about how he would explain everything to Nicola. He knew that she would have to come and see him, and that 'even she would realize that it was no ordinary ward when she saw all the skinny young men with no bottoms shuffling about in novelty slippers being visited by loads of camp queens and caring women.' I told him that he should tell her before she visited to make it less of a shock, and he decided that he probably would.

As it was past midnight I asked him if he minded if I went home, because he seemed as settled as anyone in his predicament could be. He made me promise that I wouldn't tell anyone where he was or that he was ill. I gave him a kiss and left the ward with tears streaming down my face. I drove home knowing that the horrible nightmare of hospital visiting that I had experienced with Vaughn was about to begin again.

I called the hospital the next day and they reported that Leigh had slept all right. I went to Marks & Spencer after work and bought some flowers, fruit juice and satsumas, then made my way to the hospital. When I arrived at the ward I couldn't see him. A nurse told me that he was in a room at the end of the ward on his own.

Nicola was there, and Leigh was propped up in bed with a drip in his arm. He winked at me and said 'she knows our little secret'. Nicola was much more together than I imagined she would be. A couple of years earlier, Leigh had told her that he was positive just to test her reaction. She had burst into floods of tears and got hysterical, so he had decided that she wouldn't be able to cope with the knowledge and to her relief said that he had made it all up to test her. But she had had her suspicions about what was wrong with Leigh, so it wasn't too much of a shock for her when she walked into the ward. She told Leigh that she had wanted to warn him that he 'might be HIV positive'. 'Give me the good news, why don't you?' was his caustic reply.

Nicola left, as she was working at Lucian's. This was to be the pattern of our visiting – Nicola in the day, me at night. At this point I thought that gradually Leigh would let more people know and he would have a steady stream of visitors, even thinking that it might turn into a bit of a party, but I was wrong. For the next four weeks, Leigh's only visitors were to be me and Nicola.

Leigh explained why he was in the single room. A nurse had been looking at his notes and had asked him if he knew the performance artist Leigh Bowery; she had been very disappointed because she had tickets to see him at the Freedom Café, but it had to be cancelled due to too much filth. The king of liars must have been feeling ill, because he told her that he was Leigh Bowery. It worked in his favour, as she arranged for him to have a side room so that he could have his privacy. He insisted that she keep his concocted name on all his notes and not tell the other nurses.

Leigh seemed more ill than he had done the day before, but we put it down to the vast amounts of antibiotics that were being pumped into him. We thought that he would soon begin to get better and that this was the pain before the gain. However, each day I visited he seemed sicker and more uncomfortable than the day before. He couldn't really eat, and when he did, he threw up. He had terrible diarrhoea. Whenever a new symptom appeared he was prescribed more drugs. It seemed like an endless chain – the drugs to cure the meningitis caused vomiting, the drugs to cure the vomiting caused diarrhoea, the pill to cure the diarrhoea caused water retention. Altogether they made him feel terrible. He kept saying to the nurses that they just seemed to be treating the cosmetic symptoms while the meningitis still seemed to be raging. They then found out that he was allergic to the original antibiotic that he had been given, so he had to be given it in another form. He was on a strong drip for eight hours at a time, with only small spells off it in between. His head was incredibly painful and he kept asking me and Nicola to rub it to try to wipe the pain away. Nicola was very good at this, but I was useless. I kept trying to cheer him up by saying that he was surrounded by his three favourite things (piss, shit and vomit), but unsurprisingly this didn't give him much comfort.

After a couple of days people were beginning to wonder where he was. I thought it would be better for him if he could talk about his illness with other people besides me and Nicola, but he wouldn't allow it. After a week in hospital he realized he wouldn't be out as soon as he hoped, so he said that we could tell people that he had meningitis, but we were not to say which hospital he was in. Matthew Glammore had visited me at work to ask where Leigh was. He had heard that he was in the London Hospital and had been round there visiting every ward trying to find him. I made up some story about how he must have missed him. Nicola had been collecting all the messages from Leigh's answering machine and he phoned up a few people from the payphone and explained about the meningitis. Of course they wanted to visit, but he put them off by saying he was infectious. He phoned Rifat Ozbek and boasted that he was in a private clinic in Switzerland as Lucian had paid for the best treatment available.

After about a week, Leigh's good friend Baillie Walsh called me to question me about the mystery illness. He was very insistent about getting all the details, said he didn't believe me, and asked straight out if Leigh was HIV positive. I just started crying and told him the whole story, because I needed someone to talk to even if Leigh didn't. Baillie couldn't really take it all in, and said that for years he and Leigh had been having long conversations about what it would be like if they had AIDS. 'I really wondered what had been the point of us talking on the phone for at least two hours a day for the last seven years. I couldn't believe that he had married Nicola and had kept his illness from me.' As he and Leigh were great friends, he said I should tell Leigh that he knew and ask if it was all right to visit. In my innocence I thought that it was a good idea, as I've always thought the more people you tell about something really dreadful the less dreadful it gets.

So off I went to the hospital, confident that Leigh would be pleased that Baillie knew. How wrong can you be? When I mentioned that Baillie had guessed, Leigh exploded: how dare he suggest such a thing? The last thing he wanted was him up there with 'his bloody Chinese medicines'. He demanded that I get the phone for him as he was 'going to put that interfering poof right'. I was in a terrible panic; I had already told Leigh that I had told Baillie that it was true, but he seemed to ignore that fact. He said he was going to show me how a true liar worked. I thought that perhaps I should call Baillie first to warn him, but I didn't know his number off by heart. I went to look for the phone but decided to pretend that it was in use to give me more time to think. Of course Leigh didn't believe me and asked the nurse to get it. As he dialled Baillie's number I was sitting at the side of the bed, feeling really sick. He seemed to forget his illness and became the old Leigh, shouting and bawling at Baillie. I was dreading that Baillie was going to insist that Leigh had AIDS, but he's pretty bright, and from what I could gather, he simply agreed with everything Leigh said. When Leigh put the phone down he looked at me triumphantly and said, 'That's how it's done. Remember that when anyone else asks you questions.'

As soon as I got home I called Baillie, who was shell-shocked. He said that he thought I had gone mad and was playing some evil trick on him, and that Leigh was so convincing he almost thought he had dreamt the phone call with me. This was to be the last time that the two of them spoke, but after that I talked to Baillie every day and let him know how Leigh was.

By now my brother was wondering why I was going round to Leigh's house every night, so I told him about the meningitis but not the AIDS. It wasn't until about three weeks later that I finally told him the truth. He was wondering why I was so stressed and kept telling me to take a break from hospital visiting, so the only thing I could do was tell him. I knew that I could trust him not to tell anybody.

The next couple of weeks were very up and down. One day Leigh would be very optimistic as he was given lumbar punctures that seemed to indicate that the disease was going away, but then there would be setbacks when he was sick all day. He was hardly eating, which was amazing for him. Nicola took him things during the day and I made him meals for the evening, but nothing seemed to stay down. He kept kicking his legs in the air, admiring their new slimmer shape.

After a while he asked if he could go home for the night. The hospital said it would be OK as long as he came back the next morning. I drove him home and he seemed quite cheerful, but as soon as he got into his flat he seemed to go to pieces. After the big wards and high ceilings of the hospital, his flat seemed very small. He didn't seem to know what to do with himself, and curled up in a ball under the cutting table. He asked me if I could get him a gun, because he couldn't bear to carry on like this. I don't know where he thought I was going to get it from, but I told him not to be so stupid and that he would get better soon. I waited until Nicola arrived back from Lucian's and then left them.

At about 11 a.m. the next morning, I phoned the ward to see how he was, and they were very concerned because he hadn't arrived back. I immediately phoned his flat, but there was no answer. I called the hospital again. They were extremely worried about him and asked if maybe I could go round to check he was all right and bring him back, as he was due an urgent treatment. I was at work at the time and it was a bit tricky to leave, so I decided to keep trying to call for the next half hour and then go. After phoning about ten times with no answer I got more and more worried and imagined he had jumped off the balcony. Finally he answered ... what a relief. He said he didn't feel like answering the phone but was now on his way back to hospital.

One day when I went to see him Leigh was in a terrible state, as the man in the room next door had just died. This man had been very confused – he kept wandering into Leigh's room and having garbled conversations with him. Despite his mind having gone, he had seemed quite healthy, but he had had a sudden brain haemorrhage. This event really made Leigh dwell on what was happening to him. We both sat in his room sobbing for about five hours. He said that he knew he was dying, but I tried to convince him that he would get better. It was the first time that he had seemed to give up hope.

Leigh started getting quite deep, which is a place I never like to go. He was analysing why we were friends. Most of his friends were artistic in some way and had big ambitions, but I was happy to go plodding along in the Jobcentre and had achieved my ambitions – to go to America and to go to Heaven on a Saturday, when girls weren't allowed in – ten years earlier. I had done both of these with the help of Leigh. He decided that we were friends because he could never quite control me (I refused to wear the ridiculous make-up he tried to make me wear – he once painted my lips bigger than they were and I slapped him round the face) and I kept him in touch with real life. He had told me about his illness because I was the person he knew who was most like his family. It was a really horrible evening, but enlightening as well. I kept running out of the room to go to the toilet with tears pouring down my face and heaving because I couldn't breathe properly. Between us, we probably got through a week's supply of toilet paper. He told me that he never wanted anyone to know that he had died of AIDS and that when he did die I was to tell everyone that he had gone to Papua New Guinea to help the natives.

The next day Leigh seemed more positive and said he definitely was going to recover because there were so many things he had to do. He wanted at least two more years to really make his mark. A new Irish nurse was on duty, and as she changed his drip Leigh said to her, 'What a lovely accent you have. What part of Ireland are you from? You've got such a lovely sing-song voice.' When she left the room, he was laughing at himself and saying 'What a wanker I am. Fancy talking to her like that, these bloody drugs are turning me into a nice person!'

In the middle of December, Lucian had arranged a showing of four of his paintings among the old masters at the Dulwich Picture Gallery. The new painting *Leigh under the Skylight* was to be debuted, as was a painting of me on a sofa and one of Nicola crouched on a chair, along with a portrait of Susanna Chancellor. There was to be a private view, to which Nicola, Leigh and I had been invited. Leigh was desperate to go, so he arranged with the hospital to go out. I arrived on the ward all dolled up to find Leigh still in the bath. Nicola got him ready and he crept back into the room. He said he had been really frightened in the bath: he had heard this terrible wailing and thought it was me because the nurse had told me that he was about to die. He was very relieved when he found out that I had just arrived and we discovered that the culprit was an African woman who was on the ward.

Leaving his room was a major operation, because a couple of days earlier I had seen a friend of a friend admitted and Leigh was dreading that he would see him and tell everyone he was there. I could see him through the porthole of the room, so I had to spy out and say when he was looking the other way and we made a dash for it. Leigh hid his bandaged wrist in his pocket and hoped that if the boy did see him, he would think he was a visitor. He did not put on his wig, but stuffed it in his pocket to put on later, because he hadn't been wearing it while he was in the hospital and he thought the nurses would laugh if he suddenly sprouted a full head of hair. This was rich coming from a man who was quite happy to walk around nightclubs naked or walk through the West End dressed as a birthday cake.

We drove to Dulwich and arrived rather late. This was the first time Leigh was to see people he knew since he had been in hospital: Lorcan O'Neill, his boyfriend Johnnie Shand Kydd, who Leigh had become friendly with, and Cerith would be there, and by now they knew he had meningitis, so he hoped that explanation would be enough. He was attached to a pump that gave a steady dose of anti-sickness drugs, but Nicola had sewn a handy pocket to the front of his T-shirt to transport it in. We must have looked an odd threesome. Nicola was very elegantly dressed in a short velvet dress with long dangly earrings, I was lolloping along in 'Victoria', my long, velvet blue dress, which I was wearing over 'Vivienne', a flowery, long-sleeved Lycra top that had a look of Westwood about it, and Leigh was propped up between us in his Antony Price suit, which had the most massive shoulders. He didn't look too ill, so nobody asked any awkward questions. He managed to walk around a bit, but had to have regular rests on some of the antique furniture that was dotted about. Luckily, it was a very quiet affair – there were only about fifty people there, plus a few waitresses going around with crisps and wine. We were introduced to David Hockney and the Duke of Beaufort. Lorcan O'Neill was obsessed with the Duke's hand-made shoes, which seemed to give him far more pleasure than the paintings. Lucian was hosting a dinner at his new favourite restaurant, St John, but Leigh didn't feel up to going, so we decided to go back to the hospital.

On the way back Leigh decided he was hungry, so we went to TGI Fridays in Covent Garden. They were a bit slow with the service, so Leigh decided to make use of his illness. He made sure his bandaged hand could be seen and kept shouting out, 'Why are we waiting, I'm a sick man.' The poor waitress was very distressed as he continued to bang on the table like a petulant schoolboy. To add extra pathos, he slipped his wig over one ear. It was good to see that he could still manage to play his old tricks. I saw it as a sign that he was recovering, and never thought that it would be his last restaurant meal.

I think Lucian had been glad to see Leigh, because he didn't really know how he was. At first we had just said that he was a bit poorly, and then, to explain the fact that he wasn't turning up to sit, we said that he had meningitis. But as Nicola and I hardly saw each other – we were working at different times and doing different shifts at the hospital – sometimes our stories didn't tally. We told Lucian that Leigh was in different hospitals, but luckily Nicola had a reputation for getting the wrong end of the stick, so Lucian put it down to her scattiness. Once he found out about the meningitis, Lucian was on the phone to his private doctors and said he would pay for Leigh to have private treatment. Of course, Leigh didn't want this, because it would mean Lucian knowing his secret, so he refused his offer. Lucian didn't think this was strange: he liked his privacy, too. At the time he was painting Nicola sitting in a little box in the attic and me lying on a sofa. She worked in the evenings and I did the day shift on Saturdays and Sundays. Most of the time Nicola had tears streaming down her face, and I often started crying looking at the paintings of Leigh in the studio. He looked so alive and vibrant in them, which was a great contrast to how he was in the hospital.

Lucian gave me £50 to buy some flowers for Leigh, but when I took this magnificent bouquet in, Leigh just said I should have kept the cash and we could have split it. I had thought he would like the flowers because he kept wistfully talking about his love of gardening, which I had never heard mentioned before.

Christmas was approaching, and Leigh was getting more and more concerned about what he was going to do with his family. They were coming over for the holidays as a way of trying to get over his mother's recent death. It seemed like a nightmare scenario. Here they were, coming to see their successful son and brother in London, only to find him in hospital with a terminal illness. Hardly a Merry Christmas. To make things more complicated, it wasn't just his dad, sister and her boyfriend coming, but his cousin and his girlfriend too. Originally, Leigh had thought that he would be out of hospital ages before they arrived, so he wouldn't have to tell them. There was also the question of where they were all going to sleep, as they were all supposed to be staying at his flat. He had seen a day bed he liked in Heal's, so Nicola was sent off to order that. He didn't have enough bed linen but that problem was easily solved, as there were piles of beautiful white cotton sheets hanging around the ward – every time Nicola left he'd slip a pair into her bag. When we had been to IKEA to buy the blinds for Minty's show he had seen a glass-topped table that he wanted. I brought him in a copy of the IKEA catalogue and he made a list of all the other things he needed, such as chairs and bedding. Despite the fact he was very ill, he was still concerned about his family and wanted them to be as comfortable as possible. So I went off to IKEA to get his order, but had to keep making fraught telephone calls to him in his little room because I wasn't sure about the table and dreaded the consequences if I got the wrong one.

Eventually everything was ordered and delivered. He now had the living arrangements sorted out, but he was worried sick about what he was going to tell them. He decided it would be best to tell Bronwyn first and leave her to break the news to his dad. He wanted me to phone her, so we sat with the payphone in his room, armed with about £5 in loose change. We tried her home and her office, but we couldn't reach her. Leigh left a message to tell her he was in hospital and to ring back.

Next time I went to the hospital, she had phoned back and he had explained his illness to her, but I could never really get out of him what had been said and if he had told her the whole truth. He had partly told Bronwyn two years earlier in a very drunken phone call, but it had never been discussed again.

Leigh's family were due to arrive on 22 December, and he wanted to be there to greet them, so he got a taxi home and arranged for me to come to his flat to pick him up. I was dreading it, as I wasn't sure how much they knew. It was the first time I had seen them since Evelyn died, and when other people are upset I always get upset myself. I got home from work and tried to pluck up the courage to drive round to Ronald Street, but I found any excuse not to set off, even resorting to hoovering, one of my most hated tasks. Eventually Leigh rang up asking where I was, so I couldn't put it off any longer. I slowly drove over to East London, feeling sicker with each mile travelled.

When I got to the flat it wasn't nearly as bad as I had imagined. I'd thought that everyone would be sitting around sobbing, but there was a strange feeling of normality in the air. I still couldn't make out who knew what, so I thought I had better pretend that nothing was wrong and not mention anything. Nicola was making cups of tea for the family, while Leigh was hovering around in his workroom and seemed keen to get back to the hospital. By now he had become slightly institutionalized and felt much safer being at the Middlesex. Also, as he said, 'there will be more room for the family if I stay at the hozzie'.

I went to see Leigh for the last time before Christmas on 23 December, as I was going to my parents' house for the holidays. The ward had a big Christmas tree up and decorations festooned everywhere, but it only made the place seem more depressing, because this was probably the last Christmas for a large proportion of the patients. The patients didn't seem to talk to each other much; they just lay on their beds, lost in their own misery. Leigh had warned me not to buy him anything for Christmas because it would be a waste of money. This was usual for him – ever since he had spent his first Christmas in London hiding in his bedsit he had hated the holiday and had done his best to ignore it. So I was really surprised when he produced a huge jar of Cadbury's Roses, which Nicola had bought, and asked me to give them to the nurses. He then asked me if I had anything he could write on. As it happened I had a spare, quaint little Christmas card in my bag. Normally he would have torn it up into tiny pieces and tossed it out of the window, but he said it was really nice, so I asked him since when did he think hedgehogs dressed in Father Christmas outfits were 'nice'. He wrote a note inside thanking the nurses for all their help and signed it 'John Waters'. It seemed so weird that he was still keeping up the charade of John Waters. It was almost as if by calling himself a different name all these dreadful things were happening to someone else. I left the room sobbing uncontrollably because the whole scenario was so out of character for him, and shoved the chocolates into a nurse's hand in a cloud of tears and wet tissues.

Leigh's family were able to visit him over the holidays, so Nicola and I didn't feel too bad about visiting our own families. We both kept in contact by phone, and Leigh seemed in fairly good spirits. It was good to have a break from the claustrophobic hospital visits and by Boxing Day I was beginning to feel a bit more relaxed. My twitchy eye had subsided a bit and the further away from the hospital I was, the less real it seemed.

But as I drove back on the 27th, the reality of the situation struck again. I got more and more miserable as I drove along the M4 towards London. I popped into the hospital before going home, just to see how Leigh was. Nicola was there for her first visit after the holidays and she said that he seemed in a very odd mood, as they had started giving him morphine to help the pain. This seemed very serious to me. When I got home I phoned up the nurses (I always preferred to do this as it seemed easier than talking to them face to face) and they told me not to worry, it was just to make him more comfortable.

When I got to the hospital that night, I couldn't believe my eyes. Leigh was in the best mood ever, singing and dancing round his room in his usual garb of baggy chewing-gum-white Calvin Y-fronts, saying he felt great. He was complimenting me, saying, 'Oh, Sue, you look so great. Who made that beautiful jacket for you?' When I told him he'd made it, he looked awestruck and went on and on about what a great bloke he was, so talented and so clever. He got back into bed and proceeded to tell me a long story about his sister being a foundling, squashed into a little bit of land between Australia and Tasmania. This story took about half an hour to tell and even as he was struggling to tell it, he knew it was rubbish. He kept saying, 'We're going to have such a laugh tomorrow remembering this crap. God, morphine is a fantastic drug, no wonder people go mad for it.'

Leigh continued telling jokes and dancing about all evening, and for once I had tears of laughter rolling down my cheeks instead of tears of despair. As the evening went on he began to get more sleepy as more morphine got into his system – every time the pump put a bit more into him, I could see his eyes roll as it kicked in. At about 11 p.m. he passed out, so I crept off home, feeling much better about the whole situation. It was as if the old Leigh had returned for a couple of hours.

17

Dying

On 28 December I had to go and work at Lucian's. I arrived at about 7.45 a.m., had a chat, then lay on the battered flowery sofa for a day's sitting. Lucian asked me how Leigh was and I mumbled something about him being a bit better. I said that he had been in a very jolly mood the previous evening. I left at about 3 p.m., as the light was going, and went home.

At about 6 p.m. Nicola called in a terrible state. She said that I had better come to the hospital at once, as Leigh had taken a terrible turn for the worse and they thought that he might die fairly soon. This was the first time that either of us truly thought that he might really die. We knew that he probably only had two or three years left, but the nurses had been so optimistic we were sure he would get better from the meningitis eventually. Nicola was very worried about letting down Lucian, as she was supposed to be sitting that evening. We couldn't telephone, as we didn't have his number, so I said that I would go round and let him know that Nicola wouldn't be able to sit. We decided that we should tell him the whole story, as we were sure that Leigh would like to see him before he died.

I became a bit hysterical, and didn't really know what to do, so my brother offered to drive me to Lucian's and then to the hospital. When we arrived at Lucian's I rang the doorbell furiously. When he answered I ran up all the stairs in one go, which I had never managed before. I fell into the flat, huffing and puffing, and blurted out the whole story. Lucian looked very shocked; he shed a couple of tears, which he tried to hide from me by hovering in the corner of the kitchen, and then lit one of the many cigar stubs that he always had lying around. I get very embarrassed when other people are emotional, so I just told him where the hospital was, gave him the phone number and said that I had better be off. I raced down the stairs and my brother dropped me off at the hospital.

I walked into the ward and was just going to talk to the nurses at the desk when I heard a little voice saying 'Sue, Sue'. I couldn't make out where it was coming from at first; then I noticed a figure wearing an oxygen mask in the bed nearest the nurse's station. Leigh had been moved out of his single room so that the nurses could keep an eye on him, as he was now a high-risk case. I went over and chatted to him, but it was hard for him to reply because he had the mask on, and when he took it off he started to talk gibberish because his brain was being affected by the lack of oxygen. Nicola had been in the kitchen, and when she reappeared I told her what had happened at Lucian's.

We were very worried about contacting Leigh's dad, who had gone away to visit relatives in Wolverhampton because he, like us, had not realized the seriousness of the situation. Luckily, he phoned to see how Leigh was, so we were able to tell him what was going on. He decided not to return that night and to wait until the next day because he thought that Bronwyn might turn up (she and her boyfriend Steve had gone on a tour of Britain).

It was much more interesting being in the main ward, as we could see everything that was happening, instead of being locked away in Leigh's chosen solitary confinement. There was a security guard on duty to look after a man who had been sectioned but could not be looked after in a psychiatric ward because he needed specialist AIDS treatment. The guard was a very stern-looking woman who spent the night eating the vast amount of Roses and Quality Street chocolates that had been given to the nurses for Christmas. The poor man just seemed like he needed someone to talk to, so I let him tell me about all his problems – his broken marriage, his estranged children and his illness.

At about 10 p.m. Lucian phoned to say that he was coming over. I arranged to meet him in the lobby and show him where to go. He arrived after first having gone to University College Hospital around the corner – Nicola and I had told so many lies about Leigh's whereabouts that Lucian had thought he was at UCH. We had nervously told Leigh that Lucian was coming, thinking that he might be angry with us for breaking the vow of silence, but he seemed quite pleased. He tried to sit up when Lucian arrived, and managed to have a small chat with him, but it was difficult because he had to keep having oxygen. Lucian was very keen on nurses, so when they came to change the drips he didn't move so that he could be nearer to them. He was rather disappointed that they weren't wearing starched uniforms.

The nurses and doctors kept coming over and prodding Leigh to check on his responses. They were quite cheerful and still seemed to be optimistic. Nicola said that she would stay the night, so I decided to go home in order that at least one of us would have had some sleep. I arranged to return very early the next morning so that Nicola could go and have some rest.

I went back at about 8 a.m. to find that Leigh had slept sporadically and his condition had worsened. Nicola went to Leigh's flat to have a nap, so I was left alone with him. I had never been at the hospital during the day before, so I was fascinated by the amount of activity going on. I kept being sent away while they gave Leigh more tests. When I was sitting with Leigh he kept trying to tug off the oxygen mask and talk. Hanging above the beds were brackets to hook televisions on. He went on and on about a show he had invented concerning these brackets – he was going to hang off them and then stick some sculpture on the back hinge. It was very complicated and it took ages to get the words out. He was getting confused due to lack of oxygen as he kept pulling the mask off because it was irritating him.

At about midday the auxiliary brought some lunch round, and I managed to give Leigh some soup. It felt horrible feeding this great strong man like he was a baby. The doctors came back for more prodding and then the one who had originally booked Leigh into the ward five weeks earlier called me into his office. He said that the situation was very serious, as further complications had set in. He said Leigh was going to die, but if I thought it was a good idea they would take him to Intensive Care, where he would have one-to-one nursing. He doubted that they could save him, but it might make him more comfortable. This is the only time in my life when I have been totally speechless. I tried to speak but the words just stuck in my throat. I was opening my mouth like a goldfish, but nothing came out. Tears started to tumble down my face. He said Nicola should come back to the hospital, and he offered to ring her, but I said I would do it just to get out of the room.

He showed me to another little room and I managed to phone Nicola. She had been dozing, but rushed back to the hospital. I tried to pull myself together and went to sit with Leigh. I explained that he was going to go upstairs to Intensive Care. He seemed to take this in and muttered that he would get better up there. He was getting more and more confused by now. He still kept pulling the oxygen mask off, and seemed to be struggling to tell me something really important. Eventually I understood what he was saying – 'I am not the son of Eva Peron'. He repeated it about three times, as if it was the most shocking secret he had ever had to tell me. Despite the desperation of the situation he still made me laugh, and I managed to put his mind at rest and explained that although people had often made up stories about him, no one had ever actually thought that he was the son of Eva Peron.

Nicola arrived and gave Leigh one of his favourite Tesco ice lollies. It was sad that in a lifetime of gourmet eating, a 10p lolly was to be his last taste of solid food. The doctor warned us that once Leigh was in Intensive Care he would be heavily sedated to make things easier for him. In a sick kind of way I was a bit excited to be going to Intensive Care. I have always had a fascination with hospitals, and as it was unlikely I would ever be able to watch an operation this was the nearest I would get to real medical drama. Nicola and I went up in the lift with Leigh. It was a horrible journey, with the nurses trying to be cheery, but there wasn't much to be cheery about. It was like a whole new strange world in the Intensive Care Unit. Naked people lay in beds that seemed to be dotted all around the place. There was a cacophony of beeps, hisses and whooshes as a variety of machines pumped air into and monitored the progress of these very sick people.

Leigh was put into a bed near the door and we were asked to wait in the relatives' room while they settled him. This was a very strange place, with people dozing on sofas, making fraught phone calls or weeping quietly to themselves as the television flickered in the corner showing *Neighbours*. There was so much emotion in such a little place, and an endless supply of tea and sweet biscuits – the English way of dealing with any tragedy. The mugs had an open invitation to steal them printed on them: 'Do not remove. Property of Middlesex Hospital Intensive Care Unit'.

We went back to see Leigh, who had been wired to a variety of machines and screens that measured all bodily functions. We couldn't really understand why, as we were under the impression that he was about to die, but the nurses said that there was still some hope. We were very confused by now and not sure if he was dying or not. They decided to put a tube up his nose that would go straight into his stomach so that they could administer medication more easily. It was ghastly watching them try to insert it, as Leigh kept flinching. When they had finished they brought the Mobile X-ray round to check that the tube was in the right place.

Nicola had called Cerith while she was at Leigh's, as she had decided that there was no point keeping the secret any longer and she knew that Cerith would want to see Leigh as they had been friends for so long. I went to meet him in the foyer and we returned to Intensive Care together. By now Leigh was covered in even more tubes and wires and had about six bags of various liquids going into him. He also had a strap-on oxygen mask that forced the gas into him. It really was a fantastic look, and if he had seen someone else with it, we were sure that he would have soon been wearing it to nightclubs. It seemed such a pity that he couldn't enjoy his greatest fashion triumph. When he saw Cerith, Leigh tried to smile, and said 'My lights are still on, you know.'

The nurses were very good and explained everything, so all three of us suddenly became medical experts, thinking that we could understand every little bleep on the screen. They then decided to put Leigh into a side room on his own because they were scared of cross-infection. We were dispatched to the relatives' room while this went on.

The room seemed to have been taken over by various members of one family. There was a very rough-looking woman of about sixty with a scar crossing from one side of her face to the other, bisecting her mouth in the process, and two girls of about twenty-eight dressed in the ubiquitous fashion of leggings and baggy shirts. They seemed to have taken up residence and tried to make us welcome, as if we were being admitted to some exclusive club. They told us that they had been there three days. Apparently the older woman's son had been mucking about with his girlfriend (one of the twenty-eight-year-olds) on the balcony of their sixth-floor flat after having a 'bit to drink' when he had fallen over the edge and ripped off his arm. Mum filled us in with all the details. They had managed to sew the arm back on – 'He was really shocked when he saw it was still there when he woke up.' He also had other terrible wounds. 'He's got two clots you know, one is right in his bladder, they had to stick a tube right up his penis to try and melt it.' They asked why we were there. Nicola replied 'My husband has got AIDS and there's not much hope.' Mother looked very sympathetic and said 'Aaaah, bless him!'

We then returned to Leigh's room, where he had been made comfortable on a special air bed. He was propped up and, despite all the tubes, he looked exactly as he does in Lucian's painting of him. We were given special instructions that every time we went into the room, we had to put on a yellow plastic apron and wash our hands with special pink liquid to stop infection. We couldn't really understand how a small plastic pinny could stop infections, but we were thrilled to go along with it as it made us feel more medical and any little thing that would take our minds off the horror of what was happening to Leigh was welcome. Cerith and I became obsessed with the man with the sewn-back-on arm and kept going out into the main ward to see if we could spot him. I was thrilled to see him, his bandaged arm resting on a bedside cabinet with a handwritten note stuck to it saying 'Do Not Move'.

A rather handsome young male nurse was assigned to look after Leigh for the night shift. He was very chatty and explained what was going on. Cerith took to him in a big way, but we couldn't work out if he was gay or not. Cerith arranged to meet Angus and his boyfriend Jonathan in a local pub, so I decided to go with him. Angus had fallen out with Leigh a while previously and although Leigh had left him a message wishing him a happy birthday he hadn't bothered to call back – he had sent him to Coventry, as he is very prone to do. He was sitting in the pub with a crumpled face, staring at his knees. Jonathan just looked uncomfortable. I tried to cheer them up, but it was very difficult. Angus wanted to see Leigh, so we went back to the hospital and Jonathan kindly went to the shops to buy sandwiches and drinks for me, Cerith and Nicola.

By now Nicola was in charge and was taking her duties as Leigh's wife very seriously. It was up to her who could visit and who couldn't. She was sensitive to Leigh's needs, and didn't want anyone to upset him. She also realized that some people would be so upset themselves it would be wrong for them to come, but realized that other people needed to see him. She told Leigh that Angus was coming in as he didn't want there to be any 'bad blood' between them. Angus just sat disconsolately in a chair at the side of the room. At this point Leigh was heavily sedated, but if you asked him to squeeze your hand, he would. As 11 p.m. approached Angus left, leaving just me, Nicola and Cerith, who was a bit drunk. He kept telling the male nurse how much he admired him and what a fantastic job he was doing. Then Lucian turned up and spent a long time holding Leigh's hand. As there were enough people there, I decided to go home to get some sleep. At about midnight Lucian and Cerith went down to see the nurses on the Charles Bell ward. Jonathan had bought a half-bottle of whisky, so Cerith decided to share that. He was very tired and emotional and kept the nurses talking most of the night.

I returned very early the next morning to find that Nicola and Cerith had got a bit of sleep huddled on chairs in Leigh's room. They hadn't been able to sleep in the rest room as the rough mother had commandeered it as her own – she had got changed into her nightie and made the settee up as a bed for herself – but both of them were used to being uncomfortable for long periods of time, as they had both sat for Lucian. The young male nurse was relieved of his duties by a pleasant young girl who, besides being a nurse on an Intensive Care Ward, was a full-time student studying for a degree so she could get out of nursing. There seemed little change in Leigh's condition, but we were told we would find out what was happening when the doctors did their morning round.

At one point, Cerith and I were standing at the side of Leigh's hi-tech bed, posing in our lovely yellow aprons, when he opened his eyes and looked right at us. He shook his head and stared at me, as if he was saying, 'How many times have I told you that yellow is not your colour'. It was weird that although he was extremely ill and close to death he could still sometimes understand what was going on around him.

At 11 a.m., about six people came into the room. They were introduced as an assortment of specialists. The doctor in charge had a strong resemblance to a panda, as he had such dark rings under his eyes. While they did various tests we retreated into the visitors' room, hoping to catch up on the latest news of the armless wonder. Apparently he had been taken off sedation and he had managed to mumble a few words, so there was great rejoicing in his family. We had asked the night nurse about him, and he said it was very unusual for them to have such an extreme accident – the hospital was a central location, so the cars didn't go fast enough for any dreadful smashes and there was no heavy industry nearby. The most exciting cases they usually got were stabbings, which were pretty routine. The family were discussing if it was going to be in the local paper, and which one it might be – the *Camden Journal* or the *Ham and High*?

After the doctors had finished their examination, they called the three of us into a little side room and gave us their verdict on Leigh's condition. Apparently, as most of his crucial bodily functions had given up, there seemed little point in carrying on the agony. They asked us if they should stop giving Leigh antibiotics and just give him things to make him more comfortable, such as morphine. They said we could ask him what he thought, or make up our minds ourselves. We decided that we should ask him, as he always liked to make his own decisions. Nicola volunteered to do the talking while Cerith and I sat shaking in the corner.

Nicola was very brave. She told Leigh she had something to tell him and when she had finished the nurse would remove his oxygen mask so he could say what he wanted. She told him that he wasn't going to last much longer, and asked if he wanted the healing drugs stopped and for them to continue with the ones that would make him more comfortable. We thought that he wouldn't really know what she was talking about, but he understood every word. As she spoke he got more and more agitated; the lines on the monitoring screen went all over the place. When his mask was removed he struggled to sit up and to speak, but kept whispering 'a few more days'. It was hard to imagine what was going on inside his head. What kinds of dreams must he have been having? What does it feel like when someone tells you that you are about to die? It made me realize that if I am ever in the same position I want to be kept in complete ignorance.

The nurse strapped the oxygen mask back onto him, but Leigh wouldn't settle. He kept jerking and twitching, and the monitor was still going crazy. The nurse tried to calm him down with extra morphine, but it took about half an hour before he was peaceful. Nicola told the doctors that Leigh wanted to stay on the treatment. It seemed strange to us that they should use such expensive equipment and drugs on someone who had no hope. They were even pumping him full of blood to try to raise his blood pressure and giving him very expensive liquid feed. But it was good to see that the National Health Service still had some money to spend and offered such a caring and professional service.

By now Leigh's dad had arrived back from Wolverhampton and was sitting holding Leigh's hand. It must have been so traumatic for him, all alone in a strange country with his dying son, but he was very calm and sensible throughout the ordeal.

We suddenly realized that Angus the cat had not been fed for a couple of days (although some food had been left out for him), so I volunteered to go and feed him, as I was popping out to meet my friend Mel for lunch anyway. We also thought that we should tell a few more people, since a message had gone out on Radio Four telling Bronwyn to contact the hospital because her brother Leigh Bowery was seriously ill. Leigh had several old and close friends who still had no idea that he was even poorly, and it would have been dreadful if they only heard the news on the London gossip grapevine. We found out later that several people had heard the message and were very concerned. Nicola gave me several names to call and I went home before going to feed the cat.

I called up Rachel Auburn first, because she had been a great friend of Leigh's for many years, although they didn't see each other much anymore. I didn't really know what to say, but managed to tell her. She was hysterical and just couldn't believe it. I then called Malcolm Duffy and Pearl, who were both very shocked and decided to go to the hospital straight away. My phone then started ringing; it was various people who Rachel had told, wanting to know if it was true. I was desperately trying to get hold of Lorcan and Johnnie, but I couldn't trace either. I eventually got through to Lorcan at the Anthony d'Offay Gallery and he said he would come up to the hospital later. I also left a message for Baillie. Brian Maloney, an old boyfriend of Rachel's and a good friend of Michael Clark, called to say he was going to tell Michael, but while I was talking to him the phone call was interrupted by the operator saying there was an urgent call for me. It was Cerith, who had phoned to tell me that Leigh had taken a turn for the worse and that I should get back to the hospital. So I dashed off, and poor Angus still hadn't been fed.

Leigh seemed just the same when I got back, so I didn't really see what the emergency was. I'd been told so many times in the last couple of days that he was about to die that I began to think that he would live in this state forever. I'm not a sentimental person and think that once someone is very ill and there is no hope of recovery they should die straight away and not be kept alive artificially in all sorts of agony.

The phones at the hospital had begun to go crazy: Baillie, Rifat, Rachel and various others were constantly calling. Michael Clark called from Scotland, where he was staying with his mum, to see if there was any point in coming down. We decided that there wasn't, as there was nothing he could do. Then visitors began to arrive. I was glad in a way, because up until now the nurses must have thought he was a very sad bloke with only me and Nicola as company.

Pearl arrived in an immaculately tailored suit that showed off his seventeen-inch waist to perfection. He was obsessed with making his waist as small as possible for artistic and aesthetic reasons, and was permanently trussed up in a very uncomfortable, tightly-laced corset. He was brandishing a beautiful bouquet of gerberas – Leigh's favourite flower, which he had grown in his garden in Australia. Later that evening I was talking to Pearl outside Leigh's room and could see all the nurses behind him staring and pointing. I couldn't work out why, as he was wearing the yellow pinny, which covered his tiny waist from the front. I had forgotten that from the back his waist looks about three inches wide. These nurses, who must have seen many incredible sights in their lives, were speechless. When Pearl left he took the key to Leigh's flat, as the poor cat still hadn't been fed.

Johnnie and Lorcan arrived, then Malcolm. Because there were so many people at the hospital now, we took it in turns to sit in the relatives' room. My mother phoned me while I was in there, as my brother had told her the previous evening what was going on. She had already planned to visit the Dulwich Picture Gallery that day. She said that it was so sad looking at this amazing picture of this huge strong man and knowing that he wouldn't be here much longer. Cerith and I filled everyone in on the arm accident – we were still latching onto the incident to try to take our minds off the real reason we were there. The family must have been thrilled with all these people taking such an interest in their story. Malcolm couldn't believe what had happened to Leigh: 'It was so shocking, this great big powerful man looking so helpless.' It was hard for him to take it in – he had only heard that Leigh had some kind of bad flu, and now he was in Intensive Care.

Nicola and Tom Bowery wouldn't leave Leigh's side, so the rest of us went down to the pub, where we met Angus and Jonathan. It should have been a sad time, but we all started talking about Leigh and telling stories of his ridiculous antics. We couldn't help but laugh; we spoke of the horrid things he had done as well as the amazing things. We would all miss him terribly, but he would be remembered with a tremendous amount of love.

On our return to the hospital another nurse had taken over, a rather sensible-looking girl with a homely nature. She was dressed in the usual attire of ill-fitting pyjamas in a washed-out pastel colour teamed with white clogs, but she had jazzed up her outfit with a selection of cute badges, including one spelling out her name. Lucian popped in for an hour or so and took a liking to this nurse, saying that she looked like 'she should be working in a supermarket but had studied really hard to follow her vocation and her family were probably really proud of her'.

It was very hard to know what to do. We were milling about between Leigh's room, the visitors' room and the corridor where you could have a cigarette. In the middle of the corridor by the lift there was a cardboard box marked 'HUMAN BLOOD', which we were desperate to pinch, but were too scared in case there was something in it. We got through a large supply of the yellow pinnies with our constant wanderings. At about midnight I went back into Leigh's room. He was looking weaker now, and his breathing was more laboured. Nicola insisted I sit and hold his hand, which I did. She then told him to squeeze my hand, which he did. I was so shocked I jumped, forgetting that I was in a chair with wheels on. The chair went flying across the room, making a mighty clatter as it bashed into various bits of equipment and throwing me to the floor in the process. There I was, lying on the floor, legs akimbo, struggling to get up. Leigh's lights were certainly still on – he lifted himself a good three inches off the bed and stared at this great crumpled heap on the floor. I was very happy to have given him a bit of entertainment, but I wasn't so happy to be the laughing stock of the rest of the room. Leigh seemed pretty settled for the night, so I decided to go home and get some sleep, as Lucian had persuaded me to sit the next day.

At 3.10 a.m. on New Year's Eve 1994, a couple of hours after I had got home from the hospital, Nicola called to say that Leigh had died. He had fought to stay alive until the end; he really didn't want to die, but in the end he just stopped breathing. I threw my clothes on and drove back to the hospital. It seemed so spooky and surreal. I went into the room to see him. He was lying on the bed naked, with all the tubes and wires removed. He looked truly fantastic, just like himself, but empty. It wasn't him anymore. He made a glorious corpse; he still looked powerful and strong, and the illness had left no scars on his body. The homely nurse had placed one of Pearl's gerberas in his hand to add a final poignant touch.

Nicola, Tom and I went into a small office, the same one where we had met with all the doctors, to be told of the arrangements that we had to make. We couldn't do much for about three days because of the holidays. Leigh had told me that he wanted to go home to Australia to be buried with his mother, and if there was a service he wanted no mention of God.

It was a silent and tearful drive back to Farrell House. I couldn't bear to go in, so I drove straight back home. As I was passing Russell Square I had a commemorative drive right round it to remember all the happy hours Leigh had spent there.

18

Afterwards

I was woken up for the second time on New Year's Eve by the telephone ringing. It was about 7 a.m. It was Lucian reminding me to come to work. He had already rung the hospital, so he knew that Leigh had died. He thought that if I came and sat it would take our minds off things. So off I set, crying all the way. When I arrived we just sat in the kitchen and chatted about Leigh, laughing and crying at the same time. We then did a bit of work, and I came home at about 1 p.m. to find an answering machine full of messages from people who had heard the news.

I was meant to go to a New Year's Eve party, but just couldn't face it. Still, I didn't want to stay at home on my own. Lorcan said he'd come round to cook something, but really it was a thoughtful trick to get me to go to Angus and Jonathan's flat in Long Acre. They were really kind; they had bought crates of vintage champagne and Angus had cooked some delicious food. There was me, my friend Mel, Cerith, Lorcan, Tom Bowery, Nicola and her sister Christine. I made everyone promise not to be sad – especially Angus, who I banned from looking at his knees. We managed to have quite a pleasant time, considering the circumstances. At midnight we toasted the New Year and said we hoped it would be better than

1994, at which point Nicola stood up and rather poignantly said, 'It couldn't possibly be, because Leigh won't be alive.'

Michael Kostiff phoned from Miami, which was very touching as he had gone there to get over the death of his wife Gerlinde, who had died suddenly of a brain haemorrhage two months earlier. The phone continued to ring throughout the evening and went on incessantly the next day, as the news had spread through the many New Year's Eve parties. Friends had got up on stages to give tributes to Leigh, but still a lot of people could not believe it. Leigh had always seemed so strong, so invincible, and he had been seen out just a couple of months earlier looking perfectly well.

Leigh still managed to cause trouble after he died. His last wish was to be flown back to Australia. Lucian offered to pay, so I phoned up the undertakers to try to arrange it. I explained that he had died of AIDS, because I thought that it might have some bearing on whether the body could be transported. They said that it was perfectly all right and asked how much he weighed, because the airline charged freight rates and the cost depended on body weight. When I replied 'about sixteen stone' the woman couldn't believe it. 'Are you quite sure he died of AIDS?'

Tom, Nicola, Christine and I went to the undertakers to sort everything out. They gave us a tour of the coffins. I always think that something enjoyable comes out of every tragedy, and I must say I thoroughly enjoyed looking at the coffins, especially a massive oblong one that was very deeply padded and had a Perspex box with a plastic rose inside the lid, presumably for the corpse to look at. The undertaker told us that it was very popular with Nigerian customers. They asked what clothes they should put Leigh in. There was only one option – nothing. However much he dressed up and distorted his body into the most incredible outfits, Leigh was never happier than when he was naked.

Leigh's body was shipped back to Melbourne and his father arranged a simple burial service in the hills at Macedon. He was to be buried next to his mother as he had wished. Tom was going to perform the service, but he felt he wasn't up to it, so Bronwyn led the proceedings. Leigh, as ever, had the last laugh: as they slowly dropped his coffin into the waiting hole, it wouldn't fit. However much they tried to manoeuvre it, the coffin wouldn't go in. Leigh's dad thought it was his way of telling everyone that he wasn't ready to go just yet. In the end they had to stop the proceedings and make the hole a bit larger so that he could finally be laid to rest.

When they had arrived home from the hospital after Leigh had died, Nicola didn't really know what she was doing, so she gave Tom the small painting of Angus that Leigh had stolen from Lucian, along with an etching. By the time Tom was due to leave, about a week later, Nicola regretted giving him the picture. She thought that really she should give it back to Lucian, because it was his. On the day Tom was due to return to Australia she finally plucked up the courage to ask for the picture back. Tom was furious, and thought that it was a plot between Nicola and her sister to keep the picture for themselves. Nicola went to work, so Christine was left to try to get the picture back. Tom didn't believe her story, so in desperation Christine phoned me at work, asking me to try to make Tom see reason. I tried to explain and told him that really he should give the painting back; apart from the fact it was stolen, you're not allowed to take work by important artists out of the country and he could easily be stopped at customs. In the end he agreed to give it back, but there was a problem. It was in Bronwyn's luggage, which was at Heathrow Airport waiting for her to return from Europe and then link up with her dad for the return flight to Australia.

Tom told me what time the flight was, but he wouldn't give the painting to Christine as he still didn't trust her and he didn't want to share a cab with her. So Christine came to meet me at work and we both drove to Heathrow, as I was the only one he would give the picture to. We hung around feeling like International Art Rescuers, thinking that we might be swooped on any minute. We went to the place where Tom had agreed to meet Bronwyn and found her and Steve. She was most surprised to see us and couldn't really understand the story at all. When Tom arrived he explained everything and we slunk over to a corner, where Bronwyn surreptitiously handed over the picture.

Meanwhile, Nicola had broken down at work. She was working for Bella, Lucian's daughter, and told her the story of the painting. Bella immediately told her father, who was furious. It wasn't that he didn't necessarily want Tom to have it – it was just that it wasn't finished, he wasn't happy with it and he was scared that it might end up on the open market and bring down the overall quality of his work. If we hadn't managed to get it back at Heathrow, he would have contacted Interpol.

Leigh hadn't wanted a funeral or a memorial service, but all his friends were keen to do something to remember him by, so we decided to have an exhibition at the Fine Arts Society. Johnnie Shand Kydd, who worked there, arranged it all. There were Leigh's costumes, photographs and accessories, as well as two of Lucian's paintings and a couple of etchings. Films and videos were screened downstairs. Andrew McIntosh Patrick, who was in charge of the gallery, was in his element arranging Leigh's costumes; one dress had a very full skirt and he thought it wasn't hanging properly, so he rushed upstairs to his flat and brought down a duvet and a couple of pillows, which he used to stuff it with.

The opening of the exhibition was attended by friends and admirers from all over the world. It was a chance to reflect, to meet up with old friends and to remember Leigh – not that he could possibly be forgotten. Les Child read out a poem that he had written:

> I Know a Gender Extremist
> An Inquiring, Inquisitive conversationalist
> with a wardrobe of Fancies too embellished to list
> But always with a Girlish Swish with Finish
> I know someone beyond definition
> An answer would only beg question
> 'Is it Art
> Is it science
> Reference to a domestic appliance
> Or Fashion?'
> I Know what I Know
> No!
> I Knew, now I Know
> Whether above or below
> In between in Limbo
> A Ghost in the Air
> In Earthbound Footwear
> Or beyond the Stratosphere
> On a U.F.O.
> I Know you're there Somewhere
> I Know what I Know

The exhibition continued for three more days after the opening. The dowagers of Bond Street must have been very shocked when they came in to look for a nice Victorian painting and saw Leigh's LL Cool J hat perched on the bronze bust of the founder of the gallery and a portrait of Hitler that Leigh had made from a patchwork of Lucian's paint rags. Peter-Paul Hartnett had provided a massive collage of all the Polaroids that he took at Taboo and he was in attendance most days telling the audience about them. It was the busiest the gallery had ever been, and the staff were quite sad when the exhibition had to come down.

After the opening there was a disco at Eve's Club in Regent Street. Leigh loved it there, with its tacky plastic flowers and light-up dance floor. Everyone got roaring drunk and had a great time, but there was one thing missing – the greatest disco freak of all. Clubbing felt different after Leigh died. There was a feeling that you had to behave because the king of misbehaviour was not there to lead the way.

It has been said that Leigh somehow missed his way and died leaving a lot unachieved. Ian Parker, in a large piece written for the *Observer* after attending the exhibition, argued:

> It is not clear what to make of this collection, some of it a bit dusty, some of it still startling. It was hard to know what it added up to. Bowery was a fashion designer, an expert tailor, a nightclub sensation, an art object of sorts, a model for a great painter, an aspiring pop star, a man who made his body – his presence – a life's project. And when his friends met in Bond Street, still grieving and bewildered, it was unclear if they were marking the passing of some wonderfully unflinching artistic success, or were at a wake for a life that had gone slightly

wrong, a life distracted and dogged by – or sacrificed to – the idea of making an exhibition of oneself, to adolescent habits of shock and disguise.

Leigh may well not have achieved all he wanted to in his life, but his work continued in that of his friends, many of whom pursued successful careers that they probably wouldn't have started if they hadn't been encouraged by Leigh. Every time you see a fashion show or open a magazine you can see a Leigh influence. If you look at the work of Alexander McQueen, Vivienne Westwood or Jean Paul Gaultier, you can detect Leigh's style, and Lucian's paintings of him will last forever.

Oscar Moore in his column in the *Guardian* criticized the way Leigh chose to die:

> Leigh could have had the world's most flamboyant exit, but instead the man who was at the forefront of Taboo – the Leicester Square club – became a victim of Taboo – the culture of shame. The muse of Lucian Freud became the recluse of Middlesex Hospital. I don't blame him. I blame the others ... he could have floated out on the same magic pouffe of extravagance and invention that he floated through it on.

Leigh would have been furious if he had seen this article; it was his illness, nobody else's, and he chose to manage it in the way he wanted to, not the way the campaigners wanted. The last thing he wanted to be was a professional victim, like Oscar himself or Derek Jarman. Not that he thought that they were wrong – it just wasn't right for him. He wasn't ashamed of being ill, but he wanted to be remembered alive and vibrant, with a sick mind, not a sick body.

Perhaps Leigh hasn't left much that is concrete behind him, but he left something just as important – an attitude and an inspiration for people to follow: be brave, do what you want, and don't be afraid of failure. As long as you try and try your best, it doesn't matter – just never give up.

Rachel Auburn summed up the thoughts of most of his friends and admirers in her words, 'I never met anyone like him and never will again – he was on a different level – with an incredible energy and dynamism. I miss him so much, I miss his phone calls, I miss talking to him and miss his enthusiasm and encouragement. I wish he could see what I've achieved. I want him to be proud of me.'

As Leigh was such a liar, some friends still hope that his dying was an incredibly elaborate hoax, the culmination of a life of pranks. If a tribe of natives are ever discovered in Papua New Guinea, running around with blue faces and six-inch platforms, they will know that their wish has been granted.

Legacy

It's been twenty-eight years since I wrote this book. I thought that it would be popular for a bit and then it would be forgotten about, but that hasn't been the case at all, as Leigh has continued to fascinate people since he died. I've lost count of how many times it has been optioned for a film that has never actually been made (which I don't mind, as I've met lots of very interesting people and made lifelong friends in the process). I am thrilled that it is being published again in book form, after falling out of print and being available only at inflated prices on eBay or as a digital edition on Kindle.

Leigh has had many exhibitions devoted to him since he died, a few of which I was lucky enough to attend. In 2004 there was one held in Sydney's Museum of Contemporary Art, which is right on the harbour, opposite the Opera House. It opened in late December, so I was at a party there on New Year's Eve. It was very emotional to see a huge poster of Leigh looking over the sea on the anniversary of the day he died in the country he came from. I had to walk back to my hotel as there was a taxi strike, and I wasn't quite sure where it was, so I asked a man walking his dog for directions. He looked at me and said, 'I'll tell you if you give me a hand job.' I laughed so hard, and wished that Leigh was alive so that I could tell him.

The Vienna exhibition in 2013 at the Kunsthalle was well put together, but I don't think that Vienna was ready for Leigh, as it was very poorly attended. I gave a talk and only about three people turned up. London's Victoria & Albert Museum also held an exhibition in 2013, called 'Club to Catwalk', which featured some of Leigh's looks. It was wonderful, showing how nightclubs influenced fashion runways.

I also went to Rome for an exhibition, not just about Leigh, but about famous people who had died of AIDS. I lent them a few outfits and went to the opening. It was a strange affair and everyone just seemed to want to gossip with me about everyone else who worked there, not that I minded, as I like to know what's going on. Mine and Leigh's friend, Lorcan O'Neill, has a gallery in Rome, and he came along, but was bit flummoxed by it all.

My favourite exhibition was very small, and almost didn't take place because of Covid, but opened in January 2022. It was the brainchild of Hannah Watson, a trustee of the Fitzrovia Chapel, which is the only remaining part of Middlesex Hospital where Leigh died. It is a beautiful building, and even though there were only a few costumes, they looked so amazing in their surroundings. I went to the opening and didn't even recognize some people because they were all wearing masks. In the end it was very successful, with queues of people waiting to get in. It was wonderful to get out again after being locked down for so long and it really renewed people's interest in Leigh.

In October 2024, a wonderful exhibition at London's Fashion and Textile Museum curated by Martin Green, with help from many eighties icons, displayed several of Leigh's outfits, as well as fashions from several other designers who went to Taboo. There was a mannequin of me wearing my 'Merry Queen of Scots' dress in the entrance to recreate my job at Taboo.

Now, Tate Modern is planning a February 2025 exhibition that will celebrate Leigh's daring and outrageous performances in galleries, theatres and the street, and his fearlessness in forging his own path. It will bring to life Boy George's famous quote: 'Leigh Bowery is modern art on legs.'

Boy George wrote a marvellous musical called *Taboo*, inspired of course by Leigh's great creation. The show opened in 2002 in Leicester Square, just round the corner from the club where Taboo took place. I was thrilled to be included as a character, and burst into tears when I first saw it, as my on-stage counterpart sang a song to Leigh as he was dying – not very likely in real life, as I've got the worst voice in the world. Leigh was played first by Matt Lucas (his comedy partner David Walliams had already dressed as Leigh in the sitcom *Spaced*), then by Julian Clary and Australian actor Mark Little. In the end the draw of the grease paint took over, and George himself played Leigh to great acclaim.

Matt Lucas became especially enamoured with the figure of Leigh while he was playing him: 'During the period between the workshop and the start of rehearsals I had devoured every piece of information I could find about Leigh, met up with friends and associates of his and had become attached. I felt a sense of devotion to him. And I wanted to stay and pay tribute to his brilliance and his invention.' The actress and comedian Rosie O'Donnell liked the musical so much she arranged for it to transfer to Broadway. The opening night was one of the most exciting of my life. It played for 100 performances. A new production ran for four months in 2012 in Brixton, and I have heard many rumours that the show is to be revived once more.

Leigh's influence on fashion can still be seen in the work of Alexander McQueen, Rick Owens, Jean Paul Gaultier, Pam Hogg and my favourite ever designer, John Galliano. Every season it's interesting to see which designer has referenced one of Leigh's looks in their work. The label Supreme produced a line of clothes with Leigh's image on them, which sold out very quickly. Fashion writer Charlie Porter summed up Leigh's influence:

> In a way his greatest success was failure. His influence
> on fashion has been manifold and immense, most of it
> after his death, and most of it from designers and brands
> commercializing and profiting from a vision that he himself
> never compromised. I'm sure Bowery would have loved some
> financial stability in his time. But if he had, his later influence
> would have been less. Bowery's legacy is something rare:
> pure crystalised radicalism.

And of course, Lucian Freud's monumental paintings of Leigh have been exhibited in prestigious art galleries all over the world. After seeing an exhibition of Lucian's work at the Pompidou Centre in Paris in 2010, the *Guardian*'s Jonathan Jones described Leigh as 'a cornucopian source of wonder for Freud, a marvel of nature'. I am forever grateful to Leigh for introducing me to Freud. I think that he would have been jealous when one of the paintings of me broke a world record at auction. But I'm sure that he would have taken control of the situation and told me what to wear and how to behave.

There have been a few books about Leigh and many other books mention him. Robert Violette published a great coffee-table book in 1998, and also a book of Fergus Greer's photos of Leigh, called *Leigh Bowery Looks*. And it's thanks to Robert that this book is being republished as I made a throwaway remark to him about it and next thing I knew he had negotiated a contract with Thames & Hudson. Boy George, Steve Strange, Fat Tony and even Bananarama have mentioned Leigh and his influence in their books. Only recently, Lucian Freud's daughter Rose Boyt spoke very warmly of Leigh in her memoir, *Naked Portrait*.

Meeting Leigh completely changed my life, and whenever something exciting happens to me, I can trace it back to Leigh. Because I modelled for Lucian I was asked to model for a fundraiser at the Kids Company. Because my days of stripping off have passed, the teacher asked another model, Rui Miguel Leitão Ferreira, to pose naked. Little did I know that Rui had been angling to meet me for a while, as he wanted to paint me. He told me, 'I thought that if you could put up with Leigh, you could put up with me.' We became very good friends, and ten years after we met, he had a very successful exhibition in London called 'Posing For Sue' showing pictures that he had painted of us together.

The New York filmmaker Charles Atlas made a wonderful documentary about Leigh in 2004. It shows just how much Leigh's friends loved him and still think about him. He influenced so many of them and encouraged many of them in their careers, and several of them have been very successful. Leigh was so interesting, and so fascinated in everything you did. Although he was only just over six foot, people always thought that he was much taller. I think it was because he was so full of thoughts, ideas, mischief, plans, nerves, charisma, intelligence and charm, and all of this was trying to burst out of him, giving him a huge presence.

Although Leigh wasn't really celebrated in his native Australia during his lifetime, they embraced him after his death. In 2011 the Bowery Theatre opened in St Albans in Australia. Their tagline is

'A Place To Be Bold', and they explain why they chose the name on their website:

> The Bowery Theatre is named after the late artist, Leigh Bowery who grew up in Brimbank. Leigh Bowery was one of the most influential international arts figures of the 80s and 90s. A celebrated fixture of the fashion, nightlife and avant-garde scenes in London and New York, he was known for his flamboyant get-ups, larger than life personality and bold performance art. As a creative space we are inspired by his legacy.

In Brisbane, the Stitchery Collective have held six Bowerytopia parties at the Tivoli since 2016. The evening culminates in the crowning of the Bowery Queen, and some of the looks are truly amazing.

One thing that has really changed since Leigh died are the conversations about gayness and gender. I don't think Leigh would have been bothered one way or the other by this, as he was very accepting of people, and the more different the better. He wouldn't have been an activist, as he wasn't really interested in gay politics. He was what he was and that was that. Not that Leigh ever wanted to be called a drag queen, but drag has become a very acceptable type of entertainment. *RuPaul's Drag Race* has become primetime television and Leigh is often referenced by the more forward-thinking participants. One of the winners, Bob the Drag Queen, even went on with drips on his head. I bet that Leigh would have been a guest judge.

The question that people ask me most is, 'What do you think Leigh would be doing now if he was still alive?'. Things have changed so much since he left us. The internet was brand new when he died, and no one had heard of social media. Goodness knows what mischief he could have caused with all those tools at his disposal.

Maybe he would have worked in fashion, but I couldn't imagine him running a fashion house, as there would be too much interference from investors and Leigh liked to follow his own rules. But he may well have collaborated with some designers on certain collections. Thanks to Leigh I ended up collaborating with Fendi in 2017.

Maybe he would have become a reality TV star, but to be honest I think that he was better than that. But he could have been on *Celebrity Big Brother* while it was still fresh and new, and I imagine that he would have given Pete Burns a run for his money. I can also see him on *Bake Off* – he would have taken it very seriously and practised for ages beforehand so that he could bake a great cake while still entertaining everyone.

Or maybe he would have become a performance artist with shows in contemporary galleries. Who knows? He was only thirty-three when he died, so would have had many years left to find his niche, but I think that he would have flitted about from one project to another as he never wanted to get bored and complacent.

As I was writing this I was surprised and excited to see that Leigh was the cover star on the last-ever copy of *ES* magazine. What a great honour, and there was a great article inside too.

I still miss Leigh every day, and things are always happening that I'd love to tell him about. I hope that he is pleased with everything that myself, Nicola and many of his friends and admirers have done to keep his memory alive.

February 2025

Picture Credits

Baby Leigh aged 15 months. Collection Tom Bowery.

Leigh's first publicity photo. Collection Tom Bowery.

Leigh and friends, c. 1981. Collection Nicola Bowery and Trojan.

Leigh writing postcards in Jamaica, 1983. Collection Rachel Auburn May.

Leigh, Richard Habberley and Trojan outside the U.N. building, New York, 1984. Courtesy Sue Tilley.

Leigh, New York, 1984. Courtesy Sue Tilley.

Leigh in his flat, c. 1983. Courtesy Sue Tilley.

Leigh, Trojan and Sue on the Isle of Wight ferry, 1984. Courtesy Sue Tilley.

Leigh and Jeffrey Hinton at the Schonbrunn Palace, Vienna, c. 1986. Courtesy Sue Tilley.

Leigh and Trojan in the toilets at a Max gig in Brighton, 1985. Courtesy Nazarin Montag.

Leigh Bowery, Taboo, 1988. © Dave Swindells.

Jeffrey Hinton, Leigh, Baillie Walsh and John Maybury, Christmas 1987. Courtesy Sue Tilley.

Leigh and Wigan in U4 Disco, Vienna, 1986. Courtesy Sue Tilley.

Leigh Bowery & Nicola, Daisy Chain, 1988. © Dave Swindells.

Leigh and Michael Clark, 1988. Collection Lorcan O'Neill.

Boy George and Leigh at Boy George's 'Generation of Love' video shoot, 1990. Courtesy Sue Tilley.

Leigh, Cerith Wyn Evans and Angus Cook, Cornwall, 1990. Courtesy Sue Tilley.

Leigh, Cerith Wyn Evans and Angus Cook, Trebetherick Beach, Cornwall, 1990. Courtesy Sue Tilley.

Leigh, Angus Cook and Cerith Wyn Evans in Barbara Hepworth's Sculpture Garden, Cornwall, 1990. Courtesy Sue Tilley.

Leigh Bowery posing for *Naked Man, Back View*, 1992. © Estate of Bruce Bernard.

Leigh with his parents. Collection Tom Bowery.

Leigh and Sue before Kinky Gerlinky, 1993. Courtesy Sue Tilley.

Wedding day, 13 May 1994. Collection Lorcan O'Neill.

Johnnie Shand Kydd and staff installing Lucian Freud's portrait of Leigh at The Fine Art Society, Bond Street, 1995. Courtesy Sue Tilley.

Bus poster advertising 'Take a Bowery: The Art and (larger than) Life of Leigh Bowery' at Museum of Contemporary Art Australia, Sydney, 2004. Courtesy Sue Tilley.

Index